India

WORLD BIBLIOGRAPHICAL SERIES

General Editors:
Robert L. Collison (Editor-in-chief)
Sheila R. Herstein
Louis J. Reith
Hans H. Wellisch

VOLUMES IN THE SERIES

VOLUME 26

India

Brijen K. Gupta
Datta S. Kharbas
Compilers
with the assistance of
Judith N. Kharbas
Arthur D. Lopatin

CLIO PRESS
OXFORD, ENGLAND · SANTA BARBARA, CALIFORNIA

217489

© Copyright 1984 by Clio Press Ltd.

British Library Cataloguing in Publication Data

Gupta, Brijen K.
India. — (World bibliographical series; 26)
1. India — Bibliography
I. Title II. Kharbas, Datta S.
III. Series
016.954   Z3201

ISBN 0-903450-38-0

Clio Press Ltd.,
55 St. Thomas' St.,
Oxford OX1 1JG
Providing the services of the European
Bibliographical Centre

ABC-Clio Information Services
Riviera Campus, 2040 Alameda Padre Serra,
Santa Barbara, Ca. 93103, USA

Designed by Bernard Crossland
Computer typeset by Peter Peregrinus Ltd.
Printed and bound in Great Britain by
Billing and Sons Ltd., Worcester.

THE WORLD BIBLIOGRAPHICAL SERIES

This series will eventually cover every country in the world, each in a separate volume comprising annotated entries on works dealing with its history, geography, economy and politics; and with its people, their culture, customs, religion and social organization. Attention will also be paid to current living conditions — housing, education, newspapers, clothing, etc. — that are all too often ignored in standard bibliographies; and to those particular aspects relevant to individual countries. Each volume seeks to achieve, by use of careful selectivity and critical assessment of the literature, an expression of the country and an appreciation of its nature and national aspirations, to guide the reader towards an understanding of its importance. The keynote of the series is to provide, in a uniform format, an interpretation of each country that will express its culture, its place in the world, and the qualities and background that make it unique.

SERIES EDITORS

Robert L. Collison (Editor-in-chief) is Professor Emeritus, Library and Information Studies, University of California, Los Angeles, and is currently the President of the Society of Indexers. Following the war, he served as Reference Librarian for the City of Westminster and later became Librarian to the BBC. During his fifty years as a professional librarian in England and the USA, he has written more than twenty works on bibliography, librarianship, indexing and related subjects.

Sheila R. Herstein is Reference Librarian and Library Instruction Coordinator at the City College of the City University of New York. She has extensive bibliographic experience and described her innovations in the field of bibliographic instruction in 'Team teaching and bibliographic instruction', *The Bookmark*, Autumn 1979. In addition, Doctor Herstein co-authored a basic annotated bibliography in history for Funk & Wagnalls *New encyclopedia*, and for several years reviewed books for *Library Journal*.

Louis J. Reith is librarian with the Franciscan Institute, St. Bonaventure University, New York. He received his PhD from Stanford University, California, and later studied at Eberhard-Karls-Universität, Tübingen. In addition to his activities as a librarian, Dr. Reith is a specialist on 16th-century German history and the Reformation and has published many articles and papers in both German and English. He was also editor of the *American Society for Reformation Research Newsletter*.

Hans H. Wellisch is Associate Professor at the College of Library and Information Services, University of Maryland, and a member of the American Society of Indexers and the International Federation for Documentation. He is the author of numerous articles and several books on indexing and abstracting, and has also published *Indexing and abstracting: an international bibliography*. He also contributes frequently to *Journal of the American Society for Information Science, Library Quarterly,* and *The Indexer*.

For Sheila and Anna

Contents

Contents

Contents

Introduction

'A mystery and a muddle'. This is how E. M. Forster characterised India, where he lived for many years. In many senses, India is not one country but many countries rolled into one. Over 1,260,000 square miles in area, it is the world's seventh largest nation-state, almost the size of Europe. Its 730 million people constitute one-sixth of the world's population, indeed, within the last twenty years India's population has increased by more than the entire population of the United States. Though politically a nation-state, it is a complex civilization within which are subsumed many distinct cultures, from the most tribal to the most sophisticated. India's democratic constitution recognises fourteen principal languages, each with a distinguished literary tradition. All major religions of mankind are represented within its borders, from animism to Zoarastrianism, and it is the second largest Islamic nation in the world. A country of vast contrasts, it boasts opulent palaces and magnificent temples, yet its urban slums are of unparalleled squalor. Though India has a literary tradition going back to 2000 BC the vast majority of its present-day inhabitants are illiterate. It has one of the largest air and rail transport systems, yet most of India's freight is moved on the backs of its coolies and bullock carts. It has the second largest pool of scientists and technicians in the world, but the benefits of science and technology have not yet filtered through to those who live in wretched poverty. With such variety and contrasts, authors have praised the glories, wealth and achievements of India − as A. L. Basham has done in his definitive *The wonder that was India* − or they have written in harsh tones of India's misery − as V. S. Naipaul has done in *India: a wounded civilization.*

A bibliographer intending to provide a selective and annotated bibliography of India which expresses its unique culture and its importance in the family of nations must, therefore, contend with conflicting interpretations, and, however judicious and objective he tries to be, he lays himself bare to criticism from not only one or two but practically all scholarly quarters. His task is further complicated not by the paucity of printed material about India, but by its over-abundance. India has had a rich bibliographical tradition: T. D. N. Besterman's *World bibliography of oriental bibliographies* (Oxford: Blackwell, 1975) has about 3,000 entries on India, N. N. Gidwani and K. Navalani in *A guide to reference materials on India* (Jaipur: Saraswati, 1974) have over 20,000 entries, and both these volumes exclude works entirely in Indian languages. Indeed, there is no aspect of Indian life and culture for which a bibliography has not been produced, although most of these bibliographies have not been annotated. Two years ago Maureen L. P. Patterson and William J. Alspaugh produced *South Asian civilizations: a bibliographic synthesis*, a magnificent work listing over 28,000 books and articles, mostly in English, and this they called a 'selective' bibliography. They wisely refrained from either grading or annotating the entries, perhaps to avoid criticism from India specialists who hardly agree on the relative value of a particular book.

Yet efforts, however incomplete, have been made to compile selective annotated bibliographies of India. Thanks to the financial generosity of the Carnegie Corporation of New York, J. Michael Mahar, a distinguished social scientist, brought out *India: a critical bibliography* (Tucson: University of Arizona Press, 1964), intended for those students of India who were experts in their discipline but wished to obtain a more comprehensive understanding of India. For over a dozen years now, Professor Mahar has been attempting an updated and a more comprehensive version of his 1964 bibliography, but with the enormous literature on India that appears in print year after year this is indeed a daunting task. On a less ambitious scale was *Learning about India: an annoted guide for nonspecialists*, edited by Barbara J. Harrison (New York & New Delhi: University of the State of New York, 1977), to which we contributed the substantial sections on books and on source materials. This *Guide* included several essays on how to learn about and understand India. This present selective bibliography, designed along the guidelines of the World Bibliographical Series, aims at being as comprehensive as its size will allow. Naturally it is more up-to-date than its predecessors, and we have made a particular effort to make the annotations both descriptive and analytical. The volume is designed to meet the needs of various types of reader. It will not, however, be very useful to the casual traveller, who can find all the information he needs in such guides as Fodor's, nor is it designed for the specialist who is already an expert in a particular field of Indian studies. But all other users will benefit from it, finding it an excellent introduction to learning about both traditional and modern India in general and a good starting point for locating worthwhile material on more specific subject areas.

Introduction

We believe our annotations to be reasonably exhaustive and analytical, and they will help the reader decide which books are most relevant to his needs and point out their respective merits. Librarians of academic and large public libraries, interested in building a core collection on India or asked to recommend books on a particular aspect of Indian life and culture, will find our list quite appropriate to their needs.

Our selections are thus based on the needs of the various users described above. While we have not excluded scholarly works, we have deliberately avoided those monographs and methodological studies that are highly specialized and designed only for the rigorous scholar. In fields such as art, letters, religion, and philosophy, we have chosen titles that have endured over decades, even though some of them may be faulted for not incorporating the latest scholarship — we have on the whole indicated any such shortcoming in our annotation. But in such social science disciplines as economics and politics we have included both the 'classics' and the volumes that represent latest findings and scholarship. This is because, as a developing society, modern India is undergoing rapid socio-economic and socio-political change and it is necessary that the informed reader have the latest information — we are mindful of the fact that many of the books included in sections on economics and politics are not likely to have such lasting value as the volumes included in sections on arts, letters, and philosophy. As far as possible we have chosen books that are either in print or easily available in most libraries. We make no apologies for including books in English only — the volume is designed primarily for an English-speaking audience, and publishing houses in India and abroad have very quickly produced English translations of worthwhile books published in Indian and other foreign languages. There are, of course, several Indian critics who have argued that English-language publications on India are not as penetrating as those in various Indian languages, but we reject that viewpoint. Our bibliography, however, includes all representative western and oriental (particularly Indian) scholarship. We have included controversial points of view so long as such views are respected in the scholarly community, but purely propagandist books have been ignored, whatever their popularity. While we have benefited from book reviews appearing in scholarly or popular media, the annotations represent our views based on our own reading of the books included in this bibliography.

Will India still remain a mystery and a muddle after a reader has studied all the books in this list? We hope it will — to us the joy has been in the probing of the mystery, and not necessarily in solving it. But we do hope that those who take the trouble to read some of the books from our list will become somewhat better informed, and quite a bit more appreciative of the mystical unity known as India.

Acknowledgements

A number of individuals and institutions have facilitated the preparation of this bibliography. Our sincere thanks are extended to: Bruce Bueno de Mesquita, Anthony Carter, and Neil F. McMullin for assistance in selecting items for sections on politics, anthropology, sociology, religion, and philosophy; Myra King and H. Brad Smith for help in library research; Association for Asian Studies, Prema and H. V. Janadhana, and Shashi and Ravendra Sharma for significant financial support to cover research expenses; Judith and Abhay Bhushan, Aleta and Martin Gupta, Binita and Pratap Gupta, Indira and Y. M. Jay, Kamal and Tarun Kothari, Saraswati and Lakshman Prasad, and Usha and H. K. Ramanath for additional financial support; Robert B. Hall, director of the Center for Asian Studies, University of Rochester, Ward Morehouse, president of the Council on International and Public Affairs, James F. Wyatt, director, and Janice W. Holladay, assistant director of the University of Rochester Libraries for institutional support; the Center for International Programs and Comparative Studies, University of the State of New York, for their permission to use our own materials from 'A basic bibliography', in *Learning about India: an annotated guide for nonspecialists*, edited by Barbara J. Harrison (New York & New Delhi, 1977. Foreign Area Materials Center Occasional Publications, no. 24); and Janina Nowakowska at Clio for her improvements to our manuscript.

Rochester, New York
22 August 1983

Chronology

c. 2500 BC   Harappan culture

c. 1500 BC   Migration of the Aryans to India

c. 1300-1000 BC   Composition of *Rig Veda*

c. 563-483 BC   Gautama Buddha

c. 325 BC   Alexander the Great in Punjab

c. 272-232 BC   Emperor Aśoka

c. 1st century AD   Roman trade with south India

319-540 AD   Imperial Guptas, India's Golden Age

405-11   Fa Hsien visits India

630-44   Hsüan Tsang visits India

712   Arabs in western India

c. 800   Śankara, philosopher

1030   al-Biruni in India

1206   Establishment of Islamic hegemony under the Slave dynasty in northern India

1288, 1293   Marco Polo visits south India

1336   Founding of the Vijayanagara empire in south India

Chronology

The Country and Its People

1 **India, Pakistan, Ceylon.**
   Edited by W. Norman Brown. Philadelphia: University of
   Pennsylvania Press, 1964. rev. ed. 203p. maps. bibliog.
A series of essays, written for inclusion in the *Encyclopaedia Americana*, dealing
with the geography and material resources of India and the use made of them in
developing India as a distinct culture. Achievements in philosophy, literature and
the arts are described in summary form, and information is also provided on the
history of India, its social structure, economic life, and political and legal institutions. A good handbook.

2 **The continent of Circe: being an essay on the peoples of India.**
   Nirad C. Chaudhuri. London: Chatto & Windus, 1967. 320p.
   bibliog.
An eminently readable, highly controversial, immensely opinionated, sweeping
essay on the peoples and cultures of India. The book is an attack on Indian
spirituality and the Hindu penchant for glorifying such contradictions as the
maintenance of both tradition and modernity in the body-politic. Chaudhuri
argues that Hindus and Europeans share common Indo-Aryan traits, but that the
Hindus have been corrupted by the baleful influence of India's geographical environment. Until the people of India conquer their environment and recover their
original Indo-Aryan spirit, the nation cannot hope to get out of its present
socio-economic morass.

3 **Gazetteer of India: Indian Union.**
   New Delhi: Ministry of Education and Social Welfare,
   1965-78. 4 vols. maps. bibliog.
Since 1882 the government of India has periodically issued the *Imperial Gazetteer of India*, containing an exhaustive account of the country and its people. The
1907-09 edition of the *Imperial Gazetteer* was published in 26 volumes, with the
first four volumes devoted to a discussion of the general features of Indian

1

society, culture, environment, economy, and administrative system. While the entire 1907-09 edition has not been brought up to date, the first four volumes have now been thoroughly revised and rewritten by distinguished scholars.

4 India: a reference annual.
Delhi: Ministry of Information and Broadcasting, 1953- . annual.

This standard reference annual is based on official sources and carries information on the political, constitutional, educational, cultural, scientific, and financial aspects of the country. Each chapter includes a select bibliography which directs the user to further reading on the subject. A very useful source for ready reference.

5 India: who's who.
New Delhi: INFA, 1969 - . annual.

This annual reference publication provides basic biographical information on about 2,500 eminent Indians. The work, arranged by profession, is divided into eight main sections: business, government, humanities, public affairs, sciences, applied sciences, social sciences and law, and miscellaneous. Each section is further divided into subsections. An appendix at the end gives addresses of various associations, organizations, research institutes and universities.

6 The inner world: a psychoanalytic study of childhood and society in India.
Sudhir Kakar. Delhi: Oxford University Press, 1981. 2nd rev. enl. ed. 241p. bibliog.

An incisive analysis of Indian culture from the viewpoint of contemporary psychoanalytic theory. Kakar examines the Hindu world view, including such key concepts as dharma (righteousness) and moksa (liberation), relations between mothers and infants, the extended Indian family, and major Indian myths. His thesis that Indian children have a much longer relationship with their mothers than their western counterparts, and that Indians do not place great emphasis on individualism and self-sufficiency, is very well argued.

7 The speaking tree: a study of Indian culture and society.
Richard Lannoy. London: Oxford University Press, 1974. 466p. bibliog.

An influential, yet controversial, study of major themes in the Indian ethos. Lannoy deals with aesthetic, social, and religious content of Indian art; examines the family system, particularly child-rearing, sexual relationships, and recent changes in family structure; and analyses patterns of Indian philosophical concepts, political organization, and Gandhi's influence on Indian history. There is an excellent discussion of the 'compartmentalization' habit of modern intellectuals who are caught between tradition and modernity and are unable to synthesize the two.

8 The people of India.
Herbert Risley, edited by W. Crooke. Delhi: Oriental Books
Reprint Corp., 1969. 2nd ed. 472p. maps. bibliog.
A pioneering classification of the people of India, undertaken following the 1901
census, on the basis of anthropometry. Part 1 of the book deals with the physical
types; part 2 with social types; and the remaining five parts with the origin of
caste and its relationship to religion, social institutions, folk tradition, and
nationality. Risley's book has been criticized for assuming that the process of
physical and social amalgamation has not been pervasive in India, and that various caste, linguistic, and tribal groups have continued to coexist without much
interaction with each other. Criticism has also been levelled against some of
Risley's theories on the origin of several ethnic groups. In spite of these shortcomings, Risley's anthropometric classifications continue to be of use to scholars.

9 Ethnic plurality in India.
R. A. Schermerhorn. Tucson, Arizona: University of Arizona
Press, 1928. 369p. bibliog.
A comprehensive survey of Indian minority communities. Separate chapters are
devoted to the scheduled castes, the scheduled tribes, Muslims, Jains, Sikhs,
Christians, Jews, Anglo-Indians, Parsees, and Chinese. Indian commual and eth-
nic pluralism is examined in a comparative perspective. The author also analyses
limits to integration obtaining in each group. A structuralist perspective.

10 Encyclopedia Indica.
Jagdish Saran Sharma. New Delhi: Chand, 1981. 2nd rev.
ed. 2 vols.
Designed to provide 'correct and exhaustive' information on 'all subjects relating
to India', this encylopaedia falls far short of its goals. It has good biographical
sketches, satisfactory geographical descriptions, and cogent information on a
variety of miscellaneous topics. The encyclopaedia is not altogether satisfactory,
but is quite useful and is the only work of its kind.

11 An exploration of India: geographical perspectives on society and culture.
Edited by David Edward Sopher. Ithaca, New York: Cornell
University Press, 1980. 334p. maps. bibliog.
A lively collection of essays examining the social dimensions of Indian social
order and cultural regions. Statistical results are displayed in maps, graphs, diag-
rams, charts, and tables.

12 The Times of India Directory and Yearbook Including Who's Who.
Bombay: Bennett, Coleman, 1914- . annual.
The title of this useful annual compendium has varied in past years: 1914-47, *The
Indian Yearbook*; 1948-52/53, *The Indian and Pakistan Yearbook*. Its very
extensive coverage of Indian economic, political, and social information includes
several maps and statistical tables on various aspects of life in India. The who's
who section contains biographical data on distinguished persons in various walks
of life. A separate section is devoted to states of the Union and the Union
territories. Listings of Indian diplomatic representatives abroad, foreign diplomatic

representatives in India, and membership of legislative assemblies and legislative councils of states are included. This is unquestionably one of the most useful yearbooks published in India.

13 India: an anthropological perspective.
Stephen A. Tyler. Pacific Palisades, California: Goodyear, 1973. 224p. bibliog.

A structuralist approach to the civilization of India and the Hindu view of life. One half of the book deals with analysis of the textual tradition; the other half with contemporary social organization, tribes and peasants, family and kinship, and the caste system. A well-organized and eminently readable introduction to Indian society.

Geography

General

14 India: an area study.
Surendra Nath Chopra. New Delhi: Vikas, 1977. 237p.
maps.
A short but thorough regional geography which presents information in the form
of sixty-five short essays put together under eleven conventional groupings. The
author's emphasis is on the economic and social landscape, but there is also a
chapter on Indian foreign policy written from the standpoint of geopolitics.

15 The Ganges in myth and history.
Steven G. Darian. Honolulu, Hawaii: University of Hawaii
Press, 1978. 219p. bibliog.
This book presents a comprehensive picture of the great river's cultural importance. Using materials from archaeology, art history, comparative religion,
mythology, Sanskrit and Bengali literature, classical and mediaeval European
texts, and folklore, the author explains how and why the Ganges has come to
occupy a central position in Hindu life and institutions.

16 Historical geography of ancient India.
Bimala Churn Law. New Delhi: Ess Ess Publication, 1976.
reprint of 1920 ed. 354p. maps. bibliog.
Based largely on epigraphical data, the author gives the location of places and
regions mentioned in ancient Indian and foreign texts. Of interest to students of
ancient Indian studies.

17 Geographical factors in Indian history.
Kavalam Madhava Panikkar. Bombay: Bharatiya Vidya
Bhavan, 1959. 3rd ed. 128p. maps.
A provocative essay by one of modern India's distinguished historians and diplo-
mats. Panikkar lucidly explains how India's geographical situation has moulded

5

its past and continues to shape its contemporary development. Probably the best introduction to the geopolitics of India.

18 The monsoon lands of Asia.
R. R. Rawson. Chicago: Aldine, 1969. 256p. maps. bibliog.

This introductory text contains conventional chapters on the physical and economic geography of the region as a whole. In addition there is a short and competent chapter on India and half a chapter on Kashmir.

19 The national geographical dictionary of India.
Jagdish Saran Sharma. New Delhi: Sterling, 1972. 223p.

This dictionary includes geographical place-names having historical, social, or cultural significance. Unfortunately no map of India is included. For the general public.

20 India and Pakistan: a general and regional geography.
Oskar H. K. Spate, Andrew T. A. Learmonth. London: Methuen, 1972. 3rd ed. 878p. maps. bibliog.

This volume constitutes the most complete geographical treatment of South Asia including Sri Lanka. Written in superlative prose, the work is broadly conceived and full of illustrative anecdotes and useful maps and diagrams. The land, the people, and the economy make up the first three parts of the book, and these are particularly recommended to the general reader. Part four, 'The face of the land', covers the individual regions of the subcontinent and, although packed with an abundance of useful material, is likely to be too detailed and technical for the purposes of most non-specialists. The publisher recently divided the book into two paperback volumes, *India and Pakistan: land, people and economy* and *India, Pakistan and Ceylon: the regions*, and distributed them through Barnes & Noble in the United States. These volumes, however, are now out of print, leaving only the single hardback volume currently available.

21 Asia, east by south: a cultural geography.
J. E. Spencer, William L. Thomas. New York: Wiley, 1971. 2nd ed. 669p. maps. bibliog.

This comprehensive cultural geography of monsoon Asia is divided into two main sections: systematic geography, and the regional expression of cultures. The chapters in the former, dealing with the region as a unit, contain substantial information on the society and culture of India. The second part of the book has two chapters on India, one dealing with cultural history and the second with recent economic and social developments.

Economic

22 **The state of India's environment 1982: a citizens' report.**
Center for Science and Environment, New Delhi. New
York: Council on International and Public Affairs, 1982.
200p. bibliog.

A pioneering report on India's environment. Prepared under the direction of Anil
Agarwal, it examines the impact of India's economic development policies on
land, water, forests, atmosphere, habitat, people, health, and wildlife, and pays
special critical attention to the lack of government leadership in protecting India's
ecological systems. Timely.

23 **India, resources and development.**
Basil Leonard Clyde Johnson. New York: Barnes & Noble,
1979. 211p. maps. bibliog.

A careful analysis of India's human and physical resources. Johnson discusses
such key issues as drought and water scarcity, patterns of crops, population
growth, industry and urbanization, and small-scale manufacturing, and their place
in modern India's economic development. The final chapter provides vignettes of
eight Indian cities: Pilibhit, Kolhapur, Madurai, Bangalore, Delhi, Bombay, Calcutta and Chandigarh.

24 **India's mineral resources.**
Subbier Krishnaswamy. New Delhi: Oxford & IBH, 1979.
2nd ed. 658p. maps.

A matter-of-fact descriptive text on mineral deposits, arranged alphabetically
according to the common name of the mineral. The book gives information on the
amount of production and its location in India, together with brief information on
principal locations of the mineral outside India. A chapter on Indian water-supply
and mineral springs, another on soils of India, and an additional chapter on
construction and building materials supplement the main section.

25 **Economic and commercial geography of India.**
C. B. Mamoria. New Delhi: Shiva Lal Agarwala, 1980.
523p. maps. bibliog.

A comprehensive survey of India's physical features and economic resources. Each
chapter includes up-to-date economic statistics on the production of the relevant
economic item. Chapters dealing with the industrial sector provide an historical
outline of the development of each particular industry. An indispensable almanac
for students of Indian economics.

26 **Million cities of India.**
Edited by R. P. Misra. New Delhi: Vikas, 1978. 405p.
bibliog.

A careful historical and geographic survey of the emergence of India's nine cities
with a population of one million or more according to the 1971 census: Ahmedabad, Bangalore, Bombay, Calcutta, Delhi, Hyderabad, Kanpur, Madras and
Poona. Separate chapters are devoted to each of these cities. In addition, two
introductory and two concluding chapters synthesize the findings from individual

7

studies and reflect on problems associated with the rise of the megalopolis in India.

Maps and atlases

27 **An historical atlas of the Indian peninsula.**
C. Colin Davies. London: Oxford University Press, 1959.
2nd ed. 94p. maps. bibliog.

A convenient collection of simple black-and-white line maps of India showing geographical, economic, demographic, linguistic, and political aspects of India's history. Opposite each map is a substantial statement providing background information for the map user. Useful for secondary school and upward.

28 **Indian agricultural atlas.**
Directorate of Economics and Statistics, Department of Agriculture. New Delhi, 1971. 76p. maps.

Sixty-two maps and tables dealing with India's agricultural products: locales of their cultivation, markets, and total production. Included are maps showing India's transportation routes, climatic data, soils, and population. A handy reference tool.

29 **India in maps.**
Ashok K. Dutt, S. P. Chatterjee, M. Margaret Geib. Dubuque, Iowa: Kendall, Hunt, 1976. 124p. maps. bibliog.

A graphic representation of India's political, physical, economic, and social characteristics. Maps have been arranged in seven categories including a section on cultural and demographic features. Each section has a well-written explanatory text.

30 **Early maps of India.**
Susan Gole. New Delhi: Sanskriti, Arnold-Heinemann, 1976. 126p. maps. bibliog.

An illustrated history of the early European maps of India (16th-18th centuries) together with a comprehensive catalogue of the maps of India printed between 1513 and 1795. See also the following entry.

31 **A series of early printed maps of India in facsimile.**
Susan Gole. New Delhi: Jayaprints, 1980. 56 maps.

A separate volume of reproductions, complementing the preceding entry.

32 **An atlas of the Mughal empire.**
Irfan Habib.   London: Oxford University Press, 1982. 105p.
maps. bibliog.
This atlas provides detailed regional and national maps of the Mughal empire
(1556-1857). Each map integrates political and economic information. Habib's
text includes complete references, with notes on sources and on the identification
of locations.

33 **National atlas of India: fascicule.**
National Atlas Organization.   Calcutta: Department of
Science and Technology, 1980. 2 vols. maps.
The most detailed and comprehensive atlas of modern India, containing seventy-
seven plates with brief introductions. The range of topics is impressive, from
general regional maps to maps detailing economic life, physical features, administrative divisions, population distribution, transport and communications, and climatic conditions.

34 **A historical atlas of South Asia.**
Edited by Joseph E. Schwartzberg, with the collaboration of
Shiva Gopal Bajpai (and others).   Chicago: University of
Chicago Press, 1978. 352p. maps. bibliog.
A comprehensive cartographic record of the history and culture of South Asia
from the Old Stone Age to the present. Maps and plates are divided into fourteen
principal sections followed by a similarly arranged explanatory text. The main
bibliography, listing some 4,000 items, and classified, is a substantial reference
source in itself.

Tourist guides

35 **Fodor's India and Nepal.**
Edited by Eugene Fodor, William Curtis.   New York: David
McKay, 1969- . annual.
One of the best short tourist guides, this volume provides information on the most
popular sites and major cities of India. For the uninitiated, there is a short
history of India, its architecture, music, dance, painting, sculpture, literature,
food, hotels, and inter-city and intra-city transportation. Brief information on
weather, customs regulations, foreign exchange, and health conditions is also
given. Latest edition, 1983.

36 **Hotel Guide, India: hotels, restaurants, travel agents.**
New Delhi: Federation of Hotel and Restaurant Associations
of India, 1977- . irregular. 1979 ed., 246p.
Also known as the *All India Hotel and Restaurant Guide*, this is a directory of
leading hotels and restaurants under place-names and the widely accepted star-
system of classification. Names and addresses of India's leading travel agents are
also included.

9

37 A Handbook for Travellers in India, Pakistan, Nepal, Bangladesh and Sri Lanka.
Edited by L. F. Rushbrook Williams.   New York: Barnes & Noble. irregular. 22nd ed., 1982, 762p. maps.

This is an indispensable handbook for visitors to India who want to see more than the standard tourist attractions. Originally entitled *Murray's Guide*, it was first published in 1859. The first part of the book provides general information about religion, society, and culture, and general hints to the traveller about climate, travelling conditions, and precautions to be observed. The main part of the book gives a mile-by-mile account of railroad and road journeys. Each place worthy of visit is described in detail, and for major tourist attractions good histories are provided. Floor plans of large tourist and archaeological attractions are given, and city maps included. An outstanding book for the serious traveller.

Flora and Fauna

38 Wood-yielding plants of India.
Vishnu Saran Agarwal.   Calcutta: Indian Museum, 1970.
80p. maps. bibliog.
An illustrated guide to the trees of India. The author provides lists of common names in English, Hindi, and other Indic languages (romanized).

39 Handbook of the birds of India and Pakistan together with those of Bangladesh, Nepal, Bhutan and Sri Lanka.
Salim A. Ali, S. Dillon Ripley.   New York: Oxford
University Press, 1980. 2nd ed. 10 vols. maps. bibliog.
These volumes provide a definitive account of the life history, behaviour, and biogeography of the birds of South Asia. For a shorter account see Ali's *The book of Indian birds* (Bombay: Natural History Society, 1962. 11th ed. rev. and enl. 187p. maps. bibliog.).

40 Useful plants of India and Pakistan.
Jehangir Fardunji Dastur.   Bombay: Taraporevala, 1977. 2nd
ed. 185p. bibliog.
A comprehensive survey of native plants and trees of industrial, economic, and commercial value. The local names of these plants are given and the use of each plant fully covered. A classified list of the plants according to their uses is given in an appendix. There is a companion volume, *Medicinal plants of India and Pakistan* (Bombay: Taraporevala, 1962. 2nd ed. 212p.), which provides equivalent information on plants used for drugs and remedies according to the Ayurvedic, Unani, and Tibbi systems of India.

Flora and Fauna

41 **The freshwater fishes of India, Pakistan, Bangladesh, Burma and Sri Lanka: a handbook.**
K. C. Jayaram.   Calcutta: Zoological Survey of India, 1981. 475p. bibliog.
A study of 742 species and 64 families of the fish to be found in South Asian inland waters. The habitat of each species and its distinguishing physical characteristics are included in the entries.

42 **100 beautiful trees of India: a descriptive and pictorial handbook.**
Charles McCann.   Bombay: Taraporevala, 1959. 2nd rev. ed. 168p.
An illustrated, descriptive handbook of the 100 most common trees of India. A long introduction provides an outline of the development of these trees and includes line drawings of various root and leaf systems. Illustrations, which are in colour, enhance the value of the book.

43 **Flowering shrubs.**
Benjamin Peary Pal, S. Krishnamurthi.   New Delhi: Indian Council of Agricultural Research, 1967. 155p.
An authoritative guide to the flowering shrubs of India. Illustrations accompany the text.

44 **Wild beauty: a study of Indian wildlife.**
Kailash Sankhala.   New Delhi: National Book Trust, 1973. 100p.
A short book on Indian wildlife. Habits, habitats, and other general information on Indian fauna, including those species considered to be endangered, is provided.

History

General

45 A history of India.
Koka A. Antonova, G. Bongard-Levin, G. Kotovsky,
translated from the Russian by Katharine
Judelson. Moscow: Progress Publishers, 1979. 2 vols. bibliog.
Russian scholarship on India is both old and quite new. In the 19th century
Minayeu, Shcherbatskoy and Oldenburg made significant contributions to Indology. Since 1917, Marxist scholars such as Reisner, Balabushevich, Dyakov, Osipov, and Goldberg have reinterpreted Indian history and culture. Between 1959
and 1969 Soviet historians published a four-volume *History of India*, thus breaking the monopoly in English of west European, American, and Indian (mostly
Euro-American trained) scholars on Indian historical studies. These two volumes,
drawing in part from the four-volume history, represent a Marxist view of Indian
history from its prehistoric beginnings to the present.

46 A cultural history of India.
Edited by Arthur L. Basham. Oxford, England: Clarendon,
1975. 585p. maps. bibliog.
Thirty-five essays from twenty-eight specialists. The volume is the successor to the
1937 *Legacy of India*, edited by G. T. Garratt. Contains excellent essays on
ancient, early, mediaeval and Islamic history, literature and art. The fourth section of the book dealing with India's contacts with Europe is reliable and informative. Essays on Hindu devotionalism and Mughal-British relations leave much
to be desired.

47 Dictionary of Indian history.
Sachchidananda Bhattacharya. Westport, Connecticut:
Greenwood, 1977. 963p.
This dictionary covers the ancient, mediaeval and modern periods of Indian
history. Approximately 3,000 entries include persons, places, works, and institutions, and are arranged alphabetically. A dictionary of this size covering more

than 2,500 years of Indian history cannot be exhaustive, comprehensive, or without error, but in the absence of anything similar it is of great value.

48 The United States and India, Pakistan, Bangladesh.
William Norman Brown. Cambridge, Massachusetts: Harvard University Press, 1972. 462p. map. bibliog.

Written by the late doyen of Indian studies in the United States, this is an indispensable political survey of modern India. The emphasis is less on diplomatic relations between the United States and India, more on developments in India during the last hundred years. An excellent annotated bibliography is included. For both the general audience and the specialist.

49 India: the social anthropology of a civilization.
Bernard S. Cohn. Englewood Cliffs, New Jersey: Prentice-Hall, 1971. 164p. maps. bibliog.

This book represents a combination of historical and anthropological approaches to the study of Indian society and culture. Excellent passages deal with the problem of land tenure under the Mughals and the British, town and village differences, the presence of traditional as well as modern elements in urban behaviour, and the British and Indian views of nationhood.

50 Sources of Indian tradition.
Edited by William Theodore de Bary (and others). New York: Columbia University Press, 1966. 2 vols. maps. bibliog.

India's intellectual tradition from the *Rig Veda* to the Nehru era is represented almost in its entirety in this standard and widely recommended work. The contents consists mainly of translations of Indian-language materials into English, with each section prefaced by an authoritative essay. The selections are judicious and seldom longer than a few pages. The reader should be aware that in emphasizing the literary and the 'great tradition', i.e. those elements of the culture which are widespread and long-lasting, the book largely omits the day-to-day living traditions of India. Thus the quality of Indian life is not pictured as a whole.

51 Indian Economic and Social History Review.
New Delhi: Vikas, 1963- . quarterly.

A scholarly journal devoted to social and economic history. Edited by an international board of Indian and foreign scholars.

52 Indian Historical Review.
New Delhi: Vikas, 1974- . biannual.

Each issue of the review carries six to eight articles and about seventy-five book reviews in the field of Indian history.

53 Journal of Indian History.

Trivandrum, India: University of Kerala, 1921- . thrice yearly.

Though often delayed in publication, this is India's foremost journal covering all aspects of Indian history. Most of the contributions are from scholars teaching in Indian universities. A reasonably good book review section.

54 The Indian heritage.

Humayun Kabir. New York: Asia, 1970. 3rd ed. 164p.

There are two schools of thought on the nature of Hindu and Muslim interaction in India during the last thousand years. One school emphasizes the separation of society in India into two communal groups; the other emphasizes a synthesis of the values of the two communities. Kabir surveys India's history from the latter point of view and thereby articulates the secular view current in India's government circles.

55 A concise history of ancient India.

Asoke Kumar Majumdar. New Delhi: Munshiram Manoharlal, 1980. 3 vols. maps. bibliog.

A three-volume set dealing with the history and culture of India. The first volume covers political history; the second, political theories, administration, and economic life; and the third, society, religion and philosophy. Majumdar rejects 650 or 1200 AD - the most widely accepted dates - as the terminal date for the 'ancient' period, and in these volumes covers Indian history up to ca. 1500. In the first volume there is an excellent discussion of the principal sources of ancient Indian history.

56 An advanced history of India.

Ramesh Chandra Majumdar (and others). Delhi: Macmillan, 1973. 3rd ed. 1,126p. maps. bibliog.

The standard complete political and social history of India, widely used in Indian colleges. The authors divide Indian history into three periods: Hindu (ancient), Muslim (mediaeval), and British (modern), a scheme which leaves much to be desired. The book is relentlessly empirical. It underemphasizes the role of south India in the course of Indian history, making it necessary to supplement this book with Nilakanta Sastri (q.v.).

57 The history and culture of the Indian people.

Ramesh Chandra Majumdar (general editor). Bombay: Bharatiya Vidya Bhavan, 1951-77. 11 vols. maps. bibliog.

Conceived in 1937 by Jadunath Sarkar, the then doyen of Indian historians, and Rajendra Prasad, later the first president of independent India, as the Indian response to the *Cambridge History of India*. An original prospectus called for a twenty-volume definitive history of India, written primarily by Indian scholars. After the death of Jadunath Sarkar, the original project was taken over by the Bharatiya Vidya Bhavan, with R. C. Majumdar replacing Sarkar as the general editor, and K. M. Munshi, later governor of Bombay, as the patron and producer of the series. The subtitles of these volumes are: 1. *Vedic age (up to 600 BC)*; 2. *Age of imperial unity (600 BC-320 AD)*; 3. *Classical age (320-730)*; 4. *Age of imperial Kanauj (730-1000)*; 5. *Struggle for empire (1000-1300)*; 6. *Delhi sultanate (1300-1526)*; 7. *The Mughal empire*; 8. *The Maratha supremacy*; 9.

British paramountcy and Indian renaissance (1818-1905), part 1; 10. *British paramountcy and Indian renaissance (1818-1905), part 2;* 11. *Struggle for freedom (1905-1947).*

58 Calcutta.
Geoffrey Moorhouse. New York: Harcourt, 1972. 376p. map. bibliog.

A historical portrait of the second largest city in the British empire, and the fourth largest city in the world. Moorhouse uses Calcutta to portray how the British empire was created in India, and what happened to India when the empire ended. The picture painted is of a city both monstrous and marvellous, violent and yet cultured, a child of the Industrial Revolution yet the most representative of the third world.

59 The discovery of India.
Jawaharlal Nehru. Bombay: Asia, 1969. 582p. maps. bibliog.

Written during Nehru's last imprisonment, this is a rich but subjective interpretive essay on India's history, written from the Indian nationalist point of view. Nehru is at his best discussing movements like Buddhism, Indo-Muslim syncretism under Akbar, and the failure of the British to extend the fruits of the Industrial Revolution. The book also marks Nehru's emergence as a leader of liberal nationalism and reflects a corresponding moderation of the socialist emphasis found in his earlier writings, *Toward freedom* and *Glimpses of world history.*

60 A history of south India from prehistoric times to the fall of Vijayanagar.
K. A. A. Nilakanta Sastri. New York: Oxford University Press, 1976. 3rd ed. 521p. maps. bibliog.

This is the most objective history of India south of the Indo-Gangetic plain - a region neglected in many Indian history textbooks. It provides an authoritative introduction to the region in which India's oldest native cultures continue to subsist. While the emphasis is on social and political trends, additional attention has been given to the arts and letters. An excellent supplement to Majumdar (q.v.) and Smith (q.v.).

61 The cultural heritage of India.
Ramakrishna Mission, Institute of Culture. Calcutta: Advaita Ashram, 1953-79. 2nd rev. ed. 5 vols. bibliog.

A detailed, topical, encyclopaedic survey of Indian history, social customs, philosophies, religion, and languages and literatures, written by foremost Indian scholars. Volume subtitles are: 1. *The early phases: prehistoric, Vedic and Upanisadic, Jaina, and Buddhist;* 2. *Itihasas, Puranas, Dharma and other 'sastras';* 3. *The philosophies* ; 4. *The religions;* 5. *Languages and literatures.*

62 **Cambridge History of India.**
Edited by E. J. Rapson (and others). Cambridge, England: Cambridge University Press, 1922-53. 5 vols. + supplement. bibliog.

Conceived along the lines of the *Cambridge Modern History*, this multi-volume set, by primarily British scholars, was expected to be the definitive survey of Indian history. Three interesting events marred this hope: the discovery of the Indus Valley civilization in 1921 led to the issuance of a supplement by Sir Mortimer Wheeler in 1953; the second volume was never published because the manuscript was allegedly destroyed upon the intervention of the British government; finally, in the sixth volume, additional chapters had to be improvised on the period 1919-47, by R. R. Sethi. The subtitles of the volumes are: 1. *Ancient India*; 3. *Turks and Afghans*; 4. *Mughal period*; 5. *British India, 1497-1858*; 6. *Indian empire, 1858-1918, with additional chapters on the last phase, 1919-47, by R. R. Sethi*; supplement 1. *The Indus civilization*.

63 **A new history of the Marathas.**
Govind S. Sardesai. Bombay: Phoenix Publishing, 1957-58. 3 vols. maps. bibliog.

Between the decline of the Mughals in the late 17th century and the establishment of British hegemony in the 19th, the Marathas of western India were the paramount power in the country. Sardesai's definitive study of the Maratha period is based on records available to historians like Grant-Duff and Kincaid as well as on the *peshwa daftars* (records of the Maratha *peshwas*) edited by Sardesai himself.

64 **National biographical dictionary of India.**
Jagdish Saran Sharma. New Delhi: Sterling, 1972. 302p.

The dictionary includes short biographical sketches of about 5,000 persons and covers almost 5,000 years of Indian history. Kings, military leaders, literati, artists, sportsmen, and martyrs are included. Despite its inadequate coverage of south and west India, the dictionary's usefulness lies in the inclusion of hard-to-find biographical sketches of past and present eminent Indians. It complements Bhattacharya's *Dictionary of Indian history* (q.v.) by including less well known persons from the modern period.

65 **The Oxford history of India.**
Edited by Vincent Arthur Smith, Percival Spear. London: Oxford University Press, 1981. 4th ed. 945p. maps. bibliog.

The first edition of this book, published in 1920, originated the now standard division of textbooks on Indian history into ancient, mediaeval, and modern sections. Originally written by Smith himself, this latest edition has been revised by four leading British specialists: Wheeler, Basham, Harrison, and Spear. Except for the prehistory section by Wheeler and the modern section by Spear, there is very little revision of the original text. The section by Spear is outstanding.

66 India, Pakistan and the west.
Thomas George Percival Spear. New York: Oxford University Press, 1967. 4th ed. 186p. bibliog.
A short interpretation of the course of Indian history, written from the point of view of a European liberal. Extremely readable and informative, and a useful corrective to the nationalist point of view expressed by Humayun Kabir (q.v.).

67 City of gold: the biography of Bombay.
Gillian Tindall. London: Temple Smith, 1982. 265p. maps. bibliog.
An evocative history of the growth of Bombay, India's most cosmopolitan city, in the 18th and 19th centuries. According to Tindall, Indians and Europeans alike flocked to Bombay to make their fortunes and to participate in the benefits of the Industrial Revolution and western culture. The position of women, the growth of cultural institutions, the construction of palatial houses, and the emergence of the modern tradition in Indian journalism are described, with emphasis on the contributions of a host of prominent individuals.

68 History of mediaeval Hindu India.
Chintaman Vinayak Vaidya. New Delhi: Cosmo, 1979. 3 vols. maps. bibliog.
Originally published in 1921, these volumes continue to provide the most detailed account of local and regional Hindu kingdoms that flourished between 700 AD (after the fall of Harsha's empire) and 1300 (conquest of Deogiri by Allaudin Khilji). Vaidya has utilized both Hindu and early Muslim historical sources for his narrative, and the entire text is organized on the principle of causes and effects of certain formative events.

69 A new history of India.
Stanley A. Wolpert. New York: Oxford University Press, 1982. 2nd ed. 472p. maps. bibliog.
This introductory survey is intended for the general reader. The most detailed coverage is given to the Mughal empire, British rule, and India's independence and partition. Concluding chapters provide an adequate summary of the achievements of the Nehru and Indira Gandhi governments. An unannotated but graded (in importance) bibliography is reasonably comprehensive.

Travellers' accounts

70 Travels in the Mogul empire, A.D. 1656-1668.
François Bernier, translated by Archibald Constable, second rev. ed. by Vincent A. Smith, based on the version by Irving Brock. Delhi: Chand, 1972. 3rd ed. 497p. maps. bibliog.
Descriptions of Surat, Agra, Delhi, Gwalior, Golconda, Gujarat, Mathura, Lahore, Assam, and Chittagong by a 17th-century French traveller. Bernier also includes the history of Emperor Shah Jehan's reign, and notes on Mughal admi-

nistration, Hindu social customs, and Indian military organization. The original translation of Bernier's *Histoire de la dernière révolution des états du Gran Mogul* was made by Irving Brock in 1891 and subsequently improved and annotated by Constable. In 1916, Smith revised the Constable-Brock version. The current edition is a reprint of the Smith edition published by the Oxford University Press in 1916.

71 **Alberuni's India: an account of the religion, philosophy, literature, geography, chronology, astronomy, customs, laws, and astrology of India about A.D. 1030.**
al-Biruni, translated by Edward C. Sachau. Ann Arbor, Michigan: University Microfilms, 1980. reprint of 1887 ed. maps. bibliog.
An invaluable source for the study of 11th-century India, Hindu religion and customs, mathematical, astronomical, and other sciences, and general political history. The 11th century marks the beginning of the mediaeval period in Indian history with the decline of Hindu hegemony and gradual Islamic domination. There is an abridged version by Ainslie T. Embree *Alberuni's India* (New York: Norton, 1971. 246p. maps. bibliog.).

72 **Travels of Fa Hsien (399-414 A.D.), or record of the Buddhist kingdoms.**
Fa Hsien, translated by Herbert Allen Giles. Westport, Connecticut: Greenwood, 1981. 96p. maps.
A description of the Buddhist centres in India and Sri Lanka, such as Ladakh, Taxila, Peshawar, Mathura, Kanauj, Kosala, Kapilvastu, Vaisali, Gaya, Patna, Banaras, Champa, and Magadha, by the Chinese traveller Fa Hsien. The description is valuable for the study of the Gupta period of Indian history.

73 **Early travels in India, 1583-1619.**
William Foster. New York: AMS, 1975. reprint of 1921 ed. 351p. maps. bibliog.
This volume includes travel accounts by Ralph Fitch, John Mildenhall, William Finch, Nicholas Withington, Thomas Coryat, and Edward Terry. Taken together they form an excellent picture of India from the foothills of the Himalayas to Cape Comorin in the south, and from Ahmedabad in the west to Chittagong in the east.

74 **Travels of Ibn Batuta, A.D. 1325-1354.**
Ibn Batuta, translated with revisions by Hamilton A. R. Gibb, from the Arabic text edited by C. Defremery, B. R. Sanguinetti. Cambridge, England: Cambridge University Press, 1958-71. 4 vols. maps. bibliog. (Hakluyt Society, 2nd series, nos. 110, 117, 141).
The third volume is especially valuable for an understanding of Indian social and economic life of the 14th century. Ibn Batuta discusses the Indian postal service, the custom of widow-burning (*suttee*), Delhi and other historical places, the fort at Gwalior, Muslim rulers, and provinces.

75 Travellers' India: an anthology.
H. K. Kaul.   Delhi: Oxford University Press, 1979. 535p.
bibliog.

This anthology contains nearly 400 selections from 170 travel accounts about India from the earliest times to the beginning of the 20th century. Arranged in twenty-four subject areas such as history, geography, philosophy, and religion, the book provides intriguing glimpses of India seen through outsiders' eyes. British travellers of the 19th century are heavily represented.

76 India in the fifteenth century: being a collection of narratives of voyages to India.
Edited by Richard Henry Major.   Delhi: Deep Publications,
1974. reprint of 1857 ed. 130p. maps. bibliog.

Narratives of the travels of Abdul Razzak (Arab), Nicolo Conti (Italian), Athanasius Nikitin (Russian) and Hieronimo di Santo Stefano (Portuguese), in the century preceding the discovery of the Portuguese route to India by Vasco da Gama. These accounts fuelled European interest in India and Indian opulence.

77 The classical accounts of India: the Greek and Roman accounts of ancient India.
Edited by Ramesh Chandra Majumdar.   Calcutta: Firma
KLM, 1981. 504p. maps.

Since the ancient Indians themselves wrote no history, the writings of foreign travellers and historians are an important source for the study of India. The present collection, originally published in 1960, includes all the classical texts having a bearing on India. Subjects covered include political administration, trade and commerce, military science, geography, religious beliefs, and social practices. Authors include Arrian, Strabo, Pliny, Ptolemy, Priaulx, and others.

78 Storia do Mogor or Mogul India, 1653-1708.
Niccolao Manucci, translated by William Irvine.   Calcutta:
Editions Indian, 1965. reprint of 1907 ed. 4 vols. maps.
bibliog.

A late 17th-century account particularly rich in descriptions of south India, a region generally ignored by other European travellers. These are first-rate accounts of Hindu religion, manners and customs, and of the Mughal empire. Manucci, an Italian, served as a physician to the court of Emperor Aurangzeb for forty years.

79 On Yuan Chwang's travels in India, A.D. 629-645.
Thomas Watters.   San Francisco: Chinese Materials Center,
1975. reprint of 1904-05 ed. 2 vols. maps. bibliog.

A reprint of the 1904-05 edition, this account is valuable for understanding the political and economic transformation of India between the 5th century AD (as reported by Fa Hsien, q.v.) and the final Hindu hegemony under Harsha in the 7th century. There is a useful discussion of the Hindu-Buddhist synthesis during the resurgence of Hinduism under Gupta patronage.

Early history

80 The rise of civilization in India and Pakistan.
Raymond Allchin, Bridget Allchin. New York: Cambridge
University Press, 1982. 379p. maps. bibliog.

Using ethnographic, linguistic, and historical evidence, as well as archaeological
records, the authors trace the origins and development of Indian culture in the
subcontinent from its roots in the palaeolithic era, through the rise, efflorescence,
and disintegration of the Indus civilization. The emergence of regional cultures in
the Indo-Gangetic plains and in the Deccan and the spread of Indo-Aryans
throughout India are discussed in admirable fashion. The volume concludes with
an examination of the appearance of city states in the early Buddhist period.

81 A sourcebook of Indian archaeology.
F. Raymond Allchin, Dilip K. Chakrabarti. New Delhi:
Munshiram Manoharlal, 1979. 354p. maps. bibliog.

These readings, the first of a projected three-volume sourcebook, show the development of Indian archaeology from its late 18th-century beginnings to the
present. Excerpts from the most important of older as well as the best of contemporary research on each topic are included. The first volume includes materials
grouped under four headings: historical background to Indian archaeology; earliest
researches; geography, climate, and early man; and domestication of plants and
animals.

82 Daily life in ancient India, from approximately 200 B.C. to A.D. 700.
Jeannine Auboyer, translated from the French by Simon
Watson Taylor. New York: Macmillan, 1965. 344p. map.
bibliog.

A fascinating, very readable description of the social and human aspects of
ancient Indian civilization. The author skilfully uses literature, archaeological discoveries, folklore, and anecdotes to portray the social, economic, and political
structure of the classical civilization of India.

83 India and China: a thousand years of cultural relations.
Prabodh Chandra Bagchi. Calcutta: Saraswat Library, 1981.
298p. map. bibliog.

A readable survey of Sino-Indian cultural contacts and mutual influences. Bagchi
discusses the role of Buddhist missionaries to China and Chinese pilgrims to India
in promoting Sino-Indian contacts. The influence of Buddhism in promoting
Indian traditions in philosophy, literature, and arts and sciences is carefully
delineated. An appendix includes short sketches of Indian scholars who lived in
China before the 12th century AD. Bagchi's volume should be supplemented with
Hu Shih, 'East and west: the Indianization of China: a case study in cultural
borrowing', in the Harvard Tercentenary Conference of Arts and Sciences
Independence, convergence, and borrowing (Cambridge, Massachusetts: Harvard
University Press, 1937. 272p.).

84 **The wonder that was India: a survey of the history and culture of the Indian subcontinent before the coming of the Muslims.**
Arthur Llewellyn Basham. London: Sidgwick & Jackson, 1979. 3rd rev. ed. 568p. maps. bibliog.

Perhaps the most comprehensive and scholarly survey of pre-Muslim India. Written in brilliant prose by one of the foremost authorities on ancient India and designed primarily for readers with little or no background in Indian history, the book is used widely in schools and colleges. The approach is topical: history, political life and thought, religion and philosophy, everyday life, language and literature, the arts, social order, and India's contributions to the sciences and technology. Over 200 plates and illustrations and a topical bibliography add substantially to the book's value. A minor classic which should be acquired by everyone interested in India.

85 **Harsha: a political study.**
D. Devahuti. Oxford, England: Clarendon, 1970. 295p. map. bibliog.

An important study of the last great Hindu emperor of India, who died in 647 AD. Utilizing records of Chinese Buddhist pilgrims as well as Sanskrit textual evidence, Devahuti greatly improves the earlier monograph on Harsha by R. K. Mookerji (*Harsha*. 1926. 3rd ed., Delhi: Motilal Banarsidass. 203p.). Her narrative and analysis includes an examination of the sources for this study, Harsha's political, social, economic, and religious achievements, and Harsha as a great Sanskrit dramatist.

86 **Studies in Indian history and culture.**
Upendra Nath Ghoshal. Bombay: Orient Longman, 1965. 2nd rev. ed. 385p. bibliog.

Seventeen major essays by one of India's leading Indologists. The first of the four parts analyses the Indian historiographical tradition from Vedic times to Kalhana's *Rajatarangini*, and is the least controversial. The second part challenges the current schematic division of the periods of Indian history. The third part is concerned with several different aspects of the ancient Indian political system, the area of the author's principal expertise, and is perhaps the most controversial. The last part deals with topics of general interest such as the institution of slavery.

87 **Arthasastra.**
Kautilya, translated by Mahamahopadhyaya Arthasastravisarada Vidyalankara Panditraja R. Shamasastry. Mysore, India: Mysore Printing and Publishing, 1967. 8th ed. 494p.

A work on political philosophy, written in the 4th century BC, and of the highest importance for the study of Indian law and public administration, written by Kautilya, political advisor to India's first emperor, Chandragupta Maurya. The duties of kings, ministers, and other officials are explained in detail. Shamasastry describes the pre-eminence of the *Arthasastra* in India's secular literature and its influence on the development of later treatises on not only politics, but such disparate subjects as erotics, ethics, and poetics. Comparable in importance to Machiavelli's *The Prince*.

88 The culture and civilization of ancient India in historical outline.
Damodar Dharmanand Kosambi. New Delhi: Vikas, 1970. 243p. maps. bibliog.

A striking and thought-provoking study of Indian history until 500 AD. The author, a mathematician by training, utilizes a neo-Marxian and functionalist approach, combining history, archaeology and anthropology to provide a first-rate analysis of the formative period of India's civilization.

89 The imperial Guptas and their times: cir. A.D. 300-550.
Sachindra Kumar Maity. Delhi: Munshiram Manoharlal, 1975. 286p. bibliog.

The period of Gupta rulers has been popularly known as the Golden Age of Indian history, rivalling the Periclean age of Greece. Maity's comprehensive summary is among the latest, and takes into account recent discoveries of inscriptions, coins, and archaeological materials. The chapters in this volume are topical, and in addition to political history deal with public administration; social and economic life; religion; education; and literary, artistic, and cultural achievements.

90 Hindu colonies in the Far East.
Ramesh Chandra Majumdar. Calcutta: Firma KLM, 1963. 2nd ed. 280p. maps. bibliog.

A comprehensive discussion of the large-scale emigration of Indians to Southeast Asia from the 2nd century AD onwards. Majumdar reviews oral, literary, and artistic evidence to establish dates of principal Hindu and Hinduized dynasties in the Malay peninsula, Java, Bali, Champa, Kambuja and Thailand. The book integrates the political and cultural aspects of Hindu expansion.

91 Chandragupta Maurya and his times.
Radha Kumud Mookerji. Delhi: Motilal Banarsidass, 1966. 4th ed. 263p. bibliog.

A carefully researched analysis of the achievements of the first imperial dynasty in India. Based on Greek accounts and the testimony of a political treatise known as *Arthasastra* (q.v.), this book examines the Mauryan political system, social and economic policies, and military organization. Written in 1941, the evidence contained in this authoritative volume has been substantially supplemented by later research, but Mookerji's main conclusions have remained intact.

92 Foreign trade and commerce in ancient India.
Prakash Charan Prasad. New Delhi: Abhinav, 1977. 255p. maps. bibliog.

An erudite account of trade and commerce between India and the Near East, Greece, Rome, and the Far East. The history of cities which were *entrepots*, modes of transport and communication, media of exchange, commercial banking, and import-export organization are described in detail. The period covered is from the third millenium BC to the first century AD.

93 Encounters: the westerly trade of the Harappa civilization.
Shereen Ratnagar. Delhi: Oxford University Press, 1981.
292p. maps. bibliog.
A major contribution to Indian archaeology. In six chapters the author examines geographical scope, articles of trade, technologies of overland and sea transport, the significance of clay seals, and institutional organization of the urban Harappan civilization that flourished in the Indus basin between 2500 and 1500 BC. Recent archaeological discoveries which indicate a much larger territory within the confines of the Indus Valley civilization than previously assumed have been fully exploited by the author in documenting her views.

94 India and the Greek world: a study in the transmission of culture.
Jean W. Sedlar. Totawa, New Jersey: Rowman & Littlefield, 1980. 381p. maps. bibliog.
A work of great erudition, based on European-language sources, that surveys cultural contacts between the Indian and Greek world from ca. 400 BC to the 7th century AD when Islamic expansion in the west and barbarian invasions of India disrupted this intercourse. The author argues that Indian influences upon the Greeks were slight during the pre-Hellenic period but expanded tremendously thereafter. Among the topics discussed are Christian-Buddhist affinities, Krishna-Christ analogies, and neo-Platonism and Indian philosophical similarities.

95 Indian feudalism, c. A.D. 300-1200.
Ram Sharan Sharma. Delhi: Macmillan, 1980. 2nd ed. 265p. bibliog.
A survey of the political and economic aspects of feudalism in northern India between 300 and 1200 AD. Based on an examination of royal charters, the author traces the emergence of Indian feudalism to the Gupta and post-Gupta practice of giving land grants to Brahmans, temples, and monasteries. Later such grants came to be given to military vassals in appreciation of their services, leading to the assumption of revenue, judicial, and other administrative rights by the grant-holders. A competent study of a controversial subject.

96 Asoka and the decline of the Mauryas.
Romila Thapar. Delhi: Oxford University Press, 1973. 2nd ed. 285p. maps. bibliog.
A thorough reinterpretation of existing materials on the reign of Asoka, India's most beloved emperor, who gave India its first political unity in the 3rd century BC. Thapar critically examines sources for the history of Asoka, and the emperor's attitude toward Buddhism, the political philosophy of *Arthasastra* (q.v.), and the expansion of Indian cultural influences overseas. Included in the book are new translations of Asoka's rock, pillar, and copper edicts.

97 A history of India, volume 1.
Romila Thapar. Harmondsworth, England: Penguin, 1966. 381p. maps. bibliog.
A solid survey of the history of India from ancient times to the advent of the Mughals. Thapar's analysis of ancient and mediaeval history emphasizes economic

rather than religious factors, an interesting departure from the traditional approach to the writing of Indian history.

Period of Islamic domination

98 An intellectual history of Islam in India.
Aziz Ahmad. Chicago: Aldine, 1969. 226p. bibliog.
In nine brief chapters the author summarizes the intellectual history of almost nine centuries of Indian Islam. The first five describe its unity and variety - the orthodox, sectarian, mystical, legal, and classical movements. The discussion of folk movements and beliefs is noteworthy. Two chapters on literature, one on the arts, and one on education complete the book. It is the author's conclusion that Hinduism and Islam coexisted in India, without ever achieving a synthesis.

99 Akbar.
Laurence Binyon. New York: Nelson, 1939. 165p. maps. bibliog.
Written with the sensitivity of a poet and the scholarship of an orientalist, this is a vivid and convincing portrait of India's most popular Mughal emperor. Binyon deals with the multitude of contradictions in Akbar's personality and uses them to discuss the emperor's achievements as a warrior, constructive ruler, mystic, patron of the arts, and seeker of a syncretic universal religion of brotherhood. While other detailed biographies have become available, none is more readable than Binyon's.

100 Influence of Islam on Indian culture.
Tara Chand. Lahore: Book Traders, 1963. 1st Pakistani ed. 322p. bibliog.
Originally published in 1922. Promotes the thesis that during the era of Islamic political domination, an Indo-Muslim synthesis in religion, social customs, architecture and painting, and other arts took place, blending Hindu practices with Near Eastern and Central Asian traditions. Tara Chand examines the Islamic influence on Hindu religious reformers of south India, on mystics like Kabir, Guru Nanak, and other 16th-century saints, and on north Indian temple and court architecture.

101 The history of India as told by its own historians: the Muhammadan period.
Henry M. Elliot, John Dowson. New York: AMS, 1966. 8 vols. bibliog.
Originally published between 1867 and 1877, these are translations into English from the Persian and Arabic of Indo-Muslim historians and travellers who wrote between 850 and 1850 AD. Many of the texts are included in their entirety, others are excerpted. The indispensable worth of this collection is marred by Elliot's personal view that mediaeval Muslim society was morally inferior and its rulers were tyrants. For a detailed critique of this collection see Shahpurshah Hormasji Hodivala, *Studies in Indo-Muslim history: a critical commentary on*

History. Period of Islamic domination

Elliot and Dowson's 'History of India as told by its own historians' (Bombay: Popular, 1939-57. 2 vols.).

102 The great Moghuls.
Bamber Gascoigne. New York: Harper, 1971. 264p. maps. bibliog.

A magnificently illustrated digest of the contributions of the first six Mughal emperors of the 16th and 17th centuries. Gascoigne tells a great deal about the personal lives of these emperors, their contributions to arts and letters, architecture and city buildings, and above all their religious attitudes. The section on Akbar's religious synthesis is particularly illuminating. Much of the book's worth lies in its readability and its beautiful monochrome photographs.

103 An atlas of the Mughal empire.
Irfan Habib. New York: Oxford University Press, 1982. 120p. maps. bibliog.

The most detailed maps of South Asia in the 16th and 17th centuries. Each region of the subcontinent is covered by separate political and economic sheets. The political maps show district and state boundaries and include more than 4,000 place-names. The economic maps show geographical features and economic activities. Detailed bibliographic and explanatory notes accompany each map.

104 Cities of Mughul India.
Gavin Hambly, photographs by Wim Swaan. New Delhi: Vikas, 1977. 168p. maps. bibliog.

During the 16th and 17th centuries, the Mughals, at the zenith of their political and economic power, rebuilt the cities of Delhi, Agra, Fatehpur Sikri, and Lahore, to provide the setting for a brilliant court life, the envy of Europe. Hambly's lavishly illustrated volume shows patronage of the arts, urban and court life, and manners provided by the Great Mughals. The author's text also sheds considerable light on the daily life of the Mughal emperors and the members of their court.

105 Muslim civilization in India.
Sheikh Mohamad Ikram, edited by Ainslie T. Embree. New York: Columbia University Press, 1964. 325p. maps. bibliog.

It is not easy to write a history of the impact of the Muslims on the history of India (see comments under Kabir, *Indian heritage*, q.v.). Ikram has here written one of the best and most impartial surveys. He delineates carefully both the assimilative and the separatist tendencies in the Muslim encounter with India. The section on the Mughals is particularly illuminating. In the final part he concludes that the creation of Pakistan was inevitable because partial assimilation in India did not lead to a creative Indo-Muslim synthesis.

106 **Some aspects of religion and politics in India during the thirteenth century.**
Khaliq Ahmad Nizami. Delhi: Idarah-i Adabiyat-i Delli, 1974. 2nd ed. 421p. maps. bibliog.

A major contribution on the interaction between religion and politics in early mediaeval Muslim India. Nizami argues that Sufi mystics of the 13th century accepted royal favours in the hope that they could influence the kings for the good. Later the alliance between the princes and the saints broke down, leading to the dispersal of the Sufis. The book includes a balanced assessment of Sufi contributions to Indian culture and Hindu religious life.

107 **The Indian response to European technology and culture, A.D. 1498-1707.**
Ahsan Jan Qaisar. Delhi: Oxford University Press, 1982. 225p. bibliog.

Building on Irfan Habib's monographs on the social history of Indian technology, this book examines the Indian response to a wide variety of European technological devices in naval architecture, navigation, land transport, printing, chronometry, and glass-making. Qaisar also discusses the Indian response to European innovations in painting, architecture, music, food, costume, and marriage customs. There are twenty-four pages of carefully selected plates of drawings and miniatures.

108 **A short history of Aurangzib, 1618-1707.**
Jadunath Sarkar. New Delhi: Orient Longman, 1979. 426p. maps. bibliog.

Based on Sarkar's five-volume definitive study of the last of the Great Mughals, this abridged volume covers the campaigns that enabled the emperor to extend the frontiers of his empire to its largest extent on the one hand, but which sowed the seeds of rebellion and regional and local uprisings on the other. A few of the twenty chapters deal with Aurangzeb's personality, character traits, economic system and policies, and attitude towards the arts.

109 **The crescent in India: a study in medieval history.**
Shripad Sharma. Bombay: Hind Kitabs, 1966. 3rd rev. ed. 747p. maps. bibliog.

A magisterial survey of the history of Islamic religious and political influence on India from the 8th century to the fall of the Mughal empire in the 18th century. Chronological in organization, and generally concentrating on political history, the book has adequate coverage of the social and cultural contours of this period. The text has extensive quotations from contemporary observers and distinguished academic authorities. Sharma is sympathetic to those political rulers and religious leaders who sought accommodation with the Hindu majority.

Modern history

110 Conquest of violence: the Gandhian philosophy of conflict.
Joan Valerie Bondurant. Berkeley, California: University of California Press, 1967. rev. ed. 271p. bibliog.

An orderly exposition of Gandhian thought, the technique of *satyagraha* (popularly known as civil disobedience), and village-based democracy. This comprehensive and rigorously analytical volume also examines the relationship of Gandhian political philosophy to certain liberal and anarchistic strands in modern political thought. Bondurant concludes her brilliant book by examining the relevance of Gandhian techniques in a totalitarian setting.

111 Freedom at midnight.
Larry Collins, Dominique Lapierre. New York: Simon & Schuster, 1975. 572p. maps. bibliog.

A dramatic book about the eclipse of British rule and the birth of independent India. The emphasis is on the period from New Year's Day 1947, when Lord Mountbatten was chosen to be the last Crown proconsul in India, to February 1948, when Gandhi's ashes were dispersed in the Ganges - thirteen months of tumultuous transformation in India. The authors have added several introductory chapters to discuss politics and life in India before 1947. The portraits of Nehru, Gandhi, Jinnah, Mountbatten, and princely life are outstanding. The book is flawed, however, by its open partisanship for Mountbatten.

112 Peasant struggles in India.
Edited by Akshayakumar Ramanlal Desai. Bombay: Oxford University Press, 1979. 722p. bibliog.

India's nationalist movement, unlike China's, was not a peasant-based one, yet the Indian peasantry played a crucial, if not decisive, role in shaping the politics of India. In this volume, thirty-nine articles examine tribal and peasant struggles in India both before and after independence. This book's strength lies in bringing to light movements and events that are important but likely to be ignored as not meriting a full-length monograph.

113 Curzon in India.
David Dilks. New York: Taplinger, 1970. 2 vols. maps. bibliog.

A vivid and well-written biography of Lord Curzon, one of the greatest viceroys of India. Dilks brings out all of the complexities and dichotomies of Curzon's character: a person who loved India immensely, yet criticized its classical literature as useless; one who suppressed Indian nationalists, yet counselled the British government to extend to Indians the right to self-government; one who loved the company of Indian princes, yet considered them irrelevant to India's political future. The contribution of Curzon to archaeological investigations in India, to the growth of Indian education, and to other socio-economic measures is carefully documented.

114 India's search for national identity.
Ainslie T. Embree. Delhi: Chanakya, 1980. Indian ed.
144p. bibliog.

This is a skilful analysis of the relationship of the pattern of British administration to the evolution of India's national identity. The author suggests that the use of Hindu values and symbols by the Indian National Congress was responsible for the growth of Islamic separatism. Besides being one of the best introductions to the study of modern South Asia, this is an excellent book for those studying nationalist movements from a comparative perspective.

115 Land control and social structure in Indian history.
Edited by Robert Eric Frykenberg. New Delhi: Manohar,
1979. 1st rev. Indian ed. 277p. bibliog.

Indian land tenures and related socio-political structures, dominated by caste groups, have been vastly different from those encountered in the west. This volume describes and analyses the diverse landholding and social structures in various parts of India prior to the British conquest and the changes introduced by the British in the 19th century. Frykenberg's masterly introduction is followed by three case studies from north India, three from south India, and four broad-based essays.

116 Political ideas and movements in India.
Sankar Ghose. Bombay: Allied, 1975. 558p. bibliog.

A well-written survey of socio-political ideas and ideologies that have shaped Indian history during the last one hundred years. Ghose examines the early bipolarity between the extremists and the moderates, the Gandhian synthesis transcending them both, socialist and communal challenges to Gandhian non-violence and secularism, and the eventual partition of the subcontinent along communal lines. The author argues that the legacy of these earlier events continues to shape the contemporary Indian struggle to maintain a centrally planned, parliamentary, social democratic government in the face of regional, communal, radical communist, ultraconservative religious, and extreme free-enterprise challenges.

117 Sirajuddaullah and the East India Company, 1756-1757: background to the foundation of British power in India.
Brijen K. Gupta. London: Brill, 1966. 2nd ed. 172p. maps.
bibliog.

A rigorously researched analytical study of the mid-18th century watershed in Indian history. The author points out that Clive's victory at Plassey in 1757 had a profound effect on the future course of Indian history and politics. Not only did it mark the beginning of the British empire in India, but it also altered Indo-European economic relations causing capital to flow from India to the west for the first time. Included is a thorough examination of the Black Hole incident of 1757.

118 The Muslims of British India.
Peter Hardy. New York: Cambridge University Press,
1972. 306p. maps. bibliog.

A detailed picture of the Muslim community of India in recent times, this book complements Embree's study (q.v.). Muslim reaction to the impact of British rule is carefully surveyed. The last chapter on India's partition is particularly good and is more balanced than Embree's presentation.

119 Nationalism and communal politics in India.
Mushirul Hasan. Delhi: Manohar, 1979. 372p. bibliog.

A carefully researched study of the alliance between Muslim organizations and the Indian nationalist movement, and the eventual disintegration of the alliance between 1916 and 1928. The study focuses on three provinces - Bengal, Punjab, and the United Provinces -and shows that the Muslim response to nationalism differed from province to province depending on their socio-economic conditions. Hasan finds the all-India nationalist leadership to be élitist and unconcerned with local and provincial issues.

120 The great divide: Britain, India, Pakistan.
Henry Vincent Hodson. New York: Atheneum, 1971. 563p. maps. bibliog.

A study of the simultaneous breach between Britain and its Indian empire, and between Pakistan and India. Much of the book is devoted to the five-year period 1942-1947, and is based on the private papers of leading British participants in the drama of independence and partition such as Sir Stafford Cripps, Lord Mountbatten, Lord Ismay and V. P. Menon.

121 People, princes and paramount power.
Edited by Robin Jeffrey. Delhi: Oxford University Press, 1978. 396p. maps. bibliog.

Twelve essays examine the interaction between the princes of India, their native subjects, and the British overlords, before the integration of the princely states into the Indian Union. Taken as a whole these essays shed considerable light on why nationalism developed so slowly in these states. Topical essays deal with the causes and consequences of bureaucratic modernization in Baroda (by David Hardiman), in Travancore (by Robin Jeffrey), in Alwar (by Edward Haynes) and Hyderabad (by Karen Leonard), religious forces in and around the princely states of Punjab (by Barbara Ramusack), and the cause of the demise of the princely order in Mewar (by Rajat Ray) and Rajkot (by John Wood).

122 Nationalism on the Indian sub-continent: an introductory history.
Jim Masselos. Melbourne, Australia: Thomas Nelson, 1972. 227p. maps. bibliog.

A convenient summary of the history of Indian nationalism and the impact of British rule in India. The author's main thesis is that imperialism and imperial institutions inevitably sowed the seeds of nationalism. Communalism and other divisive forces in modern Indian history are covered.

123 Story of the integration of Indian states.
Vapal P. Menon. New York: Arno, 1972. 511p. maps. bibliog.

A carefully documented study of the integration of over 500 quasi-autonomous princely states into the Republic of India, written by a civil servant who played a key role in bringing about this integration. In addition, the author carefully analyses the causes of the Indo-Pakistan dispute over the integration of Kashmir into India and also provides in-depth documentation of the role of the Indian deputy prime minister, Sardar Patel, in obtaining this integration with all possible speed. Unfortunately Menon has very little to say about the viewpoint of those princes who felt victimized by Patel's high-handedness. Originally published in 1956.

124 The Indian political parties: a historical analysis of political behaviour up to 1947.
Bankey Bihari Misra. Delhi: Oxford University Press, 1976. 665p. bibliog.

An analysis of the framework within which political parties evolved and operated in India between 1905 and 1947. Several chapters are devoted to the behaviour of these parties in provincial and federal legislative bodies, and others to the development of party ideologies. Misra argues that the primary goal of these parties was to obtain power, and that ideologies were always subservient to that goal.

125 The break-up of British India.
Bishwa Nath Pandey. Delhi: Macmillan, 1981. reprint of 1969 ed. 248p. maps. bibliog.

This survey is primarily a study of the causes of the partition of the Indian subcontinent in 1947. It examines the social and religious movements of the 19th and 20th centuries, their role in fuelling nationalism, the origins of Muslim separatism, and the struggle of Gandhian nationalists against both imperialism and communalism.

126 The partition of India: policies and perspectives, 1935-1947.
Edited by Cyril Henry Philips, Mary Doreen Wainwright. London: Allen & Unwin, 1970. 607p. bibliog.

The factors and personalities responsible for the 1947 partition of British India into the states of India and Pakistan are examined in this indispensable volume. The papers include contributions by specialists in modern Indian history, by journalists and other observers who covered the events of the period for the press, and by political notables who played secondary, yet important, roles in the politics of the day. Many of the authors had access to hitherto unpublished, and often confidential, papers of the primary actors in the events of the 1935-47 period, making their essays both durable and authentic.

127 The story of integration.
Vanaja Rangaswami. Delhi: Manohar, 1981. 392p. bibliog.

Contradicting the usual rosy picture of the integration of the princely states in the Indian Union, the author charges that the interests of the citizens of the states of Mysore, Travancore and Cochin, especially in areas such as government employment and civil liberties, were subordinated to the larger interests of the Congress Party. Rangaswami argues her case strongly with a wealth of detail and a massive bibliography.

128 **The emergence of Indian nationalism: competition and collaboration in the later nineteenth century.**
Anil Seal. London: Cambridge University Press, 1968.
416p. maps. bibliog.

A significant contribution to the understanding of the embryonic phase of Indian nationalism. Seal examines the special roots of élite groups in both the British administration and Indian national politics, and finds that both these groups, while maintaining a façade of powerfulness, were really engaged in shadow-boxing. The book has very little to say about the progressive nature of British rule (which the rulers claimed) or its harsh political effects (which the nationalists opposed).

129 **Dictionary of national biography.**
Edited by Siba Pada Sen. Calcutta: Institute of Historical Studies, 1972-74. 4 vols.

This dictionary covers the period 1800-1947, and includes over 1,300 biographical sketches of persons from various walks of life, written by 350 contributors. Persons from areas now part of Pakistan and Bangladesh have also been included. At the end of each entry is a select bibliography for further research. The most commonly used English spelling for a given surname determines the alphabetical order of the entries - the 'rational manner' in the view of the editor. Subsequent supplements, the first of which will cover the twenty-five years after independence, will include only persons living in what is now India.

130 **Eighteen fifty-seven.**
Surendra Nath Sen. Delhi: Publications Division, Ministry of Information and Broadcasting, 1958. 468p. maps. bibliog.

This carefully researched, well-written account, issued by the government of India on the centennial of the Great Revolt of 1857, presents the orthodox nationalist viewpoint on the causes, extent, and significance of the Sepoy uprisings. One school of thought sees this rebellion as the last-ditch stand to restore princely rule, anachronistic social traditions, and pre-commercial society, the other as the first serious attempt to shake off gradual European domination. Sen maintains a delicate balance between the two viewpoints, yet suggests 1857 was an important nationalist watershed. For a more popular account, see Richard Collier, *The great Indian mutiny: a dramatic account of the Sepoy rebellion* (New York: Dutton, 1964. 384p. maps. bibliog.).

131 **The Nabobs: a study of the social life of the English in eighteenth century India.**
Thomas George Percival Spear. London: Curzon, 1980.
213p. bibliog.

A book of rare beauty, this work examines the metamorphosis in the social life of the English in India in the 18th century. Spear points out that the cosmopolitanism of the English residents of India in the mid-18th century, when both the foreigners and upper-class Indians had social intercourse with each other and adopted each other's manners, gave way to a splendid isolation in the late 18th century, with foreigners assuming the role of master race. This change in social attitude was the result of the collapse of Indian political authority and the emergence of British control in various parts of India.

132 **English utilitarians and India.**
Eric Stokes.   Oxford, England: Clarendon, 1963. 350p.
bibliog.
A critical examination of the impact of utilitarian trends, both liberal and
authoritarian, in England on the British administration in India. Stokes examines
the role of James Mill, his utilitarian interpretation of Indian history, and his
'minutes' on Indian affairs as an India Office functionary; the dispatches of
Charles Wood; the educational and legal minutes of Macaulay; and, above all,
the climactic role of Sir James Fitzjames Stephen in shaping utilitarian administrative policies.

Historians and historiography

133 **Historiography in Indian languages.**
Edited by J. P. DeSouza, C. M. Kulkarni.   Delhi: Oriental,
1972. 275p. bibliog.
A study of historical sources in Indian languages. Twenty-three essays survey
historical writings in Bengali, Gujarati, Kannada, Malayalam, Marathi, Punjabi,
Tamil and Telugu, and supplement the four essays on Bengali, Hindi, Marathi,
and Urdu sources contained in Philips' *Historians of India, Pakistan, and Ceylon*
(q.v.). Coverage includes both epigraphical and literary sources, and national as
well as regional history. There are four essays discussing research in progress and
areas worthy of future investigation.

134 **Historiography in modern India.**
Ramesh Chandra Majumdar.   Bombay: Asia, 1970. 61p.
bibliog.
A broad, yet incisive, essay on historians of India. Majumdar argues that 18th-
century British historians of India were biased against the Hindus and India's
pre-Islamic history. With Sir William Jones, ancient Indian history began to be
taken in earnest, helped in part by German and Russian studies of Indian religion. According to the author, the direct and not-so-direct attempts of the present
government of India to support a nationalist and secular view of Indian history is
as pernicious to the growth of Indian historiography as was the imperial bias in
the early stages of Indian historical investigations.

135 **Ancient historians of India: a study in historical biographies.**
Vishwambhar Sharan Pathak.   Bombay: Asia, 1966. 184p.
bibliog.
This thorough analysis of ancient Indian historiography and of four early mediaeval texts throws new light on the traditional Indian historical mentality and
suggests new ways to reconstruct India's mediaeval past. The author argues that
to write the history of the past, modern historians must understand the ancient
and mediaeval worlds in their own terms without imposing contemporary modern
values.

136 **Historians of India, Pakistan and Ceylon.**
Edited by Cyril Henry Philips. New York: Oxford
University Press, 1961. 504p. bibliog.

A comprehensive and critical assessment of the various historical writings that have been published since antiquity, but especially during the last four centuries. There are essays on historians of different nationalities such as Portuguese, Dutch and Danish. Other essays deal with such principal authorities as Kalhana, Mill, Elphinstone, and Moreland. There are four essays on regional language materials in Hindi, Urdu, Bengali, and Marathi. At least one essay examines western and Indian historians writing on ancient India.

137 **Survey of Indian historiography: mediaeval period.**
Jagdish Narayan Sarkar. Calcutta: Jadavpur University
[n.d.]. 81p. bibliog.

A brilliant essay on gradual changes in the study of the history of mediaeval India (1000-1757 AD). The author traces the utilitarian roots of early British historians who studied this period, the efflorescence and maturity of Indian scholarship during th 1940s, the development of liberal-national-secular and separatist schools during the last thirty years, and the emergence of 'sociological' studies of recent years. A well-annotated critical bibliography follows the text.

138 **Historians and historiography in modern India.**
Edited by Siba Pada Sen. Calcutta: Institute of Historical
Studies, 1973. 464p. bibliog.

Forty essays assessing the work of eminent historians of India - thirty-three Indian and seven European - give a full account of the development of Indian historiography from the mid-19th to the mid-20th century. Special emphasis is placed on the work of the 19th-century pioneers and their influence on 20th-century historians. Papers are grouped in four categories: ancient, mediaeval, modern, and regional (Maharashtra, Gujarat, Rajasthan, and Punjab). An admirable survey.

139 **Sources of the history of India.**
Edited by Siba Pada Sen. Calcutta: Institute of Historical
Studies, 1978-80. 3 vols. bibliog.

A thorough description and analysis of archaeological, epigraphic, numismatic, and written records covering ancient, mediaeval, and modern periods of regional and national Indian history, with contributions by distinguished historians. The first volume covers Karnataka, Andhra Pradesh, Maharashtra, and Goa; the second, Rajasthan, Haryana, Meghalaya, Uttar Pradesh, and Jammu and Kashmir, and the third, Assam, Sikkim, and Tamil Nadu. Each section deals with the extent and dependability of the different categories of source materials and the extent to which they have been utilized.

140 **A bibliography of Mughal India (1526-1707 A.D.).**
Sri Ram Sharma. Philadelphia: Porcupine Press, 1977.
reprint of 1938 ed. 206p. bibliog.

A careful survey of original sources for the study of Mughal India. Sharma groups these sources into twelve categories: official records, official histories, royal autobiographies, non-official histories, provincial or local histories, biographies and memoirs, gazetteers, private letter books, administrative manuals, literary works, foreign accounts, and archaeological, epigraphic, and numismatic evidence. It should be supplemented with D. N. Marshall, *Mughals in India: a bibliographical survey, volume 1: manuscripts* (Bombay: Asia, 1967. 634p.), a detailed survey of manuscripts in various languages bearing on Mughal history.

141 On historiography.
Shripad Ramachandra Tikekar. Bombay: Popular, 1964. 79p. bibliog.

A study of the research of three eminent Indian historians: Jadunath Sarkar, G. S. Sardesai, and P. K. Gode. Tikekar carefully reviews the attacks made upon Sarkar and Sardesai by the Poona group of the Maratha biographers who could not accept any unflattering criticism of Maratha history. He considers Gode to be a different type of historian, who wrote about 475 papers, very few of them of great individual significance but taken as a whole representing meticulous research in Indian chronology.

Population and Family Planning

142 **Population control in India: policy - administration - spread.**
A. P. Barnabas. New Delhi: Indian Institute of Public
Administration, 1977. 121p. bibliog.
An overview of population control programmes and policies of the Indian government since 1947, the book describes and discusses the relationship between demographic growth and economic development. The author faults India's socially
unresponsive bureaucracy for its failure to have a successful family planning
programme.

143 **Family planning in India: diffusion and policy.**
Piers M. Blaikie. London: Arnold, 1975. 162p. bibliog.
A fresh look at India's family planning programme in the context of spatial
diffusion theory and its use in policy-making. Blaikie argues that Indian family
planners suffer from two handicaps - a geographical bias due to uneven demographic data from various regions, and inaccurate information on the rate of
'innovation-adaptation' in family planning in rural India. The author argues that
unless the social advantages of a large family are reduced, small family norms
will not become widely accepted.

144 **India: population, economy, society.**
Robert H. Cassen. New York: Holmes & Meier, 1978.
419p. bibliog.
A fascinating and comprehensive study of India's population and its impact on
the nation's economy and society. Following a brief introductory chapter, the
second chapter looks at present and future characteristics of India's population -
fertility, mortality, and migration; the third deals with current and projected
family planning programmes. In the fourth chapter there is a lively discussion of
interrelationships between economic development and population change. The last
chapter includes reflections on the problems associated with population growth
both in India and China. A useful glossary of demographic terms is provided.

145 **Abortion in a crowded world: the problem of abortion with special reference to India.**
S. Chandrasekhar. Seattle, Washington: University of Washington Press, 1974. 184p. bibliog.

Written by India's foremost demographer, this book deals with the controversial issue of abortion, its social, ethical, psychological and demographic implications in the context of India's burgeoning population. Chandrasekhar's evaluation of this emotional topic is infused with his concern for enhancing the quality of human life in India.

146 **Human fertility in India: social components and policy perspectives.**
David G. Mandelbaum. Berkeley, California: University of California Press, 1974. 132p. bibliog.

A book of uneven quality but rich in data. The first part has an excellent discussion of how social and cultural factors and traditional methods of birth control have affected human fertility in India. The second part deals with the problems of fertility but fails to provide any analytical perspective on these problems.

147 **India's population: aspects of quality and control.**
Asok Mitra. New Delhi: Abhinav, 1978. 2 vols. bibliog.

The work's central thesis is that effective population control requires commitment to an enhanced quality of life rather than high economic growth rates or great material prosperity. Low infant mortality, female literacy, and employment opportunities outside the home can all be accomplished within prevailing economic constraints. However, it is imperative that there be a concerted effort to mount effective land reforms so that gross inequalities are eliminated and scarce capital is freed for necessary investments in social overheads. Mitra blames both the bureaucracy and the intelligentsia for thwarting the required democratic decentralization along socialist lines. The work is a mine of information.

148 **Census of India 1971: series 1, India.**
Office of the Registrar General. Delhi: Manager of Publications, 1972-75. 3 vols. maps. tables.

Three papers summarize some of the key data from the 1971 census. *Paper 1 of 1972: final population* gives population figures for the country, states, districts, subdivisions, police stations, development blocks, and towns. It also gives the population of scheduled castes and scheduled tribes. *Paper 2 of 1972: religion* gives the distribution of population by major religions, broken down for each district and each city with a population of 100,000 and above. *Paper 3 of 1972: economic characteristics of population* gives the educational characteristics of India based on sample surveys, and the distribution of population by nine broad industrial categories of workers, and cross-classified by eight broad age groups.

149 **Population Review.**
Madras: Indian Institute of Population Studies, 1957- . biannual.

Edited by the famous Indian demographer S. Chandrasekhar, this biannual contains articles on population problems, family planning, birth control, and other

Population and Family Planning

demographic issues in non-technical language for the informed public. Emphasis is on India and Asia.

150 Dynamics of population and family welfare in India.
Edited by K. Srinivasan, S. Mukerji. Bombay: Popular, 1979. 339p. bibliog.

A collection of sixteen essays divided into three groups: general studies in population dynamics; special groups; and studies on family welfare. Several essays in the volume merit serious attention: Mukerji's essay on the application of linear programming for estimating migration rates to urban areas, Sebastian's paper on demographic micro-simulation models, Pathak's study on the acceptance of sterilization in rural India, and Srivastava's essay on fertility differentials among Hindu and Muslim women.

151 India's population: second and growing.
Pravin Visaria, Leela Visaria. Washington, DC: Population Reference Bureau, 1981. 56p.

An overview of India's population problems, written by a World Bank demographer and his wife. The booklet provides a clear description and analysis of India's population problem followed by a discussion of the impact of population growth on India's social and economic development. The book features a description of the government of India's compulsory sterilization policies aimed at achieving a 2.5 per cent birth rate by 1984.

Languages

Grammars

152 A grammar of the Oriya language.
A. Andersen. Copenhagen: Danish Missionary Society, 1959. 134p.

A descriptive grammar for the beginner. The volume has seven parts: letters and phonetics, parts of speech and inflexion, formation of words, syntax, the verb, the sentence, and indeclinables. Examples with translation follow each section. Oriya script is used throughout; no transliteration except in the introductory section.

153 A progressive grammar of the Tamil language.
Albert Henry Arden, revised by A. C. Clayton. Madras: Christian Literature Society, 1976. 5th rev. ed. 342p. bibliog.

Traditional grammar with an introductory section on the chief characteristics of the Dravidian languages. The section on grammar deals with rules governing Tamil alphabet and orthography, parts of speech, verbal constructions, colloquialisms, and foreign words. Appendixes contain grammatical terms, calendar names, and a bibliography.

154 A progressive grammar of the Telugu language.
Albert Henry Arden, revised by F. L. Marler. Madras: Christian Literature Society, 1955. 475p. bibliog.

A pedagogical and reference grammar. The first part deals with the colloquial language and contains an introduction to the alphabet, reading and translation exercises, and model sentences. The second part deals with the parts of speech, types of sentences, and exercises. The third part deals with the literary language. *A companion Telugu reader* is appended to the grammar.

Languages. Grammars

155 A Marathi reference grammar.
Maxine Berntsen, Jai Nimbkar. Philadelphia: University of Pennsylvania, South Asia Regional Studies, 1975. 206p.
Prepared originally for American Peace Corps volunteers, this is a carefully designed volume setting forth the basic grammatical rules of Marathi. The introductory chapters deal with the Marathi sound system and the Devanagari script, and are followed by a discussion of the parts of speech. Sentence structures, unary and binary transformations, and work derivatives are explained in detail with morphophonemic rules. Roman and Marathi scripts are used.

156 A Gujarati reference grammar.
George Cardona. Philadelphia: University of Pennsylvania Press, 1965. 188p. bibliog.
Traditional reference grammar, structural in approach. Most of the book discusses phonology and the nominal and verbal systems of Gujarati. Later chapters deal with morphophonemics, the writing system, composition, derivation, and syntax. Examples follow items described.

157 The Sindhi language.
Raisa Petrovna Egorova. Moscow: Nauka, 1971. 162p.
An introduction to both the language and its grammar. The grammatical section includes phonology, morphology, and syntax. Perso-Arabic script and Romanized transcription are utilized throughout the text.

158 A progressive grammar of the Malayalam language.
Ludwig Johannes Fröhnmeyer. New Delhi: Asian Educational Services, 1979. 2nd rev. ed. 366p.
Originally published in 1913, this is a pedagogical and reference grammar. There are twenty-one lessons dealing with the alphabet, parts of speech, and sentence structure, all accompanied by graded exercises. The appendixes have examples of 'Malayalisms' and foreign words in the Malayalam language. All Malayalam material is in the Malayalee script.

159 Pali literature and language.
Wilhelm Geiger, translated by Batakrishna Ghosh. Delhi: Oriental Books Reprint Corp., 1968. 2nd ed. 250p.
A pedagogical and reference grammar. Part 1 has a short history of the Pali literary tradition, including both canonical and secular literature. The section on grammar deals with phonology, word formation, parts of speech, and thematic and athematic conjugation. Romanized transliteration is used throughout. The German edition was published in 1916.

160 A reference grammar of Punjabi.
Harjeet Singh Gill, Henry A. Gleason. Patiala, India: Department of Linguistics, Punjabi University, 1969. rev. ed. 157p.
A standard grammar of modern spoken and written Punjabi. The introductory section discusses the history of the language and earlier grammars. In the phonology section, the Punjabi language is compared to Hindi and other northern lan-

guages. The chapters on morphology and syntax discuss parts of speech, verbs, clauses, and inflexion. The final chapter is designed to teach sentence sequencing. Phonemic transcription is used throughout.

161 A reference grammar of Kashmiri.
Braj B. Kachru.   Urbana, Illinois: Department of
Linguistics, University of Illinois, 1969. 416p. bibliog.
Pedagogically oriented, introductory reference manual of Kashmiri. The introductory section deals with the origin of the Kashmiri writing system and the emergence of the Kashmiri literary tradition. Other chapters deal with phonology; word formation; word classes; noun, verb, and adverbial phrases; and sentence types. Appendixes include Kashmiri-English and English-Kashmiri glossaries.

162 Outline of Hindi grammar with exercises.
Ronald Stuart McGregor.   London: Oxford University
Press, 1977. 2nd ed. 230p. bibliog.
Traditional pedagogical and reference grammar for post-beginners. Chapters deal with nominal forms, verbs, post positions, adverbs, conjunctions, rules of *sandhi* (coalescence of final and initial letters of words), and formation of words. There are twenty-six lessons with associated vocabulary and translation exercises. Key to exercises.

163 A Sanskrit grammar for beginners in Devanagri and Roman letters throughout.
F. Max Müller.   New Delhi: Asian Publication Services, 1975. 2nd ed., rev. 300p. bibliog.
A pedagogical grammar, first published in 1866. Its superiority over other grammars in English lies in its extensive yet simplified discussion of rules of *sandhi*, declension, and conjugation. There are the usual sections on the parts of speech, verbs, tenses, compound words, and numerals. One appendix contains a list of verbs and another covers the accent in Sanskrit. An equally enduring grammar is Edward Delavan Perry's *A Sanskrit primer* (New York: Columbia University Press, 1977. 230p.), originally issued in 1885. Both these volumes use Devanagari script throughout.

164 Comparative grammar of the Prakrit languages.
Richard Pischel, translated from the German by Subhadra Jha.   Delhi: Motilal Banarsidass, 1981. 653p. bibliog.
First published in German in 1900, this reference grammar remains the most elaborate on the Prakrit languages. There is a long introduction on the history of these languages and early Prakrit grammarians. This is followed by grammatical rules dealing with sonants, vowels and consonants, and parts of speech. There is an extensive index of Prakrit words. Roman transliteration is used throughout.

165 A grammar of the Hindustani or Urdu language.
John Thompson Platts.   Delhi: Munshiram Manoharlal, 1969. reprint of 1884 ed. 399p.
A grammar that has endured since its first publication in 1870. The first part provides a short description of the orthographic system, with examples in the Arabic-Persian script, transliteration and translation. Part two covers the parts of

speech, and part three covers syntax. Examples are generally in the paradigm form.

166 A reference grammar of Bengali.
Punya Sloka Ray. Chicago: University of Chicago Press, 1966. 2 vols.

A descriptive but authoritative grammar. Introductory chapters deal with general and historical backgrounds and an outline of the history of the Bengali language. Later chapters deal with phonology, morphology, literary and colloquial language, Bengali metre, and a sketch of the Assamese language.

167 A Kanarese grammar with graduated exercises.
Harold Spencer. Mysore, India: Wesley Press, 1950. 2nd rev. ed. 452p.

Originally issued in 1914, this is a well-established pedagogical grammar with translation exercises and vocabulary lists. There are forty-six lessons. All Kanarese materials are in the standard orthography except in the first two introductory lessons where Roman transcription is included side by side. Appendixes include vocabularies, irregular verb lists, and an index in English.

Dictionaries

168 Candrakanta abhidhana: a comprehensive dictionary of the Assamese language.
Edited by M. K. Barua. Gauhati, India: Gauhati University, 1964. 2nd ed. 1,045p.

A comprehensive dictionary of the Assamese language with etymology of words and their English and Assamese equivalents. Parts of speech indicated. Illustrative sentences.

169 Bhargava's standard illustrated dictionary of the Hindi language: Hindi-English edition.
Varanasi, India: Bhargava Book Depot, 1980. rev. enl. ed. 1,280p.

Lists over 100,000 Hindi words. Though usage is not indicated for the words included, this is the best dictionary available for the purpose. Parts of speech and guides to pronunciation and grammar are included. Numerous topical appendixes.

170 English-Tamil dictionary.
Edited by A. Chidambaranatha Chettiar. Madras: University of Madras, 1965. 1,223p.

A comprehensive dictionary. Parts of speech and levels of usage are indicated. Grammatical information is provided.

171 **Marathi-English dictionary.**
Compiled by Madhav Kashinath Deshpande. Poona, India:
Suvichar Prakashan Mandal, 1979. 2nd rev. ed. 604p.

One of many standard desk dictionaries, this volume contains 26,000 words. It is
based on J. T. Molesworth *et al, Dictionary of Marathi and English*, originally
published in 1831. Parts of speech are indicated. Etymological information and
levels of usage provided.

172 **A Malayalam and English dictionary.**
Compiled by Hermann Gündert. Osnabruck, GFR: Biblio
Verlag, 1970. 2 vols.

Originally published in 1872. Entries include parts of speech, levels of usage,
cross-entries, grammatical information, and word roots. Malayalam script and
Roman transliteration used throughout.

173 **Kittel's Kannada-English dictionary.**
Ferdinand Kittel, revised and enlarged by M. Mariappa
Bhat. Madras: University of Madras, 1968-69. 4 vols.

One of the most exhaustive and useful dictionaries of ancient and modern Kannada words. The introduction traces the history of Kannada lexicography. It
includes parts of speech, pronunciation, grammatical information, and literary
references. Extensive directions for the use of the dictionary are included. Originally published in 1894.

174 **People's own dictionary: English to Bengali and Bengali to
English.**
Edited by A. S. Mahmud, compiled by M.
Quamruzzaman. Dacca: Academic Publishers, 1971.
1,665p.

A comprehensive dictionary. Numerous appendixes include proverbs, biographies,
and trade and financial information. Grammatical information and levels of usage
indicated.

175 **The modern Gujarati-English dictionary.**
Compiled by Bhansukhram Nirgunram Mehta, Bharatram
Bhansukhram Mehta. Baroda, India: M. C. Kothari, 1925.
2 vols.

One of the better standard Gujarati-English dictionaries. Etymology of words,
idioms, proverbs, quotations, botanical and other technical terms are included.
Entries include parts of speech, levels of usage, and illustrative phrases.

176 **Student's diamond dictionary of words, phrases, and idioms: Anglo-Oriya.**
Compiled by Jagan Mohan Patnaik, edited by Girija Sankar Ray. Cuttack, India: Cuttack Publishing House, 1962-64. 2 vols.
A comprehensive dictionary. Entries include parts of speech, levels of usage, and illustrative phrases. Numerous topical appendixes.

177 **A dictionary of Urdu, classical Hindi, and English.**
John T. Platts. New Delhi: Oriental Books Reprint Corp., 1977. reprint. 1,259p.
Originally published in 1884 and frequently reprinted, Platts' dictionary continues to be the best available for working with classical, and especially courtly, Urdu. Entry words are preceded by an initial code letter to indicate the language to which the word belongs (i.e. S = Sanskrit, P = Persian). Entries include etymological information.

178 **Pali-English dictionary.**
Edited by T. W. Rhys Davids, William Stede. New Delhi: Oriental Books Reprint Corp., 1975. 738p. bibliog.
Originally published in 1921 and reprinted several times in both India and Britain, this is the standard dictionary of Pali words, their etymology, uses, and English equivalents. Over 160,000 entries.

179 **Telugu-English dictionary.**
Paluri Sankaranarayana. Madras: V. Ramaswamy Sastrulu, 1967. rev. enl. ed. 1,606p.
Originally published in 1900, and revised and enlarged frequently. Telugu script is used throughout. Entries include parts of speech, levels of usage, and grammatical information. Copious English synonyms and definitions of technical terms are included.

180 **The Punjabi dictionary.**
Compiled and edited by Maya Singh. Patiala, India: Language Department, Punjabi University, 1972. 1,221p.
Originally published in 1895 and thoroughly revised in 1961, this is the standard Punjabi (Gurumukhi) to English dictionary. Words are given in Romanized form as well as in the Gurumukhi script. Both the etymology of the word and its various usages are clearly explained.

181 **Sanskrit-English dictionary: etymologically and philologically arranged with special reference to cognate Indo-European languages.**
Monier Monier Williams. Oxford, England: Clarendon, 1976. new ed. 1,333p.
The best one-volume dictionary of the Sanskrit language, with over 180,000 words. It is based on the definitive seven-volume *Sanskrit-Wörterbuch*, compiled

and published by Otto von Böhtlingk between 1858 and 1877, and revised by Ernst Leumann and Carl Cappeller.

Religion

Buddhism

182 The Buddha and his dharma.
Bhimrao Ramji Ambedkar. Bombay: Siddharth, 1974. 2nd ed. 430p. bibliog.

An unusual interpretation of the teachings of the Buddha, espoused by the leaders of the 'untouchables' in India who have led the movement for their conversion to Buddhism. Ambedkar's view is considerably different from both the Hinayana and Mahayana interpretations, but it has, nevertheless, led to the acceptance of neo-Buddhism by millions of India's downtrodden. The extent of Ambedkar's influence is examined in Eleanor Zelliot, *Dr. Ambedkar and the Mahar movement* (Philadelphia: University of Pennsylvania Press, 1969. 304p. bibliog), a well-documented study of the mass conversion of the untouchables to Buddhism and its political ramifications.

183 2500 years of Buddhism.
Edited by Purushottam Vishvanath Bapat. Delhi: Publications Division, Ministry of Information and Broadcasting, 1976. reprint of 1956 ed. 439p. map. bibliog.

A collection of essays, mostly by Indian scholars, on many aspects of Buddhism including its origin, the Buddha's life and teachings, the early councils, the role of Emperor Asoka in the expansion of Buddhism, the principal schools and sects, Buddhist literature, and art. There is a useful glossary and a good bibliography.

184 The Buddhist experience: sources and interpretations.
Stephen Beyer. Encino, California: Dickenson, 1974. 274p. bibliog.

Translations from all major Buddhist traditions, including cultic and popular materials. A companion volume to Richard Robinson (q.v.). The texts, which are organized into the divisions of *sila* (virtue), *samadhi* (meditation), and *prajna* (wisdom), give a first-hand account of all aspects of the Buddhist path. Sections on worship and the magical use of charms and 'visualization' (a special Buddhist meditation technique requiring visualization of the Buddha) add to the work. Two other equally competent anthologies are Edward Conze, *Buddhist texts through the ages* (New York: Philosophical Library, 1954. 300p. bibliog.) and Henry Clarke Warren, *Buddhism in translations* (Cambridge, Massachusetts: Harvard University Press, 1953. 496p. bibliog.).

185 Buddhist parables: translated from the original Pali.
Eugene Watson Burlingame. Ann Arbor, Michigan: University Microfilms, 1980. reprint of 1922 ed. 348p. bibliog.

A fine anthology of important parables that encapsulate the basic doctrines of Buddhism. The parables are translated from earlier Pali and later Prakrit and Sanskrit texts. Burlingame provides European parallels to many of the parables.

186 The teachings of the compassionate Buddha.
Edited by Edwin Arthur Burtt. New York: New American Library, 1963. 247p. bibliog.

A fine first book on the Buddha and his teachings. The selection from Buddhist texts emphasizes the fundamentals of the religion, and not the major aspects of Buddhist scholastic philosophy. A short introductory essay describes the essentials of the Buddha's life and his message. Good for both secondary school and college students.

187 Buddhism: its essence and development.
Edward Conze. New York: Harper, 1975. reprint of 1951 ed. 212p. bibliog.

A popular and reliable introduction by one of the most respected scholars in the field. The author traces the major doctrinal developments in Buddhism from its origins to the Tantric period. The opening forty pages are especially helpful for the general reader because in them the author places Buddhism within the context of world religions, and he specifically addresses such usually disregarded questions as 'Is Buddhism atheistic?'. The work concludes with a handy seven-page chronological chart of major dates and events in Buddhist history. Though complex for the beginner, it can be read profitably after Rahula (q.v.) and Robinson (q.v.).

188 Buddhist meditation.
Edward Conze. New York: Harper, 1975. reprint of 1956 ed. 183p. bibliog.

An outstanding collection from Pali, Sanskrit and Tibetan sources. Conze provides an explanation of Buddhist meditation, its range, its chief literary documents, and its relation to modern psychology.

189 The Buddhist tradition in India, China and Japan.
Edited by William T. de Bary. New York: Vintage Books, 1969. 417p. bibliog.

A comprehensive anthology of selections from Indian, Chinese, and Japanese Buddhist materials. Excerpts have been taken from the basic scriptures and from the writings of major Buddhist philosophers, with the editor's commentaries. For the most part the texts included are recognized by Buddhist scholars as representing the mainstream of their religion.

190 **Buddhist monks and missionaries in India.**
Sukumar Dutt. London: Allen & Unwin, 1962. 397p. bibliog.

A thorough and definitive study of the Buddhist monastic community (*sangha*) in ancient India. Dutt traces the growth of the *sangha* from its earliest days and establishes its connection with the tradition of *sanyasins* (wandering ascetics) of India. Included is a history of the rise and fall of the great Buddhist monastic universities of India and their curricula.

191 **In the footsteps of the Buddha.**
René Grousset, translated from the French by Mariette Leon. San Francisco: Chinese Materials Center, 1976. 352p.

Based on the sixteen-year (629-45 AD) pilgrimage taken by Hsüan Tsang as he retraced the footsteps of the Buddha, the Buddha's disciples, and later Buddhist saints. Grousset's text provides history, adventure, art, archaeology, and above all a careful exposition of Mahayana mysticism. Originally published in 1932.

192 **Women under primitive Buddhism: laywomen and almswomen.**
Isaline Blew Horner. Delhi: Motilal Banarsidass, 1975. reprint of 1930 ed. 391p. bibliog.

A pioneering study of the position of women in India before and during the growth of Buddhism. Horner shows that in spite of the early reluctance of the Buddha himself to accept women into the *sangha* (community of monks), women enjoyed an honoured place in the religion, and their social status was vastly improved by the spread of Buddhism. The roles of mothers, daughters, wives, widows, and women workers are highlighted.

193 **The central philosophy of Buddhism: a study of the Madhyamika system.**
T. R. V. Murti. London: Allen & Unwin, 1980. 372p. bibliog.

A thorough study of the Madhyamika school of Buddhist philosophy, established by Nagarjuna who declared that everything is 'empty' or 'void'. Murti examines Nagarjuna's central concepts in the light of the criticisms of Stcherbatsky (*Conception of Buddhist nirvana*, q.v.) and Chandrakirti (*Prasannapada madhyamak-avrtti*. Translated into French by Jacques May. Paris: Maisonneuve, 1959. 539p.), and draws parallels, often contrived, with Kantian categories.

194 **What the Buddha taught.**
Walpole Rahula. London: Fraser, 1978. rev. ed. 151p. bibliog.

This is the best available treatment of the basic teachings of early Buddhism. It is much more extensive than Burtt (q.v.) and much less philosophical than Conze (q.v.). Nowhere else are such difficult-to-understand doctrines as *annata* (no self) expounded so clearly. Explanations are illustrated with appropriate quotations from Buddhist scriptures. Both secondary school and college students can read this book with profit.

195 Guide to Buddhist religion.
Frank E. Reynolds, with John Holt (and others). Boston, Massachusetts: G. K. Hall, 1981. 415p. bibliog.

A comprehensive, annotated bibliography on Buddhism, containing several thousand entries grouped under twelve headings: historical development; religious thought; authoritative texts; the arts; social, political and economic aspects; religious practices and rituals; hagiography, mythology; sacred places; soteriological experiences; and research aids. There are author/title and subject indexes.

196 The Buddhist religion: a historical introduction.
Richard H. Robinson, Willard L. Johnson. Belmont, California: Dickenson, 1982. 3rd ed. 290p. bibliog. (Religious Life of Man Series).

This short book, of great beauty, is one of eight in a series on world religions intended for the general reader. First published in 1970, the book includes personal interpretations of various aspects of Buddhism by Robinson, one of America's foremost Buddhist scholars. Following an initial chapter that describes the present religious scene in various Buddhist countries, there is a traditional presentation of Buddhism and the life and teachings of Gautama, a chapter on the development of Indian Buddhism, and a chapter on developments outside India. This book is more readable but less sophisticated than Conze (q.v.).

197 The Buddha's way.
H. Saddhatissa. London: Allen & Unwin, 1971. 139p. bibliog.

One of the simplest and most easily understood introductions to the teachings of the Buddha. The author includes translations from the Pali canon. The final chapter deals with Buddhist meditation and the role of tranquility and insight in achieving a good life.

198 Buddhist ethics: essence of Buddhism.
H. Saddhatissa. New York: Braziller, 1971. 1st American ed. 202p. bibliog.

The author examines the integral relation among the three pillars of the Buddhist 'trinity' - Buddha, *dhamma* (teachings), and *sangha* (community of monks) - and presents Buddhism as fundamentally an ethical philosophy that requires arduous spiritual discipline before nirvana (beatitude) can be attained.

199 Indian Buddhism.
Anthony Kennedy Warder. Delhi: Motilal Banarsidass, 1980. 2nd rev. ed. 627p. maps. bibliog.

A definitive study of Buddhism in India by a leading Pali scholar. Following an introductory section in which Warder examines Indian civilization before and during the Buddha's lifetime, the author attempts to separate the probable facts about the Buddha's life from the legends that have grown up over the years. Two lengthy chapters discuss Buddhist teachings and Buddhist schisms.

200 **The Buddhist nirvana and its western interpreters.**
Guy Welbon.   Chicago: University of Chicago Press, 1980.
320p. bibliog.
A scholarly discussion of western Europe's contacts with and impressions of
Buddhism between 1800 and the early 20th century. Focusing on the central
concept of nirvana (cessation of pain) in Buddhism, Welbon examines the role of
principal European scholars of the 19th century and thereafter in interpreting and
misinterpreting Buddhism. Superb bibliography.

Christianity and Judaism

201 **The Church as Christian community: three studies of north
Indian churches.**
Edited by Victor E. Hayward.   London: Lutterworth, 1966.
353p. bibliog.
These three studies - one on the Church in Delhi (by James Alter and Herbert
Jai Singh), another on the Church in the Punjab (by Ernest Campbell) and the
third on the Church in the Kond Hills (by Barbara Boal) - discuss the historical
background of the Church in India, the religious and social life of Indian Christians, and the encounter between Hinduism and Christianity. Especially useful for
understanding the incorporation of non-Christian elements into Indian Christianity.

202 **A history of Christianity in India from early times to St.
Francis Xavier, AD 52-1542.**
George Mark Moraes.   Bombay: Manaktalas, 1964. 320p.
bibliog.
A thoroughly documented, exemplary Church history. Moraes discusses the relations between India and the west in antiquity; the history of the Syrian and St.
Thome Christians to the 13th century; the establishment of the Catholic Church
in India by the Latin Mission of France; Portuguese efforts at evangelization; the
establishment of hospitals under Church auspices; and the achievements and failures of the Christian churches up to the mid-16th century.

203 **The story of the Christian Church in India and Pakistan.**
Stephen Charles Neill.   Grand Rapids, Michigan:
Eerdmans, 1970. 183p. bibliog.
The development of Christian Churches in India and their prospects in independent India are the issues discussed in this slim volume. The author discusses the
influence of the Church of St. Thome, the Roman Catholic missions, and the
Anglicans and other Protestant denominations in the promotion of the Christian
faith on the subcontinent. He concludes that while the Roman Catholics seem to
be gaining ground, the Protestants are in decline.

204 **The Bene Israel of Bombay.**
Schifra Strizower. New York: Shocken, 1971. 176p.
bibliog.

A socio-religious analysis of the Bene Israel Jews who constitute over 80 per cent of the Indian Jewry and live predominantly in Greater Bombay. Strizower discusses both the religious and social differences between and among the Bene Israelites, the Baghdadi Jews, and the Cochin Jews. Their claim to be descended from the Ten Tribes of Israel is examined, as is their lack of knowledge of the Pentateuch, the Talmud, Hebrew, and traditional synagogue rituals.

Hinduism

205 **Modern trends in Hinduism.**
Philip H. Ashby. New York: Columbia University Press,
1974. 143p. bibliog.

Up-to-date information on major recent institutional developments in Hinduism. Ashby substantiates the view that the modernization of India has enhanced the importance of Hinduism in the beliefs and practices of the younger generation.

206 **The Tantric tradition.**
Agehananda Bharati. Westport, Connecticut: Greenwood
Press, 1977. 349p. bibliog.

An innovative examination, based on Sanskrit and Tibetan sources, of the Tantric tradition in both Hinduism and Buddhism. Bharati begins with a short discussion of the philosophy of Tantra, but the major portion of his study is devoted to a trenchant analysis of Tantric terminology. A thirty-page bibliography is included.

207 **The religion of the Veda.**
Maurice Bloomfield. Delhi: Indological Book House, 1972.
300p. bibliog.

A compilation of six general lectures on Vedic thought delivered in 1906-07. Bloomfield is the best starting point for the study of the Vedic religious tradition. For a more advanced study see Arthur Berriedale Keith's *The religion and philosophy of the Vedas and Upanishads* (Cambridge, Massachusetts: Harvard University Press, 1925. 2 vols.), which includes discussions on Vedic mythology and rituals.

208 **Guide to Hindu religion.**
David J. Dell (and others). Boston, Massachusetts: G. K.
Hall, 1981. 461p. bibliog.

A comprehensive, annotated bibliography on Hinduism that contains several thousand entries grouped under twelve headings: history of Hinduism; Hindu religious thought; authoritative and sacred texts; popular practices; the arts; Hinduism in social life and politics; rituals; ideal beings; mythology; sacred locations; soteriology; and research aids. There are author, title and subject indexes.

209 **Classical dictionary of Hindu mythology, religion, geography, history and literature.**
John Dowson. London: Routledge & Kegan Paul, 1979. 411p.

First published in 1879, this still remains a useful reference aid in dictionary form of names and terms from Hindu mythology and religion. Short descriptions are given of Indian deities, classical Sanskrit works and their authors, and geographical names and places.

210 **Hinduism and Buddhism: an historical sketch.**
Charles Eliot. London: Routledge & Kegan Paul, 1971.
reprint of 1922 ed. 3 vols. bibliog.

A reliable, objective, and detailed survey. The first section describes the general characteristics of Indian religion and religious life in pre-Buddhist India. The second section deals with the emergence of Saivism and Vaisnavism. The sections on Buddhism examine the development of this religion in India and its expansion abroad.

211 **Modern religious movements in India.**
John Nicol Farquhar. New York: Garland, 1980. 471p.

An indispensable guide to the major religious movements, both Hindu and non-Hindu, that developed in India during the British hegemony. Farquhar classifies these movements according to their response to western influences, ranging from total westernization to ultra-orthodoxy. Writing in 1915, the author did not anticipate that the then prevalent religious chauvinism might be defeated by a secularist and tolerant Hinduism which has emerged in recent years.

212 **An outline of the religious literature of India.**
John Nicol Farquhar. Delhi: Motilal Banarsidass, 1967. 451p.

An indispensable guide to the basic contents of principal Hindu, Buddhist, and Jain writings, from the Vedas to about 1800 AD. Chapters are arranged by schools of thought within historical periods. Editorial remarks include basic information on the characteristic features of each period.

213 **Vedic literature.**
Jan Gonda. Wiesbaden, GFR: Harrassowitz, 1975. 463p.
(History of Indian Literature, vol. 1, fasc. 1).

This is the first volume of a projected ten-volume series on the ancient, mediaeval, and modern literatures of India, which is designed to bring standard books, such as Winternitz (q.v.), up to date. Volume 1 is limited to Vedic *Samhitas* and *Brahmanas*. Gonda's discussion of the *Rig Veda*, which occupies one-half of the volume, is both rigorous and well balanced.

214 **Visnuism and Sivaism: a comparison.**
Jan Gonda. London: Athlone, 1970. 228p. bibliog.

A valuable study of the Vedic and post-Vedic origins of India's two principal gods, Visnu and Siva, and of the religious traditions associated with their names. Gonda includes information on temple rituals, popular religious practices, and sectarian texts. The text is supplemented by seventy-five pages of detailed notes and references.

215 The Hindu religious tradition.
Thomas J. Hopkins. Encino, California: Dickenson, 1971. 156p. bibliog.

A widely used college text. The volume has two major parts: the first deals with development up to 900 AD when, according to Hopkins, the Hindu tradition reached its classical zenith, and from then to the present, a period during which only minor changes in that tradition have taken place.

216 Dayanand Sarasvati: his life and ideas.
S. T. F. Jordens. New York: Oxford University Press, 1979. 368p. bibliog.

An accurate, comprehensive account of the founder of the Arya Samaj, a Hindu reform organization, and his influence on Hinduism in 19th-century western India and on 20th-century Hindu nationalism. Jordens examines Dayanand's novel interpretations of the Hindu scriptures and argues that these have to be taken seriously. Excellent and thorough bibliography.

217 History of Dharmasastra.
Pandurang V. Kane. Poona, India: Bhandarkar Oriental Research Institute, 1968. 2nd rev. ed. 5 vols. bibliog.

A monumental scholarly achievement. The author, an attorney by profession, undertook to examine nearly all Sanskritic literature on the social and religious duties and practices of the Hindus from ancient times to the early modern period. The result is an encyclopaedic set that contains enormous information and is buttressed with extensive quotations and thorough primary and secondary source citations.

218 The presence of Siva.
Stella Kramrisch, photographs by Praful Patel. Princeton, New Jersey: Princeton University Press, 1981. 514p. bibliog.

A unique critical study of the myth, metaphysics, and artistic expressions of Lord Siva, perhaps the most elusive member of the Hindu pantheon, by a leading art historian. Kramrisch handles a huge variety of literary and archaeological materials with imagination and delicacy. She narrates and interprets Saivite myths on both ontological and metaphysical levels. A work of wisdom.

219 Hymns from the Rigveda.
Translated by A. A. Macdonell. Delhi: YMCA Publishing House, 1966. 98p.

A reprint of the 1922 edition, this selection of forty major hymns from the oldest extant Hindu scriptures is readable and reasonably accurate. The entire corpus of the *Rig Veda* has been translated by Ralph T. H. Griffith, *The hymns of the Rig Veda* (Benares: E. J. Lazarus, 1896-97. 2 vols.), but the Griffith translation, though often anthologized, has several unsatisfactory features.

220 **Indian theism: from the Vedic times to the Muhammadan period.**

Nicol MacNicol. Delhi: Munshiram Manoharlal, 1968. 2nd ed. 292p. bibliog.

The most authoritative book on Indian theism. The first part deals, in the main, with mediaeval *bhakti* movements. The second discusses theological views and controversies, and the third evaluates Indian theistic movements from the standpoint of Christianity.

221 **Puranic encyclopedia: a comprehensive dictionary with special reference to the epic and Puranic literature.**

Vettam Mani. Delhi: Motilal Banarsidass, 1975. 922p.

This Puranic encyclopaedia is an English translation, by a committee of five scholars, of Vettam Mani's original Malayalam work which was first published in 1964. Though the coverage of Puranic literature is not comprehensive the encyclopaedia is, nevertheless, a major reference source for Hinduism in general and Hindu mythology and south Indian Hinduism in particular. It is superior to John Dowson's *Classical dictionary of Hindu mythology* (q.v.). Useful geneological charts are appended.

222 **The lord of the autumn moons.**

Radhakamal Mukerjee. Bombay: Asia, 1957. 167p.

Krishna, the great incarnation of Visnu, is the most important deity in the Hindu *bhakti* (devotional) tradition. One of the great myths associated with Krishna is his *rasa* dance with milkmaids. In this eminently readable book Mukerjee has collected and interpreted the many-sided erotic-spiritual love myths popular among the Krishna devotees.

223 **Development of religion in south India.**

K. A. Nilakanta Sastri. Bombay: Orient Longman, 1963. 148p. bibliog.

A discussion of the encounter between Aryan and Dravidian religious and cultural traditions, and their synthesis in south India. Sastri is particularly helpful for an understanding of the *bhakti* movements and their institutional context. Written by a historian, this book concentrates especially on the golden periods of the Sangam and Vijayanagar dynasties.

224 **Asceticism and eroticism in the mythology of Shiva.**

Wendy D. O'Flaherty. New York: Oxford University Press, 1973. 386p. bibliog.

An important, original, stimulating, and convincing interpretation of sexual excitement and repression both by gods and ascetics in the Indian tradition. Based on a wide array of Puranic and epic texts and myths, the book explores stories associated with Siva and Kama, using psycho-sexual interpretations.

225 **Hindu samskaras.**

Raj Bali Pandey. Delhi: Motilal Banarsidass, 1969. 2nd rev. ed. 327p. bibliog.

An exposition of the principal Hindu 'rites of passage'. Pandey presents the history of each of these rites from the Vedic period to the present, and in his concluding chapter examines the totality of these rites within the universal context of human life.

226 **History of the Brahmo Samaj.**

Shiv Nath Sastri. Calcutta: R. Chatterji, 1974. 2nd ed. 642p.

Brahmo Samaj was a Hindu reform movement that arose in 19th-century India under the impact of western, and particularly Christian, influence. This book carefully describes the religious history of the Samaj and its major leaders, Ram Mohun Roy and Keshab Chunder Sen.

227 **Hinduism: new essays in the history of religions.**

Edited by Bardwell L. Smith. Leiden, the Netherlands: Brill, 1976. 231p. bibliog.

A careful examination of selected aspects of Vaisnava *bhakti* and mythology principally in Bengal. Included are two essays on Caitanya, another two on Ramakrishna, one on the pilgrimage to Ramadevra in Rajasthan, and another on the bibliography of the mediaeval *bhakti* movement.

228 **A dictionary of Hinduism, its mythology, folklore, and development, 1500 B.C.-A.D. 1500.**

Margaret Stutley, James Stutley. Bombay: Allied, 1977. 372p.

This is perhaps the most comprehensive and yet concise encyclopaedia on Hinduism. Its approximately 2,500 subject headings include rites, practices, concepts, functionaries, myths, places, literary texts, religiously significant fauna and flora, gods and goddesses, legends, symbols, music and philosophical and religious terms. The book provides comparative references from other ancient religions such as those in the Near East. Published in the United States as *Harper's dictionary of Hinduism: its mythology, folklore, philosophy, literature, and history* (New York: Harper & Row, 1977. 372p.).

229 **Basic ideas of occult wisdom.**

Anna Kennedy Winner. Wheaton, Illinois: Theosophical Publishing House, 1970. 113p.

The theosophy movement was started in 1875 by Henry Olcott and Helena Blavatsky in the United States, and expanded to India under the influence of Annie Besant, an Englishwoman prominent in Indian nationalist politics. Winner's book provides a good historical and philosophical introduction to theosophy, and carefully examines the impact of eastern mystical traditions upon Judeo-Christian traditions within the theosophical synthesis.

Islam

230 Muslim self-statement in India and Pakistan, 1857-1968.
Edited by Aziz Ahmad, Gustav E. von
Grünebaum. Wiesbaden, GFR: Harrassowitz, 1970. 240p.
bibliog.
An anthology of the theological and religio-political thought of major 19th- and
20th-century Muslim schools of India. Selections are included from Sayyid
Ahmad Khan, Shibli Nu'mani, Amir Ali, Abul Kalam Azad, Muhammad Iqbal,
Muhammad Ali Jinnah, A. A. A. Fyzee, Abul Ala Madudi, and Ghulam Ahmad
Parwez. These scholars are critically analysed in Aziz Ahmad's *Islamic moder-
nism in India and Pakistan, 1857-1964* (London: Oxford University Press, 1967.
294p. bibliog.) which was written from the standpoint of 'integral humanism'
(*anthropocentrisme réfléchi*), an attitude unknown in traditional Islamic theology.

231 Sufis of Bijapur, 1300-1700: social roles of Sufis in medieval India.
Richard Maxwell Eaton. Princeton, New Jersey: Princeton
University Press, 1978. 358p. bibliog.
A superb book dealing with the role that the Sufi orders played in spreading
Islamic popular culture to south India - a topic that is generally neglected in
other historical surveys. Eaton examines the lives and times of the various Bijapur
Sufis and their relationship with the *ulema* (Islamic doctors of law), the Bijapur
court, and the Hindu population. His chapter on saint-worship and the tomb-cult
of the Indian Sufis is perhaps the most literate account on the subject.

232 The Shía of India.
John Norman Hollister. New Delhi: Oriental Books
Reprint Corp., 1979. 2nd ed. 440p. bibliog.
A religious and historical account of the growth of the Shia sect of Islam and its
major denominations, especially the *mustalians* and the *nizarians*, in India. Hol-
lister discusses the theological roots of Ithna Ashariya (those Shias who recognize
only twelve imams), the expansion of the Shia community in the south under
Bahmani and succeeding kingdoms and in the north under the Mughals, the
emergence of the Ismailiyas, and the adjustments made by the Shia with the
Hindu faith and traditions.

233 The rose and the rock: mystical and rational elements in the intellectual history of South Asian Islam.
Edited by Bruce B. Lawrence. Durham, North Carolina:
Duke University Press, 1978. 200p. bibliog. (Comparative
Studies on Southern Asia, no. 15).
Six essays. Sheila McDonough's essay shows that India's great philosopher Iqbal
was both traditional and progressive, Islamic and western, and opposed to both
secularism and rationalism. Bruce Lawrence's essay points out that Sayyid
Ahmad Khan, who is often viewed as the supreme rationalist of modern Indian
Islam, was at heart influenced by Delhi mysticism. Annemarie Schimmel's articles
analyse the role of Ameer Ali in introducing the rational element into the under-

standing of the Prophet Muhammad. Two other essays examine the mystical element in the poetry of Bedil and Ghalib.

234 The Indian Muslims.
Mohammed Mujeeb. London: Allen & Unwin, 1969. 590p. bibliog.

The author, an Indian Muslim, has portrayed the life and thought of the Muslims in India. The approach is chronological, but each period (early, middle, modern) is examined from various perspectives. The treatment of politics and politicians, poets and writers, the arts and architecture, and social life is particularly illuminating. The writer argues that the Muslims' desire to maintain the identity of faith has often come in conflict with the desire to be fully integrated in India, leading the 'separatist' elements to emphasize the former and the 'secular' forces to seek the latter.

235 Gabriel's wing: a study into the religious ideas of Sir Muhammad Iqbal.
Annemarie Schimmel. Leiden, the Netherlands: Brill, 1963. 428p. bibliog.

A critical study of 20th-century India's pre-eminent Urdu poet, nationalist leader, and Islamic philosopher. Schimmel points out that although Iqbal was publicly critical of the generally ignorant Sufi Muslim *pirs* (religious leaders), in private he relied heavily on Sufi influences.

236 Islam in the Indian subcontinent.
Annemarie Schimmel. Leiden, the Netherlands: Brill, 1980. 303p. bibliog.

A careful, balanced survey of the history and situation of Islam in India, Pakistan, and Bangladesh. Schimmel describes and evaluates the cultural activities of devoted mystical leaders who won over many Hindus to the Islamic faith and generated a Hindu-Muslim religio-cultural sythesis against the background of Islamic political tradition which was intolerant of Hinduism and which kept Hindu-Muslim tensions alive.

237 Islam in India, or the Qanun-i-Islam: the customs of the Musalmans of India.
Ja'far Sharif, translated by G. A. Herklots, revised by William Crooke. New Delhi: Oriental Books Reprint Corp., 1972. 374p. bibliog.

Written in 1832 by a Muslim *hakim* (physician), and translated by Herklots, a surgeon, this is a definitive account of the rites and ceremonies, rules of religious and social life, and the religious calendar of Muslims in India. Separate chapters deal with dress, jewellery, food, drink, intoxicants, and games common among Indian Muslims.

238 **Modern Islam in India.**
Wilfred Cantwell Smith. New Delhi: Usha, 1979. reprint.
396p. bibliog.

A vigorous Marxist analysis of Islamic religious movements and trends in the
Indian subcontinent from the latter third of the 19th century until the 1940s. The
information contained in this volume has led to a re-examination of the religious
history of the Indian Muslims by native scholars who has, in turn, provided
apologias either for the 'nationalist' interpretation of Islam, as by Mujeeb (q.v.), or
the separatist interpretation, as by several Pakistani scholars led by I. H. Qureshi.

239 **Islam in India and Pakistan.**
Murray T. Titus. Calcutta: YMCA Publishing House,
1959. rev. ed. 328p. bibliog.

Originally published in 1930, this is a cogent survey of the history of Islam in
India. Titus discusses Islam's peaceful and violent penetrations of India: its diversification into various Sunni, Shia, and Sufi communities; its impact upon Hinduism and Hinduism's impact upon it; its reactionary and modern factions in the
20th century; and contemporary Islamic apologetics.

Jainism

240 **A comprehensive history of Jainism up to 1000 AD.**
Asim Kumar Chatterjee. Calcutta: Firma KLM, 1980.
400p. bibliog.

A history of the birth and growth of Jainism in India during the formative period
from 800 BC to the early mediaeval times. Based on Vedic and Anga texts, it
provides a historical narrative on the origins, development, and contributions of
the Digambara and Svetambara sects of Jainism.

241 **Outlines of Jainism.**
Jagmandar Lal Jaini, edited with preliminary notes by F.
W. Thomas. London: Cambridge University Press, 1940.
156p. bibliog.

A compact presentation of Jaina religion and philosophy by a member of the
tradition. The volume includes a selection of texts in translation.

242 **The Jaina path of purification.**
Padmanabh S. Jaini. Berkeley, California: University of
California Press, 1979. 374p. bibliog.

A capable, scholarly, general introduction to the Jains and their religion, written
in a lucid, expository style. Jaini draws on both Digambara and Svetambara
historical traditions in order to depict the beginnings of Jainism, the life and
career of the founder, Mahavira, and the early development of the Jaina tradition. The concluding chapter discusses Jainism's historical development.

243 **A history of the canonical literature of the Jains.**
Hiralal Rasikdas Kapadia. Bombay: Gujarati Printing
Press, 1941. 272p. bibliog.

The Digambara and the Svetambara sects of Jainism are hopelessly divided on
what constitutes canonical literature: indeed, the former reject *in toto* Svetambara
canonical literature. Kapadia's carefully written volume discusses the nature and
range of the canonical literature of both the Digambara and Svetambara sects. It
examines major Indian and foreign scholarship on the texts, and it incorporates
many later discoveries not noted by German and French scholars who were
among the first to examine Jaina theology.

244 **The religion of the Jainas.**
Walther Schubring, translated from the German by
Amulyachandra Sen, T. C. Burke. Calcutta: Calcutta
Sanskrit College, 1966. 43p. bibliog.

Schubring's contributions to Jaina studies have been of major importance in the
field, and he remains one of the most distinquished authorities to this day. This
translation of *Der Jinismus* is a well-ordered, brief account of the religion. It is
more readable than his *magnum opus, Die Lehre der Jains* ('The doctrine of the
Jains'. Translated by Wolfgang Beurlen. Delhi: Motilal Banarsidass, 1962. 335p.
bibliog.), which is an indispensable work for a thorough understanding of Jainism.

245 **Jaina yoga: a survey of the mediaeval Sravakacaras.**
Robert Hamilton Blair Williams. London: Oxford
University Press, 1963. 206p. bibliog.

A superb study of the life of the laity in the Jaina community. Williams discusses
and analyses the non-canonical sources and their presentation of the rules of
conduct for the laity. A specialized work.

Sikhism

246 **Guru Nanak in history.**
J. S. Grewal. Chandigarh, India: Panjab University, 1969.
348p. bibliog.

A definitive study of the life and teachings of Guru Nanak, founder of the Sikh
religion. Grewal portrays the guru as essentially a quietist and a pietist who was
largely uninterested in political issues. On the basis of his analysis of Nanak's
morning prayer, *Japji,* and the morning hymns contained in the *Adi Granth,* the
author argues that while Sikhism was influenced by both Hinduism and Islam, it
is a distinct religion in its own right.

247 **A critical study of the Adi Granth, being a comprehensive and scientific study of Guru Granth Sahib, the scripture of the Sikhs.**
Surinder Singh Kohli. Delhi: Motilal Banarsidass, 1976. 2nd ed. 391p. bibliog.

A meticulous analysis of the influence of the Hindu *bhakti* movement on the development of Sikh religion, and of Guru Nanak's role in reshaping Hindu philosophical ideas, especially Vedantic constructs, in premodern India. Kohli draws attention to the texts in the *Upanishads* from which the guru derived many of his ideas.

248 **Guru Nanak and the Sikh religion.**
W. H. McLeod. Bombay: Oxford University Press, 1976. 259p. bibliog.

A profound, objective, and critical portrait of the founder of the Sikh religion. Though McLeod demolishes several mythical beliefs of the Sikh community about the founder of their religion, he has avoided offending Sikh sensibilities. The author's analysis of the guru's personality, the formative influences on his life and thought, his poetry, and his impact on his community is extremely competent and thoroughly convincing.

249 **A history of the Sikhs. Volume 1: 1469-1839. Volume 2: 1839-1964.**
Khushwant Singh. Delhi: Oxford University Press, 1977. 2nd ed. 2 vols. maps. bibliog.

A definitive history of the Sikhs, their religion, and their political fortunes. Singh considers Sikhism to be a *mélange* of the Hindu *bhakti* and Islamic Sufi traditions of mediaeval India. His contention that the rise of Sikhism and the resurgence of Punjabi nationalism are synonymous is not generally accepted by Sikh theologians. Appendixes contain translations of hymns from the *Adi Granth* and *Dasam Granth*.

250 **Hymns of Guru Nanak.**
Translated by Khushwant Singh. New Delhi: Orient Longman, 1978. 192p. bibliog.

A representative selection of the hymns written and sung by the founder of the Sikh religion. The hymns are arranged to the ragas (melodies) in which they were sung. Some hymns have been translated in full, others only in part. But in the case of the latter, Khushwant Singh has given prose synopses so that the reader does not miss the continuity.

251 **Selections from the sacred writings of the Sikhs.**
Translated by Trilochan Singh (and others), revised by George S. Fraser. New York: S. Wiser, 1973. 1st American ed. 288p.

Prepared by a panel of Sikh scholars and sponsored by UNESCO, this is a comprehensive anthology of Sikh writings. The translations were polished by the Irish poet George S. Fraser. An introduction by Sarvepalli Radhakrishnan, the philosopher and second president of India, explains the fundamental tenets of the Sikh religion.

Zoroastrianism

252 **Zoroastrians: their religious beliefs and practices.**
Mary Boyce. Boston, Massachusetts: Routledge & Kegan Paul, 1979. 252p. maps. bibliog.

An introduction to the Zoroastrian religion as it is practised by the Parsee community of India, written by its foremost living expert. The book provides a history of the religion and its practitioners from Indo-Iranian times to the present. It examines the influence of Zoroastrianism not only on three great Iranian empires but also on Buddhism, Judaism, Christianity, and Islam.

253 **The religious ceremonies and customs of the Parsees.**
Jivanji J. Modi. New York: Garland, 1979. 3rd ed. 484p.

Based on articles that he wrote for James Hastings' *Encyclopaedia of religion and ethics*, Modi draws heavily on archaeological and anthropological discoveries for explanations of the significance of Parsee practices, and also on the latest findings of European scholarship on Zoroastrianism.

Philosophy

254 **Temple of the phallic king: the mind of India, yogis, swamis, sufis, and avatars.**
Pagal Baba, edited by Edward Rice. New York: Simon & Schuster, 1973. 282p.
An informed survey of many contemporary Indian spiritual personalities, their cults, and their teachings. The volume is rich in detail and impressions. Some selections from mantras (religious chants) and devotional poetry are also included.

255 **The Indian theogony.**
Sukumari Bhattacharji. Calcutta: Firma KLM, 1978. corrected Indian ed. 397p. bibliog.
A brilliant study of the evolution of the major deities of India from their pre-Vedic antecedents to the present. Each section discusses one of the three principal gods of India - Siva, Visnu, and Brahma - and the minor deities related to each of them. A final section discusses general issues relating to the Indian trinity.

256 **A history of Indian philosophy.**
Surendra Nath Dasgupta. Cambridge, England: Cambridge University Press, 1965-69. reprint of 1922-25 ed. 5 vols. bibliog.
A monumental work by one of the greatest specialists in the field. The author has undertaken not only a survey of the better-known Indian philosophical systems, but also an in-depth analysis of many obscure Indian philosophical schools. The fifth volume, completed posthumously by the author's widow, examines Saivite thought. There is an abridgement of these volumes by R. Agarwal and S. K. Jain (Allahabad: Kitab Mahal, 1969. 230p.), with the same title.

257 **The philosophy of Mahatma Gandhi.**
Dhirendra Mohan Datta. Madison, Wisconsin: University of Wisconsin Press, 1972. 154p. bibliog.
Written by a disciple who spent several years in Gandhi's ashram (retreat), this is the clearest exposition of Gandhi's religious, social, political and economic

62

thought. According to Datta, although Gandhi was neither a metaphysician nor a systemizer, his philosophy had an integral unity and represented a consistent philosophical viewpoint on a number of issues from religion to social welfare.

258 The philosophy of the Upanishads.
Paul Deussen. New York: Dover, 1966. 417p. bibliog.

Written by a Kantian scholar, this definitive study of the *Upanishads* emphasizes the idealistic element in Vedantic philosophy without ignoring the variety of thought present in the texts. Part one discusses the key concept of Brahman, part two Vedantic cosmology, part three the psychology of the *atman* ('self'), and part four the concept of transmigration and salvation.

259 The Bhagavad Gita.
Edited by Eliot Deutsch. Washington, DC: University Press of America, 1982. 192p. bibliog.

A scholarly, readable translation of India's most important religious text. Deutsch has written a marvellous introductory essay about the importance of the book and its central characters, Krishna and Arjuna. A concluding chapter in four parts examines the principal message of the *Gita*. The total effect, therefore, is to present the message of the *Gita* clearly and accurately.

260 Yoga: immortality and freedom.
Mircea Eliade, translated from the French by Willard R. Trask. Princeton, New Jersey: Princeton University Press, 1970. 2nd ed. 536p. bibliog.

Probably the most comprehensive and scholarly study of yoga in all its aspects. The author knows the subject both from having studied it in India and from his personal practice of yoga. Both the classical tradition as represented in Patanjali's *Yoga sutras* and the less exalted, almost decadent, yogic practices in Tantricism are examined carefully. A brilliant chapter discusses the connection between yoga and alchemy, and the final chapter deals with yoga's relationship to aboriginal and primitive practices such as those in shamanism. Only for the serious and advanced student.

261 Outlines of Indian philosophy.
Mysore Hiriyanna. London: Allen & Unwin, 1975. 419p.

A college-level text for students of religion and philosophy. Though the scope of the volume is limited to Vedic, early post-Vedic, and other early systems culminating in the philosophy of Ramanjua, all the principal Indian philosophical doctrines are clearly delineated. Unfortunately the author, an eminent Indian philosopher, has omitted any discussion of the Tantric tradition.

262 The reconstruction of religious thought in Islam.
Muhammad Iqbal. Lahore: Ashraf, 1965. 205p.

One of the intellectually most impressive philosophical examinations of Islamic religious knowledge and the necessity for restructuring Muslim thought, especially on the Indian subcontinent. The chapter which deals with the theoretical issues of adapting Islamic law to new situations is truly brilliant.

Philosophy

263 **Journal of Indian Philosophy.**
Dordrecht, the Netherlands: D. Reidel, 1970- . quarterly.
Published in the Netherlands under the editorship of an Indian philosophy professor, this journal is the only western publication exclusively devoted to Indian philosophy. Few book reviews.

264 **Six pillars: introduction to the major works of Sri Aurobindo.**
Edited by Robert A. McDermott. Chambersburg,
Pennsylvania: Wilson Books, 1974. 198p. bibliog.
Aurobindo, a Cambridge-educated classicist, is the author of thirty volumes of religio-philosophical interpretations of Vedanta and his own teachings, and had a profound influence on modern Indian philosophy. In this slim volume, six experts examine his ideas on the spiritual transformation of the modern world; his interpretation of the *Gita*; his philosophical theories about existence, knowledge and spiritual evolution; and his long epic poem *Savitri*. The best introduction to Aurobindo.

265 **The spirit of modern India: writings in philosophy, religion, and culture.**
Edited by Robert A. McDermott, V. S. Naravane. New
York: Thomas Y. Crowell, 1974. 313p. bibliog.
A collection of principal writings of the leaders of the Indian renaissance from 1820 to 1947. Among those represented are Rammohun Roy, Tagore, Gandhi, and Ramakrishna. Selections are organized under topical headings such as education, national consciousness, aesthetics, spiritual discipline, and *karma-yoga*. Historical background to the selections is provided by editorial notes, chronological tables, and a good bibliography.

266 **The Jaina philosophy of non-absolutism: a critical study of Anekantavada.**
Satkari Mookerjee. Delhi: Motilal Banarsidass, 1978. 289p.
bibliog.
An excellent study, particularly of the Jaina notion of universals and Jaina differences from other schools of Hindu and Buddhist philosophy. Mookerjee also examines such key issues as *avidya* (nescience) and the Jaina notion of karma (action and rebirth).

267 **Encyclopaedia of Indian philosophies.**
Edited by Karl H. Potter. Princeton, New Jersey:
Princeton University Press, 1970-81. 3 vols. bibliog.
As of 1982 only three of the projected twenty-eight volumes has been published. The first volume, a bibliography of over 9,000 entries, contains complete information on Sanskrit philosophical texts and their authors, chosen for their enduring theoretical and philosophical value. The second volume deals exclusively with the Nyaya and Vaishesika philosophical systems, and commentaries on those systems upto 1350 AD. The third deals with Advaita-Vedanta, and commentaries on it, principally those of Sankara. For research scholars.

268 **The principal Upanishads.**
Translated by Sarvepalli Radhakrishnan. New York:
Humanities, 1978. 958p. bibliog.

A careful and extremely readable translation of the fifteen major *Upanishads* and five short ones. Radhakrishnan has been criticized for sacrificing literalness for readability. The translator's introductions to the texts reflect the position of the school of commentators led by Sankara, but they also include interesting comparisons with western religious ideas wherever appropriate.

269 **A sourcebook in Indian philosophy.**
Edited by Sarvepalli Radhakrishnan, Charles A.
Moore. Princeton, New Jersey: Princeton University Press,
1967. 683p. bibliog.

This anthology successfully accomplishes its two stated objectives: to supply western readers with basic source material on Indian philosophy in convenient and usable form, and to present material on all the major philosophical systems and perspectives of India. Selections from the Vedas, *Upanishads, Gita, Mahabharata, Manusmriti, Arthasastra, Carvakas*, Jainism, Buddhism, the six principal schools of philosophy, Sankara, Ramanuja, Aurobindo, and Radhakrishnan have been included. Not all the translations are original. The translation of the *Gita* is exceptionally good.

270 **Indian philosophy since independence.**
Dale Riepe. Calcutta: Research India Publications, 1979.
360p. bibliog.

An examination of the writings of major Indian philosophers and teachers of philosophy, written by an American scholar committed to dialectical and historical materialism. The author discusses foreign influences on Indian philosophy which he considers to be the major obstacle to the development of an 'Indian' tradition in philosophical analysis. Riepe's comments are as personal as they are enlightening.

271 **The philosophy of Sarvepalli Radhakrishnan.**
Edited by Paul Arthur Schlipp. New York: Tudor, 1952.
883p. bibliog. (Library of Living Philosophers).

The most important secondary source on the eminent Hindu philosopher who also served as the second president of India. In addition to articles by distinguished Indian, European, and American scholars, the book contains a response by Radhakrishnan himself and an even longer intellectual 'confession'. It includes a complete bibliography of Radhakrishnan's works to 1952.

272 **Conception of Buddhist nirvana.**
Fedor I. Stcherbatsky. New York: Wiser, 1978. 2nd ed.
246p.

Originally published in Leningrad in 1926, this work contains the great Russian orientalist's interpretation of the philosophical dicta of Nagarjuna and his 'middle path'. Stcherbatsky's views have influenced all later scholars of Buddhist philosophy.

Society

General

273 **Caste and social stratification among Muslims in India.**
Edited by Imtiaz Ahmed. Columbia, Missouri: South Asia
Books, 1978. 2nd rev. enl. ed. 314p. bibliog.
A collection of ethnographies on the variety of South Asian Muslim subcultures, focusing on the question of the existence of caste among Indian Muslims. All but one of the contributors agree that Muslim social structure in India has many but not all features of the Hindu caste system. The one critical area in which Muslims usually, but not always, have been found to differ from Hindus is the lack of a highly developed sense of the concepts of ritual purity and pollution.

274 **The divine hierarchy: popular Hinduism in Central India.**
Lawrence A. Babb. New York: Columbia University Press,
1975. 266p. bibliog.
A comprehensive structural analysis of the Hindu social ethos. The pantheon, rituals, devotional practices, and concepts of space and time as reflected in an ordinary Hindu's life cycle, and other day-to-day activities are described in simple and concrete terms. Eminently readable.

275 **Structure and cognition: aspects of Hindu caste and ritual.**
Veena Das. Delhi: Oxford University Press, 1982. 2nd ed.
147p. bibliog.
This study provides an understanding of Hindu theories of caste and ritual through structural analysis of the relevant Sanskrit texts. It is the first attempt to apply this method - previously used in the study of kinship and marriage - to the study of caste and ritual. The two key chapters on *jatis* (castes) and the sacred and the profane in Hinduism integrate textual and contextual information.

276 **India since independence: social report on India, 1947-72.**
Edited by Shyama Charan Dube. New Delhi: Vikas, 1977.
577p. bibliog.

A survey of major developments and significant trends during the first twenty-five years of Indian independence and their likely future implications. Part of the book is devoted to key sections of India's population, another to key sectors of its cultural life, and yet another to summary appraisals of such issues as public order, science and technology, and economic development. Most contributors argue that, measured against the problems confronting it, India's performance has, indeed, been creditable.

277 **Homo hierarchicus: the caste system and its implications.**
Louis Dumont, translated from the French by Mark Sainsbury. Chicago: University of Chicago Press, 1980. rev. English. ed. 386p. maps.

An intellectual and comparative analysis of the Indian caste system and western egalitarianism. Dumont argues that purity and pollution concepts underlie the caste system. The book assumes considerable knowledge of Indian sociological literature and contemporary anthropological theory. It has been criticized for ignoring the occupational dimension of the caste system. A milestone in the continuing debate on the nature of caste.

278 **An anthropological bibliography of South Asia together with a directory of recent anthropological field work.**
Compiled by Elizabeth von Fürer-Haimendorf, Helen Kanitkar. Paris: Mouton, 1958-76. 4 vols.

Almost 13,000 western-language items on South Asia, the bulk of them on India, are listed, though not annotated. With the exception of Indian census publications, government publications have been excluded. The volumes have one general and nineteen regional sections, each covering the following categories: cultural and social anthropology, material culture and applied art, folklore and folk art, prehistoric archaeology, physical anthropology, and miscellanea.

279 **Marginality and identity: Anglo-Indians as a racially mixed minority in India.**
Noel P. Gist, Roy Dean Wright. Leiden, the Netherlands: Brill, 1973. 161p. bibliog.

A straightforward narrative account of people of mixed British-Indian racial heritage in India, who number a little more than 100,000 according to the latest estimates. The authors examine the relations of Anglo-Indians with other Indian communities and sadly conclude that these people while only culturally marginal to the British are both culturally and socially marginal to the Indians.

280 **Western sociologists on Indian society: Marx, Spencer, Weber, Durkheim, Pareto.**
Gurmukh Ram Madan. London: Routledge & Kegan Paul, 1979. 399p. bibliog.

Written by a prominent Indian sociologist, this book consists of chapters on the views of Marx, Spencer, Weber, Durkheim and Pareto about Indian society. In addition there are separate interpretive chapters dealing with their views on the central topics of religion and caste. Madan also deals with sociological theories about marriage and family structure, the village community, the social organization of cities, education, political organizations, economy, and the effects of colonial rule.

281 Society in India.
David Goodman Mandelbaum. Bombay: Popular, 1972. 1st Indian ed. 665p. bibliog.

A readable, reliable, and comprehensive survey of Indian society and its principal components - the individual, his family, the caste system, and village life. The author has also identified the patterns and extent of social mobility and institutional change in India. Though somewhat dated, Mandelbaum's conclusions have stood the test of time.

282 India and Ceylon: unity in diversity, a symposium.
Edited by Philip Mason. New York: Oxford University Press, 1967. 311p. maps. bibliog.

Authoritative essays on five topics: religion, language, tribes, caste, and education. Among the more useful are those dealing with the position of Muslims (by Spear), the backward castes and classes (by Beteille), the Gandhian and the neo-Gandhian views on caste (by Dalton), and Indian élites (by Bottomore). Almost all the authors agree that while caste remains an important factor in Indian society, its significance has been steadily declining.

283 An untouchable community in South India: structure and consensus.
Michael Moffatt. Princeton, New Jersey: Princeton University Press, 1979. 323p. bibliog.

This superb study of five untouchable castes in a Tamilian village argues that untouchables are among the most fervent believers in the system that oppresses them. In social terms, the untouchables have adopted a system of caste-specific roles among themselves that replicates the larger caste system. Also, culturally, untouchables believe in the same hierarchically graded pantheon as do upper castes.

284 Caste and kinship in Kangra.
Jonathan P. Parry. London: Routledge & Kegan Paul, 1979. 353p. bibliog.

A case study of how the principle of hierarchy based on religious concepts of purity and pollution permeating Indian society affects thoughts and action in India's western Himalayan (Kangra) region. The author argues that hierarchy underlies divisions within and between castes and families, as well as between men and gods. The special strength of this book is its examples of how people's ideas and behaviour are moulded by caste.

285 **Harijans in Indian society: a cultural study of the status of harijans and other backward classes from the earliest times to the present day.**
Suresh Narain Srivastava. Lucknow, India: Upper India Publishing House, 1980. 304p. bibliog.
The author maintains that most of the discriminatory practices against the harijans (untouchables) were well established by the 6th century AD. Textual evidence is cited to outline prohibitory rules and sanctions governing marriage, education, dress, occupation, and rituals. A concluding chapter discusses contemporary legislative and public efforts to eliminate discriminatory practices against the untouchables.

Family and marriage

286 **Some aspects of family in Mahuva: a sociological study of jointness in a small town.**
I. P. Desai. London: Asia, 1964. 239p. bibliog.
One of the many detailed empirical sociological studies of the village of Mahuva in Gujarat, this book examines the gradual erosion of the joint family system and the emergence of nuclear families. According to Desai there is a direct correlation between the emergence of the nuclear family and higher education, occupational variations within the family, and the development of market economy and urbanization. Yet, the author finds that kinship ties remain strong in spite of the weakened status of the joint family.

287 **The death of a marriage law: epitaph for the rishis.**
John Duncan Martin Derrett. New Delhi: Vikas, 1978. 228p. bibliog.
In 1976 the Indian parliament liberalized Hindu law to permit the dissolution of marriage by mutual consent. According to Derrett this cataclysmic change killed the traditional Hindu marriage law derived from the writings of ancient *rishis* (sages). He further argues that easy divorce has invited the philandering of immature husbands and encouraged exorbitant demands of dowry from the parents of the grooms. Derrett recommends a dual system: a 'modern' law of marriage for the élite; a traditional law for the masses.

288 **Urbanization and family change.**
M. S. Gore. New York: Humanities, 1968. 273p. bibliog.
A careful study of the changes in family structure of the Vaish Aggarwals, a subcaste of the Delhi region, based on interviews and sample data. Gore, a student of the Bombay school of Indian sociology, examines the impact of both urbanization and industrialization, and such other attributes as education, occupational variations, and migration, on the gradual evolution of the urban nuclear family, with strong kinship ties, from the traditional rural joint family. He notes that the pace and scope of change has been slow and limited.

289 **Marriage, religion and society: pattern of change in an Indian village.**
Giri Raj Gupta. New Delhi: Vikas, 1974. 187p. bibliog.

A thorough study of marriages in rural India based on an analysis of 321 marriages since 1936. Gupta gives ethnographic information on marriage rituals. He finds that as of ca. 1970, child marriages, in contravention of state laws, were still prevalent, and that remarriage and polygamy were generally restricted to lower castes. There is an analysis of expenditures on marriage. The author estimates these to be in excess of a year's family income.

290 **Family web: a story of India.**
Sarah Hobson. Chicago: Academy, 1982. 1st American ed. 284p.

A sensitive and evocative account by a British journalist who participated in, as well as observed, the life of a joint family in rural Karnataka. Much of the text consists of the family members' own words as they discuss such topics as kinship ties, village politics, the role of women, sex, family planning, birth, female encounters with the supernatural, and changing roles.

291 **Kinship organization in India.**
Irawati Karve. New York: Asia, 1968. 3rd ed. 431p. maps. bibliog.

First published in 1953, this is a comprehensive survey of national patterns and regional differences in Indian kinship organization. The book begins with a discussion of caste and family and examines kinship usages as detailed in ancient and historical literature. Subsequent chapters discuss regional and intra-regional variations in kinship organization and the Hindu law of property, inheritance and succession in various areas of India.

292 **Family and kinship: a study of the Pandits of rural Kashmir.**
T. N. Madan. London: Asia, 1966. 259p. maps. bibliog.

A detailed account of the Kashmiri Brahman families of a particular village in northern India. Madan pays special attention to the role of the household, the smallest and most discrete group, in the kinship system. He finds that kinship groups do not act collectively in the economic, political, and juridical activities of the village.

293 **Himalayan polyandry: structure, functioning, and culture change: a field study of Jaunsar-Bawar.**
Dhirendra Nath Majumdar. New York: Asia, 1962. 389p. maps. bibliog.

An anthropological study of polyandry in the Jaunsar-Bawar region of the Himalayan foothills. Majumdar, founder of the Lucknow school of Indian sociology, examines the impact of this institution on family life and regional culture. There is a section on the limited impact of state-run community development programmes in the region.

294 **Husband-wife communication and motivational aspects of population control in an Indian village.**
Thomas Poffenberger (and others). New Delhi: Central Family Planning Institute, 1969. 117p. bibliog. (Monograph Series, no. 10).
This study, one of several carried out in the village of Rajpur in Gujarat, examines communication patterns between spouses, focusing on such issues as family planning and other personal domestic matters.

295 **The household dimension of the family in India: a field study in a Gujarat village and a review of other studies.**
A. M. Shah. Berkeley, California: University of California Press, 1974. 281p. bibliog.
The ideal typical Hindu joint family is a coparcenary unity comprising at least three generations in which each male member acquires a share at birth and the right to claim it as soon as he reaches the age of maturity. Based on a detailed analysis of over a century's research data as well as extensive field work in Gujarat, Shah argues that this type of family is characteristic only of the high castes. He also argues that, contrary to general opinion, the household size in India has not decreased during the last 100 years. The book includes a 100-page annotated bibliography on family in India.

296 **Punjabi century, 1857-1947.**
Prakash Tandon. Berkeley, California: University of California Press, 1968. 274p. map.

297 **Beyond Punjab, 1937-1960.**
Prakash Tandon. Berkeley, California: University of California Press, 1971. 222p.

298 **Return to Punjab, 1961-1975.**
Prakash Tandon. Berkeley, California: University of California Press, 1981. 211p.
The above three entries constitute the autobiography and family history of the Tandons, a family of western Punjab, written by a leading business executive. The first volume deals with the changing urban lifestyle in north India under British rule, the second with the author's spectacular rise in the Indian corporate universe, and the third with his tenure in state-controlled banking and trade enterprises. While substantial portions of these volumes deal with corporate organization and behaviour, there is a wealth of information on family life in India during the last 150 years.

299 **I give thee my daughter: a study of marriage and hierarchy among the Anavil Brahmins of south Gujarat.**
Kloss W. Van der Veen. Assen, the Netherlands: Van Gorcum, 1972. 307p. bibliog.
This study of marriage and caste concentrates on two villages in the Surat district of western India: one of predominantly high caste Brahmans, and the other of

lower caste ranking. By painstaking study of marriages arranged in these villages since 1930, the author shows how and why the non-Brahmans have tried to marry their daughters into poorer but ritually higher Brahman families.

Social change

300 India's ex-untouchables.
Harold Robert Isaacs. New York: Harper & Row, 1974. 188p. bibliog.

A well-written account of India's lowest castes and the impact of political legislation and social change upon them in urban India. Isaacs points out that some progress is being made because the motivation to become salaried employees - especially teachers and clerks - is strong among urban untouchables. However, the progress of untouchables in 'village India' where the bulk of them live has been minimal. An evocative study, originally published in 1965.

301 Democracy in search of equality: untouchable politics and Indian social change.
Barbara R. Joshi. Atlantic Heights, New Jersey: Humanities, 1982. 200p. bibliog.

A study of the drive of India's lowly 'scheduled' castes to obtain social equality in India. Joshi argues that the mobilization of these castes and their guaranteed representation in federal and state legislatures as well as in administration have helped them achieve a modicum of political equality. However, they continue to be discriminated against both socially and in private employment, and most particularly in rural areas where the benefits of land reform have not been fully extended to them.

302 The changing Brahmans: associations and elites among the Kanya-Kubjas of north India.
Ravindra S. Khare. Chicago: University of Chicago Press, 1970. 251p. bibliog.

A micro-sociological account of this principal north Indian Brahman subcaste and the efforts of its members to cope with changing socio-economic realities. Khare examines the role of caste associations in promoting the interests of the erstwhile priestly group and sponsoring caste-specific welfare programmes. He finds that these associations can somewhat deparochialize sectarian tendencies in Indian society but that they are unable to create a truly democratic society.

303 Change among India's harijans: Maharashtra, a case study.
Sunanda Patwardhan. New Delhi: Orient Longman, 1973. 239p. bibliog.

This readable study provides an historical account of the movement to liberate harijans from the stigma of untouchability during the 19th and 20th centuries. In addition, the author reports the changes that have taken place among five untouchable castes in the state of Maharashtra. She shows that the poorer an economic area, the more emphasis is placed on social stratification, but in industrial-urban areas caste organization has been weakened.

304 **Social movements and social transformation: a study of two backward caste movements in India.**
M. S. A. Rao. Delhi: Macmillan, 1979. 279p. bibliog.
Case studies of the genesis, growth, and dynamics of two backward caste movements: one state-wide and the other regional. The regional SNDP (Sri Narayan Dharma Paripalana) movement is an example of conflict between untouchables and 'clean' Hindu castes, while the Yadava movement exemplifies conflict between non-Brahman upper castes in northern India. These movements are analysed according to the conceptual categories of sociology of movements: relative deprivation, ideology and identity, leadership organization, and internal schisms.

305 **When a great tradition modernizes: an anthropological approach to Indian civilization.**
Milton Singer. New York: Praeger, 1972. 430p. bibliog.
A careful and empirical rejection of the view that traditional Indian society is resistant to change. Using Madras as a case study, and utilizing information on the industrial leadership of the city, on the one hand, and on the Vaisnavite tradition on the other, Singer concludes that the Indian tradition has utilized adaptive strategies for several centuries. He points out that, given the long history of the Hindu civilization of India, the process of modernization is likely to be complicated and not easily discernable.

306 **Caste in modern India and other essays.**
Mysore N. Srinivas. London: J. K. Publishers, 1978.
reprint of 1962 ed. 171p. bibliog.
According to Srinivas, three processes of social change are active in modern India: Sanskritization (the gradual availability of higher caste rituals to the untouchables), westernization, and secularization. The author argues that westernization and secularization, with the help of urbanization, have reduced the differences between the subcastes but the progress in Sanskritization continues to be painfully slow in modern India.

307 **Dimensions of social change in India.**
Edited by Mysore N. Srinivas, S. Seshaiah, V. S. Parasarathy. Bombay: Allied, 1977. 518p. map. bibliog. (National Seminar on Social Change, Bangalore, India, 1972).
A collection of consistently excellent papers dealing primarily with social change among caste, tribal, and religious groups. After establishing the constituents of socio-economic development, the authors examine changes in rural power structure, social stratification, the concept of dominant caste, status of women, and the place of Muslims in Indian society.

308 **The Marwaris: from traders to industrialists.**
Thomas Timberg. New Delhi: Vikas, 1978. 268p. maps.
bibliog.

An outstanding study of the emigrant businessmen from the semi-arid regions of
Marwar in modern Rajasthan, who now control between one-half and two-thirds
of all industrial assets and production in the 'private sector' of India. The
Marwari diaspora began in the 18th century and gained momentum in the late
19th and early 20th when many of them came to control business houses in
Calcutta and Bombay. Timberg provides regional details of their migration, their
business methods, and particularly information on changes in their attitudes,
values, and social and kinship structure.

Social problems and social welfare

309 **Greater universe of Kota: stress, change, and mental disorder
in an Indian village.**
G. Morris Carstairs, R. L. Kapur. London: Hogarth Press,
1976. 176p. maps. bibliog.

A study of the epidemic presence of psychiatric symptoms in a large sector of the
population of a southern coastal village, Kota. The authors discovered that over
36 per cent of persons in their sample survey had one or more psychiatric symptoms and more than 15 per cent required psychiatric treatment, thereby establishing that psychiatric disorders are as widespread in simpler third-world societies as
in complex industrialized nations.

310 **Prison as a social system: with special reference to
Maharashtra state.**
R. N. Datir. Bombay: Popular, 1978. 438p. bibliog.

A historical and structural study of the Indian prison system, based on information derived from prisons in the state of Maharashtra. The author examines the
evolution of the Indian prison system, changes in the theory and practice of
punishment, the uneasy balance between punishment (as a deterrent) and rehabilitation, and the limits of rehabilitation in India's prisons. A liberal criminologist,
the author is critical of the capacity of prisons as presently organized to function
successfully as rehabilitative institutions.

311 **Pills against poverty: a study of the introduction of western
medicine in a Tamil village.**
Göran Djurfeldt, Staffan Lindberg. Delhi: Macmillan,
1980. 232p. bibliog.

A study based on field-work in a coastal village twenty miles south of Madras,
inhabited mostly by untouchables. The book describes the incidence of disease
and mortality, the use of indigenous and western-allopathic systems of medical
practices, and the minimal success of the family planning programme in the
village. Especially valuable is the examination of the relationship between the
indigenous medical system and local religious values, and of the relationship of
the values of the dominant urban policy-makers to the western medical system.

312 Encyclopedia of social work in India.
Delhi: Publications Division, Ministry of Information and Broadcasting, 1968. 3 vols.

This encyclopaedia, issued by the government of India's Planning Commission, describes the social conditions of the Indian people. It is divided into seven parts. Part one consists of scholarly articles on various aspects of social problems and social work; part two provides biographical sketches of eminent but deceased social reformers; part three provides social statistics. The remaining parts contain information on social welfare agencies, scheduled castes and tribes, and other aspects of social work and welfare.

313 Social welfare: legend and legacy.
Edited by S. D. Gokhale. Bombay: Popular, 1975. 432p. bibliog.

An evaluation of the past performance, present status, and future prospects of social welfare work and agencies in India. The first of the five sections provides a retrospective view of the Indian Conference of Social Work. The next two sections deal with emerging concepts and concerns of social change and development. The last two examine trends in social work and social action. The book is critical of the use of foreign, especially American, consultants in the field of social work and of the poor quality and irrelevance of advice received by Indians in the field of welfare studies and research.

314 Indian Journal of Social Work.
Bombay: Tata Institute of Social Sciences, 1940- . quarterly.

One of the oldest Indian quarterlies, devoted to 'the promotion of professional social work'. Contains articles on various social issues including child welfare, juvenile delinquency, labour welfare, physically and mentally handicapped, criminology. Some book reviews.

315 Readings in social defence: a study of crimes and corrections in Indian society.
Edited by Navin Chandra Joshi, Ved Bhushan Bhatia. Allahabad, India: Wheeler Publishing, 1981. 271p. bibliog.

The book is divided into six sections: social services in India, immoral traffic in women, juvenile delinquency, beggary problems, study of crimes, and prison system. All articles discuss the taxonomy and etiology of social deviance, and suggest ameliorative measures.

316 Shamans, mystics, and doctors.
Sudhir Kakar. New York: Knopf, 1982. 306p. bibliog.

A fascinating descriptive analysis of mystical cults, shamans, indigenous doctors, and the 'sacred' component of Indian culture, concerned with 'healing' mental disorders in India. Kakar explores in depth the healing practices of a Sufi saint, a Tantric mystic, and an Ayurvedic doctor in the context of modern psychotherapy. Written by a western-trained Hindu psychotherapist, the book finds that modern psychoanalysis and other psychiatric therapies are of only marginal relevance to the mental health situation in India.

317 **Dynamics of crime: spatial and socio-economic aspects of crime in India.**
S. Venugopala Rao. New Delhi: Indian Institute of Public Administration, 1981. 201p. bibliog.
While attempting to examine the relevance of western criminological theories to India, the author provides a thorough overview of the problem of crime and disorder in India. The nature and magnitude of crime, the reliability of crime statistics, national trends, female criminality, juvenile delinquency, regional variations and their causes, urban crime, the economics of crime, and the penal system are some of the topics covered. The author believes that the incidence of crime in India, which has been rising steadily in recent years, has been consistently low compared to the west.

318 **Violence erupts.**
Edited by Udayan Sharma. New Delhi: Radha Krishna, 1978. 148p. bibliog.
Twelve narrative accounts of intercaste and intercommunal rural and urban riots between May 1977 and June 1978, supplemented by two analytical essays. The book supports the thesis that rising expectations of an untouchable rural proletariat and low caste agrarian *kulaks* (rich farmers), the defensive reaction of high caste families, the unscrupulous 'pandering' of parochial politicians, and the bumbling partiality of local bureaucracy have resulted in a trend of rising social violence in contemporary India.

Tribal life

319 **Tribalism in India.**
Kamaladevi Chattopadhyay. New Delhi: Vikas, 1978. 302p.
A popular account of tribal life intended for the lay reader, based on the experiences of the author who lived with various tribes while helping them to develop their crafts. Chattopadhyay has essays on nineteen different tribes from almost all parts of India. She believes that, in spite of many surface differences, tribal life throughout different areas of India is the same - with a high degree of psycho-social integration, high standards of craftsmanship, the blending of the sacred and profane, and complex kinship systems.

320 **Tribal heritage of India, volume 1: ethnicity, identity and interaction.**
Edited by Shyama Charan Dube. New Delhi: Vikas, 1977. 212p. bibliog.
The first of a projected four-volume encyclopaedic inventory on the scheduled tribes of India. The six essays included in this volume focus on the theme of ethnicity in the tribes of India, particularly its expression in their corporate self-identity. The authors examine how ethnic self-identity has led tribes to seek a larger share in scarce national development resources and has often caused violent conflicts in Indian society.

321 The kingdom of the young: abridged from *The Muria and their ghotul.*

Verrier Elwin. Bombay: Oxford University Press, 1968. 261p. maps. bibliog.

The author's abridgement of his 1947 definitive study of the Muria Gond tribe of central India. In the *ghotul* or youth dormitory, all boys and girls live together and are socialized into adult psycho-sexual life. Elwin discusses the membership rites, discipline, recreation, sexual attitudes, moral standards, and marriage of this tribal community, especially its young.

322 The tribal world of Verrier Elwin: an autobiography.

Verrier Elwin. New York: Oxford University Press, 1964. 356p.

The life story of an extraordinary scholar and human being. Born into a deeply religious evangelical home and educated at Oxford, Elwin journeyed to India where he came under Gandhi's influence. Inspired by the Gandhian ideals of service, he devoted his life to working among and studying and serving the tribal people of India. Instrumental in shaping the Indian government's policy towards the tribal peoples, he was awarded India's coveted honour, the Padma Bhushan.

323 Races and cultures of India.

D. N. Majumdar. New York: Asia, 1973. 4th rev. enl. ed. 457p. bibliog.

A basic anthropological text. Part 1 deals with the racial background of Indian culture and examines the role of environment and race in shaping culture. Part 2 examines tribal culture, economy, social institutions, and other ethnographic traits. In the concluding part, Majumdar deals with changes in the tribal societies resulting from increasing contacts with Hindu caste society.

324 The Santals, a tribe in search of a great tradition.

Martin Orans. Detroit, Michigan: Wayne State University Press, 1965. 149p. bibliog.

An account of the shifting historical pressures for and against acculturation and assimilation, and of the impact of a spreading market economy and industrialization on the Santal tribe of eastern India. Based on field-work on Santal migrants to the industrial town of Jamshedpur, the book examines the role of the 'great tradition' (those elements of Indian civilization that have persisted almost all over the subcontinent over an enormously long period of time) in modifying the 'little tradition' (elements that are local, fleeting, and accepted only by particular groups) but without totally destroying the distinctiveness of a tribal culture.

325 The Korwa of Palamau: a study of their society and economy.

Abanindra Narayan Sandhwar. Vienna: E. Stiglmayr, 1978. 341p. bibliog. (Acta Ethnologica et Linguistica, Series Indica).

This volume, part of the *Acta Ethnologica et Linguistica* series edited by L. P. Vidyarthi and Anna Hohenwart-Gerlachstein, deals with a small tribe living in the Palamau district of eastern India. Sandhwar discusses the social organization and economic, political, and social life of the tribe. He also provides short biographies of his informants and summaries of tribal cases dealing with marriage, divorce, and intertribal marriage.

326 The tribal culture of India.
Lalita Prasad Vidyarthi, B. K. Rai. Delhi: Concept, 1977. 487p. maps. bibliog.

A well-written survey of Indian tribal life. Topics covered include tribal dimensions of India, tribal economic, political, religious, and kinship structures, tribal art and folklore, settlement patterns of various Indian tribes, and cultural change induced in tribal areas by government-sponsored programmes. There is also a fascinating chapter on the growth of Indian anthropological studies, first under British influence, and lately (since 1950) under American influence.

Village life

327 Hindus of the Himalayas: ethnography and change.
Gerald Duane Berremen. Berkeley, California: University of California Press, 1972. rev. ed. 440p. bibliog.

Detailed anthropological examination of the role and significance of kinship, caste, and community in a village of the Garwhal region in the Himalayan foothills. The culture of the villagers is examined within the broad context of north Indian traditions. The revised edition includes observations on the return visit to the village ten years after the initial field survey and the lack of social progress in the intervening period.

328 Caste, class, and power: changing patterns of stratification in a Tanjore village.
André Beteille. Berkeley, California: University of California Press, 1971. 238p. map. bibliog.

A pioneering and detailed study of a south Indian village in the Tanjore district, written from a Marxian and Weberian point of view by an Indian sociologist. The author postulates that power, prestige, and wealth have become detached from caste status in recent years, and concludes that, as a result of rapid economic change, caste stratification will be seriously damaged, leading to a new and mobile balance among castes.

329 Patronage and exploitation: changing agricultural relations in south Gujarat.
Jan Breman. Berkeley, California: University of California Press, 1974. 287p. bibliog.

Case studies of two villages showing how the traditional system of labour exchange (*jajmani*) has broken down and has been replaced by the employer-employee relationship, with its inherent conflict. According to Breman, the social and economic position of the service castes has deteriorated, and government intervention in village social and political life has not mitigated the condition of the village landless poor.

330 **Elite politics in rural India: political stratification and political alliances in western Maharashtra.**
Anthony T. Carter. London: Cambridge University Press, 1974. 207p. maps. bibliog.
A descriptive analysis of political stratification and political alliances in rural western India. Carter argues that there is a fundamental difference between factions, which are relatively stable and hierarchically organized, and alliances between faction leaders which change frequently according to calculations of personal advancement.

331 **Development and change in Basudha: story of a West Bengal village.**
Ajit K. Danda, Dipali G. Danda. Hyderabad, India: National Institute of Community Development, 1971. 132p. maps. bibliog. (Diffusions of Innovations in Rural Societies, Report no. 20).
A village in West Bengal is the locale of this study of the relationship between planned change and social structure. The authors find that although it appeared that the villagers' level of participation in adopting social innovation was high, their real influence and participation was superficial, especially for the poor and low castes. The key role of the Village-Level Worker in the Community Development Programme as the link between villagers and administrative system is highlighted.

332 **Indian village.**
Shyama Charan Dube. London: Routledge, 1965. 248p. bibliog.
A classic account by an eminent sociologist of social structure, ritual activities, and extra-village activities in the late 1940s. The beginnings of change, as it affects family, caste, and village justice, are documented. According to Dube, growing individualism leads to frequent migration, the diminished authority of tradition, occupational diversification, weakened hereditary principles and paternalistic justice.

333 **Village studies: data analysis and bibliography. Volume 1: India 1950-1975.**
Edited by Claire M. Lambert. Epping, England: Bowker, for the Institute of Development Studies at the University of Sussex, Brighton, 1976. 329p. bibliog.
A bibliography of individual research studies undertaken in rural areas of India. The focus is on the information obtained and analyses completed of individual villages between 1950 and 1975. In addition to the annotations, the compilers have given computer-coded, numerical classification to the various categories of village life explored in these studies.

334 **My village, my life: portrait of an Indian village.**
Prafulla Mohanti. New York: Praeger, 1974. 230p.
An Indian, domiciled in England but constantly pulled back to his village in India, simply describes various aspects of life in his village. The joint family,

festivals, caste, the economic system, foods, religion, women, education, the cow, are all included. Village India comes alive through the author's technique of letting each villager speak for himself. Insight into the difficult concepts of dharma, karma, the economic interdependence of caste, and much else will come easier after reading this book. Excellent for newcomers to Indian studies.

335 Gaon: conflict and cohesion in an Indian village.
Henry Orenstein.   Princeton, New Jersey: Princeton University Press, 1965. 341p. bibliog.

Historical reconstruction and contemporary observation are used to develop a theory about the relationship of political, economic and social power to patterns of conflict and cohesion in a western Indian village. According to Orenstein, the *jajmani* system of hierarchically ordered labour exchange contributed to social integration, in spite of caste rivalries, in traditional India. However, modernization has introduced a new set of factors and has exacerbated social and caste conflicts along economic lines.

336 The politics of inequality: competition and control in an Indian village.
Miriam Sharma.   Honolulu, Hawaii: University of Hawaii Press, 1978. 262p. maps. bibliog.

An intimate view of the many subtle ways through which the dominant caste in an eastern Uttar Pradesh village exercises its authority. Sharma finds evidence that class interests have very slowly begun to replace caste as an organizing principle in the countryside. She examines the role of developing capitalist relations in agriculture and of the Green Revolution in the process.

337 Remembered village.
Mysore N. Srinivas.   Berkeley, California: University of California Press, 1976. 356p.

When the field notes of the author, a leading Indian sociologist, about Rampura village in Karnataka were burned in a fire, he decided to abandon the traditional problem-oriented monograph and revert to traditional ethnography. The result is a masterful account of a Mysore village in the late 1940s. Ecology, caste, marriage and family functions, religion, and agriculture are some of the topics addressed in this sensitive and masterful account.

338 Behind mud walls, 1930-1960: with a sequel: the village in 1970.
William H. Wiser, Charlotte M. Wiser.   Berkeley, California: University of California Press, 1973. rev. ed. 287p.

A little classic, this book describes the life of a north Indian village in which the Wisers lived for several years. The authors write movingly of the quality of Indian village life as well as of the capacity of the villagers to accept some modern advances. The concluding sequel was written by Mrs. Wiser who visited the village alone after her husband's death. A warm human document.

339 **Third class ticket.**
Heather Wood. London: Routledge & Kegan Paul, 1980.
331p. maps.
A land-owner of Bengal, in a gesture uncharacteristic of her class, bequeathed her wealth to finance an all-India railroad tour by forty of her fellow villagers. The author, a foreign research scholar, met these villagers by chance and accompanied them on part of their journey. The result is a sensitive rendering of the villagers' thoughts and feelings, at once simple and profound, and of the village life with its superstitions, phobias, and traditions. A wonderful introduction to India's village ethos.

Urban life

340 **Studies in India's urbanization: 1901-1971.**
Ashish Bose. New Delhi: Tata McGraw-Hill, 1974. 465p.
bibliog.
A series of studies on different social and demographic aspects of urbanization in India. Bose defines the term 'urban' in the context of Indian conditions, surveys the growth of urbanization between 1901 and 1971 on the basis of census data, and examines linguistic inter-state migration and dispersal. He also makes an empirical study of the emergence through land price speculation of an urban land aristocracy in the Delhi metropolis. The volume is rich in statistical data.

341 **Urban perspectives: 2001.**
Edited by C. S. Chandrasekhara, Deva Raj. New Delhi: National Institute of Urban Affairs, 1978. 284p. bibliog.
The proceedings of a multidisciplinary urban affairs symposium held in Delhi in 1977. Economic and social dimensions, urban settlement perspectives and technology, and infrastructure are the three major topical headings under which the volume's seventeen papers are grouped. The papers focus on the basic complementarity of urban and rural areas, the enormous increase in the transport needs of the society, the key role of energy in determining employment and settlement patterns, and the problems created by the unplanned and uncontrolled growth of a few metropolises.

342 **The Indian city: poverty, ecology and urban development.**
Edited by Alfred de Souza. New Delhi: Manohar, 1978.
243p. bibliog.
Eleven papers by as many scholars and bureaucrats specializing in urban affairs, from both India and overseas. These essays focus on the causes and consequences of and possible solutions to problems of urban poverty in India. Topics covered include: slums, women, nutrition, housing, community development activities, and tribal migration.

343 **From zamindar to ballot box: community change in a north Indian market town.**
Richard G. Fox. Ithaca, New York: Cornell University Press, 1969. 302p. bibliog.

This book discusses the changing relation of a small north Indian market town to the larger society of India. The author examines the reasons for the town's lack of internal social cohesion, and the role of business families and castes in promoting change. His thesis is that the nature of the town's social integration predetermines its reaction to modern political influences: when the social cohesion is weak, modern ideas penetrate the town more quickly.

344 **Indian urban scene.**
K. C. Sivaramakrishnan. Simla, India: Indian Institute of Advanced Study, 1978. 152p. maps. bibliog.

A masterful survey of India's large cities, new towns, slum areas, and the problems of the governance of urban settlements. The author argues that urban problems are only sharper manifestation of socio-economic maladies pervading India's rapidly developing but socially disruptive political economy.

345 **Kinship and urbanisation: white-collar migrants in north India.**
Sylvia J. Vatuk. Berkeley, California: University of California Press, 1972. 219p. bibliog.

An articulate study of the persistence of kinship and extended family ties among urban migrants. The author compares urban and rural norms of behaviour and shows that joint-families do not disintegrate in urban settings and that urban dwellers continue to maintain their village nexus. A readable account enlivened by anecdotes.

346 **Social life in an Indian slum.**
Paul D. Wiebe. New Delhi: Vikas, 1975. 179p. bibliog.

A comprehensive picture of the ways in which slum dwellers of Madras socially organize their lives and relate to other spatial and caste communities. Wiebe chose the slum of Chennanagar because its future held more hope than despair. He finds that the slum dwellers lived in poverty but not in a 'culture of poverty', and that caste structures and kinship ties provided them with psychological securities.

Women

347 **Elite women in Indian politics.**
Vijay Agnew. New Delhi: Vikas, 1979. 163p. bibliog.

The author argues that during the last one hundred odd years, women in the west have been primarily involved in the demand for suffrage and personal economic and professional advancement. Women in India, on the other hand, were active in the Indian independence movement, taking pride in the national culture of India which they believed to be threatened by western values. Mrs Agnew pays special attention to the role of Gandhi in bringing women into the nationalist movement. A chapter on the role of women in radical political movements sheds considerable light on a hitherto largely unexamined topic. Well written.

348 Tribal women in India.
Pratap C. Dutta (and others). Calcutta: Indian Anthropological Society, 1978. 199p. bibliog.

A collection of essays by Indian anthropologists, written in popular style, this book covers a wide range of variations in the life and activities of tribal women throughout India. Tribal women as coal miners, industrial workers, agricultural labourers, and food gatherers are discussed. Other chapters deal with tribal women's involvement in politics. In another chapter, 'Beautiful, hardy and wealthy yet weak and exploited', nomadic women are described. Included are several profiles of tribal women.

349 Women and social change in India.
Jana Matson Everett. New York: St. Martin's, 1979. 233p. bibliog.

This study traces the historical development of the women's movement in India from the late 19th to the mid-20th century, and compares it to similar movements in Britain and the United States. The key chapters analyse the campaign of Indian women for political representation and reform of Hindu personal law. The author suggests that relative to the American and British movements, Indian women enjoyed greater access to the political élite and therefore achieved greater success. However, no significant change in the social position of women, especially in rural areas, has taken place.

350 Femina.
Bombay: Bennett, Coleman, 1959- . semimonthly.

India's leading magazine for women, *Femina* carries articles on beauty, careers, clothes and fashion, cooking and home-making, and general culture.

351 Indian women.
Edited by Devaki Jain. New Delhi: Publications Division, Ministry of Information and Broadcasting, 1975. 312p.

This collection of essays by both men and women, scholars and journalists, is a comprehensive introduction to the 'woman generation' in India. The first six essays are historical, describing many aspects of Indian women's lives in the ages past, and are based on textual materials. Five more essays describe and analyse current patterns in the life of Indian women. The book's second half is devoted to studies of women in different regions, of varied religious backgrounds, and of three professions - nursing, monastic life, and prostitution.

352 Women's quest for power: five Indian case studies.
Devaki Jain, assisted by Nalini Singh, Malini Chand. Delhi: Vikas, 1980. 272p. bibliog.

Four of these case-studies deal with the efforts of low-income women to undertake co-operative income generation, and the fifth with efforts for social reform. Each case-study includes a discussion of the origins of the organization, its goals and activities, the characteristics of its organizers and members, its operational techniques, and, most importantly, an assessment of the organization's impact on the quality of women's lives. Devaki Jain's introductory essay is at once romantic and highly analytical.

353 Symbols of power: studies on the political status of women in India.
Edited by Vina Mazumdar. Bombay: Allied, 1979. 373p. bibliog.

This is the first volume in a series on women in a changing society planned by the Research Unit on Women's Studies of the SNDT (Shreemati Nathibai Damodar Thackersey) Women's University, Bombay, and the seventeen essays contained herein have a genteel Marxist flavour. Three essays deal with the broad issue of women in Indian national politics, another three examine in some depth the politicization of Indian women in the states of Gujarat, Maharashtra, and West Bengal. The last section has case-studies from ten states and presents a profile of women in state politics. Unfortunately, none of the essays deal in any significant way with the problems of sex inequality faced by rural Indian women.

354 Indian women and patriarchy: conflicts and dilemmas of students and working women.
Maria Mies, translated from the German by Saral K. Sarkar. New Delhi: Concept, 1980. 311p. bibliog.

This study, by a western scholar with long experience in India, deals with the conflicts and dilemmas of Indian women students and working women within a family system characterized as patriarchal. Biographical case-studies complement texts to reveal the role conflicts in India's changing society. Maria Mies concludes by saying that no matter how educated they are, urban women are still tied down by established patriarchal norms, and that a broad-based women's movement has not developed because urban and educated women remain unaware of the problems of rural women. A thought-provoking book.

355 Bengali women.
Manisha Roy. Chicago: University of Chicago Press, 1975. 206p. bibliog.

Through case-study accounts of the lives of upper and middle-class Hindu women in Calcutta, the author examines the psychological adjustments required of women in Indian joint families. The women describe their childhoods, marriages, lives as mothers, and old age. The author concludes that a woman's life as a wife is full of frustrations, but that as a young girl and as an elderly mother, she receives partial and indirect compensation and satisfaction. A sensitive, empirical study.

356 Status of Muslim women in north India.
Shibani Roy. Delhi: B. R. Publishing Corp., 1979. 241p. map. bibliog.

The changing position of middle-class Muslim women in the north Indian cities of Delhi and Lucknow is the focus of this scholarly study. The author argues that Muslim men fuelled the drive for Muslim women's education due to changing social norms. In turn, educated Muslim women revolted against the restrictions of traditional family life, especially sexual segregation at home and in society. In so doing these women gave up protective mechanisms inherent in traditional family life, giving rise to greater personal freedom and increased emotional insecurities.

Indians abroad

357 Roma: the Panjabi emigrants in Europe, central and middle Asia, the USSR and the Americas.
Weer Rajendra Rishi. Patiala, India: Punjabi University, 1976. 119p. maps. bibliog.

Based on a close study of etymology, linguistics, material culture, religious beliefs and practices, and historical evidence, the author validates the generally accepted belief that the gypsies, or Roma, are of Punjabi origin, most of them descending from Punjabis escaping the Muslim invaders of India. For a more complete account of gypsy life in Europe, this book should be supplemented by Jean-Paul Clebert, *The gypsies* (London: Vista, 1963. 234p.).

358 The banyan tree: overseas emigrants from India, Pakistan, and Bangladesh.
Hugh Tinker. New York: Oxford University Press, 1977. 204p. bibliog.

A survey of South Asian expatriates in fifty-three countries of the world. Tinker points out that South Asians have a poor share in the political power of the countries of their adoption irrespective of their number or economic power. He considers multiracialism as possible in Malysia but impossible in East and South Africa. The study's conclusion is pessimistic: Indians appear to be doomed to second-class status as citizens abroad due both to their refusal to integrate and to the suspicion of the majority towards Indians in the diaspora.

Politics and Government

General

359 India: government and politics in a developing nation.
Robert L. Hardgrave. New York: Harcourt, Brace, 1980.
3rd ed. 285p. maps. bibliog.
This edition brings a useful introductory text first published in 1970 up to date.
Hardgrave begins with an analysis of Indira Gandhi's stunning 1980 electoral
victory and triumphant return to power after a two-and-a-half-year eclipse. Mrs.
Gandhi is described as the only genuine all-India leader with an appeal transcending boundaries of caste, religion, and region. Hardgrave uses development
theory to highlight key issues in India's politics. The book has succinct chapters
on India's historical background, its constitution, institutional structures, interest
groups, political parties, electoral behaviour, and foreign policy.

360 Indira Gandhi's India: a political system reappraised.
Edited by Henry Hart. Boulder, Colorado: Westview, 1976.
313p. bibliog.
Nine chapters by Hart and his colleagues examine the origins, course, and likely
consequences of the Emergency proclaimed by Mrs. Gandhi in 1975. The book's
insights into the workings of India's political institutions continue to be valid.

361 Inside India today.
Dilip Hiro. New York: Monthly Review Press, 1979. rev.
ed. 338p. bibliog.
An overview of Indian urban and rural life and the impact of contemporary party
politics on Indian society. It is a neo-leftist partisan indictment of Mrs. Gandhi's
'constitutional coup' of June 1975 and of the Janata Party's non-revolutionary
and muddled overthrow of Mrs. Gandhi's régime in 1977. Mr. Hiro believes that

communists have a bright future ahead, due to the inability of the present political leadership to solve India's problems.

362 Indian Journal of Political Science.
Delhi: Indian Political Science Association, 1939- .
quarterly.
This quarterly carries scholarly articles on all aspects of politics, with primary
emphasis on India. Contributions are mainly from Indian, American, and British
political scientists. Some book reviews.

363 Politics mainly Indian.
W. H. Morris Jones. Bombay: Orient Longman, 1978.
392p. bibliog.
A useful survey of the work of this leading British political scientist specializing
on India. There are nineteen essays, and most deal with India. Of special significance is the introductory essay, written at the end of the Emergency of 1975-77,
which shows his confidence in the vitality of Indian democratic institutions.

364 Reason wounded: an experience of India's emergency.
Primila Lewis. New Delhi: Vikas, 1978. 207p.
An important contribution to the literature of the Emergency period in Indian
politics (1975-77). Ms. Lewis, a social worker, was arrested during her attempts
to organize labourers in the Delhi area. In telling the story of her arrest, she
presents a vivid picture of how the educated élite lost their belief in democracy
and corrupted even the police and judicial systems. The book belongs with Mary
Tyler's *My years in an Indian prison* (New Delhi: UBS Publishers, 1977. 191p.)
as an exposé of the corruption of power and the plight of the underclass in India.

365 A family affair: India under three prime ministers.
Ved Mehta. New York: Oxford University Press, 1982.
166p.
Another of the author's volumes of lucid reportage on contemporary India, this
one begins with Mrs. Indira Gandhi's massive 1977 electoral defeat. It chronicles
the unravelling of the Janata Party coalition that succeeded her and her triumphant return to power in 1980. The book is especially noteworthy for a revealing
interview with Janata prime minister Morarji Desai. For Mehta's pre-1977 reportage, see *Mahatma Gandhi and his apostles* (New York: Viking, 1977. 260p.)
and *The new India* (New York: Viking, 1977. 174p.), both equally readable.

366 The story of the integration of the Indian states.
Vapal Pangunni Menon. New York: Arno, 1972. 511p.
maps. bibliog.
Before independence the Indian subcontinent contained over 550 princely states,
many feeble in power and extremely limited in territory, but practically all ruled
far more autocratically than British India. After independence all of these states
were integrated into India and their rulers pensioned off. Mr. Menon was one of
the four architects of this integration - the other three were Mountbatten, the last
viceroy; Nehru; and Vallabhbhai Patel, the home minister. This lucid book
presents a detailed account of the process of integration.

Politics and Government. General

367 **Tradition and politics in South Asia.**
Edited by Robin James Moore. New Delhi: Vikas, 1979.
266p. bibliog.
Several essays analyse the concept of 'tradition' and the question of its continuing
relevance in Indian politics. Others deal with specific traditions in Indian political
history from ancient to modern times. Particular attention has been paid to
Indian responses to the challenge of modernity.

368 **The gentle anarchists: a study of the leaders of the**
Sarvodaya movement for non-violent revolution in India.
Geoffrey Ostergaard, Melville Currell. Oxford, England:
Clarendon, 1971. 421p. bibliog.
A detailed and systematic examination of the social characteristics, organization,
and opinions of the leaders of a Gandhian movement engaged in the task of social
reconstruction. The authors point out that 'revolutionary' Gandhians constitute
the vanguard of this movement, known as the Sarvodaya and dedicated to the
total reconstruction of Indian society. Though active in village affairs, the movement's senior leaders, according to the study, are generally urban-bred, highly
educated, economically well-off, and concerned with the 'ideals' of Gandhism
much more than are grass-root workers.

369 **India's political system.**
Richard Leonard Park, Bruce Bueno de
Mesquita. Englewood Cliffs, New Jersey: Prentice Hall,
1979. 2nd ed. 205p. maps. bibliog.
This revised and substantially enlarged second edition provides a brief but cogent
analysis of India's political system. In about 200 pages the authors summarize
India's history, her human and economic resources, social structure and other
traditional elements, and examine their impact on the organs, policy, and performance of the government. The value of the work is significantly enhanced by the
inclusion of election statistics, comparative international social statistics and
indicators (populations, areas, life expectancies, gross national products, per capita
incomes, etc.). A valuable select bibliography is given at the end.

370 **Politics and society in India.**
Surindar Suri. Calcutta: Naya Prakash, 1974. 338p.
bibliog.
A storehouse of information on Indian politics. The author focuses on the question of whether a society as complex as India's can achieve material progress and
maintain political stability, while remaining a parliamentary democracy. The
sweep is broad-ranging, covering the legacies of empires as well as contemporary
India's domestic problems and policies. An excellent book, suitable for reading-
lists on the government and politics of India.

Political biographies and memoirs

371 **India wins freedom: an autobiographical narrative.**
Abul Kalam Azad, introduced by Louis Fischer. New
Delhi: Sangam, 1978. reprint of 1959 ed. 262p. bibliog.

Memoirs of a nationalist Muslim who was the president of the Indian National
Congress during the crucial years between 1939 and 1946. Azad, a pragmatist,
criticizes Gandhi for being so preoccupied with moral objectives as to be blind to
political realities. He is equally critical of Nehru for acting on impulse or being
too theoretical. This reprint of the first edition has a new introduction by Louis
Fischer which helps put Azad's narrative in historical perspective.

372 **Nehru: a political biography.**
Michael Brecher. New York: Oxford University Press,
1959. 682p. bibliog.

An exhaustive examination of Nehru's life and political philosophy. Two perceptive chapters, 'Portrait of the man' and 'Portrait of a leader', at the beginning
and at the end of the life history, enhance the value of the book. This study is
not only an account of Nehru but also a careful analysis of the growth of
nationalism in India since 1885 (Nehru was born in 1889). The chapters recount-
ing the events leading to India's partition are superb.

373 **The story of my life.**
Morarji Ranchodji Desai. New York: Pergamon, 1978. 2
vols.

This two-volume autobiography of India's fourth prime minister is characteristi-
cally honest and self-righteous. Desai's differences with Mrs. Gandhi led to the
split in the ruling Congress Party in 1969, and in 1977 a loose coalition led by
him ousted Mrs. Gandhi from political power - albeit briefly. This work contains
a wealth of material on the inner workings of the Indian political élite.

374 **An autobiography: the story of my experiments with truth.**
Mohandas Karamchand Gandhi, translated from the original
Gujarati by Mahadev Desai. Ahmedabad, India:
Navajivan, 1976. 2nd ed. 392p.

Written by Gandhi during his imprisonment by the British in the 1920s, this
extraordinary autobiography first appeared serially in Gandhi's weekly news
magazine. Though the autobiography does not cover the last twenty-five years of
his life, when Gandhi stood at his political zenith, this is a remarkable book of
personal confessions that contains a frank discussion of Gandhi's human weaknesses. Ved Mehta's finely written study of the life and work of Gandhi and of
some of his disciples, *Mahatma Gandhi and his apostles* (New York: Viking,
1976. 260p.), provides a current assessment of the destiny of Gandhism in India.

375 **The Rajaji story. Volume 1: a warrior from the south.**
Rajmohan Gandhi. Madras: Bharathan, 1978- . bibliog.

Written by his grandson, this is an affectionate biography of Chakravarti Rajago-
palachari ('C. R.'), the first Indian governor-general of India. Once touted as
Gandhi's successor in Indian politics, C. R. was the first important nationalist

Politics and Government. Political biographies and memoirs

leader to recognize the existence of irreconcilable differences between Muslim and Hindu political leaders, thereby anticipating the inevitability of Pakistan. Gandhi's first volume describes the political life of C. R. until 1937 - further volumes are expected. For a complete but short biography, see Monica Felton *I meet Rajaji* (London: Macmillan, 1962. 193p.).

376 **Jawaharlal Nehru: a biography. Volume 1: 1889-1947. Volume 2: 1947-1956.**
Sarvepalli Gopal. Cambridge, Massachusetts: Harvard University Press, 1976-79. 2 vols., vol. 3 forthcoming. bibliog.

The official biography of India's first prime minister, by a distinguished Indian historian. The volumes are essentially partisan: Nehru's heroes and villains are Gopal's heroes and villains. The first volume includes a remarkable, full-length discussion of Nehru's wife, Kamala. The second volume has a reasoned discussion of Nehru's achievements and failures in foreign policy. Gopal dubs most of Nehru's associates as either 'mouldering mediocrities' or displaying 'the disadvantages of their eminence'. The last volume is due in 1983.

377 **M. N. Roy: political biography.**
V. B. Karnik. Bombay: Nav Jagriti Samaj, 1978. 656p. bibliog.

Manabendra Nath Roy was a leading operative of the Communist International and its representative in China during the 1920s. He was one of the founders of the Mexican and Indian communist parties. Expelled from the Communist International in 1929, he became a left-wing critic of Gandhian nationalism and a founder of a labour federation in India. This biography of Roy, by one of his trusted friends, is based on published sources and discusses Roy as a nationalist, communist, and humanist. Though not definitive, it is the best available.

378 **Dr. Ambedkar: life and mission.**
Dhananjay Keer. Bombay: Popular, 1971. 3rd ed. 541p. bibliog.

An unusually detailed and sympathetic biography of the leader of India's 'untouchables'. Keer carefully examines the debate between Gandhi and Ambedkar on the position and future role of the untouchables in Indian politics. He also provides an excellent analysis of Ambedkar's contribution to the framing and enactment of independent India's constitution. A major study of one of 20th-century India's important statesmen.

379 **Indira Gandhi: a biography.**
Zareer Masani. New York: Thomas Crowell, 1976. 341p. bibliog.

A detailed, but also critical, biography of India's third prime minister, and the daughter of its first prime minister, Jawaharlal Nehru. Banned in India for suggesting that Mrs. Gandhi might become a dictator, the book's great value lies in its examination of Indian socio-economic and political developments. Masani suggests that under Mrs. Gandhi's leadership *kulaks* (rich peasants) rather than the poor benefitted. The book is based on extensive interviews with Mrs. Gandhi and her contemporaries and utilizes her unpublished letters and those of her father.

Politics and Government. Political biographies and memoirs

380 **Gokhale: the Indian moderates and the British raj.**
Bal Ram Nanda. Princeton, New Jersey: Princeton
University Press, 1977. 520p. bibliog.
The biography of India's pre-eminent 'moderate' nationalist, who believed in using constitutional means to gain political rights from the British. Nanda carefully follows Gokhale from his years as a poor student in late 19th-century Bombay province into nationalist politics and his various social reform and political activities. Written for the specialist, the book includes several rare photographs.

381 **The indomitable Sardar.**
Kewalram Lalchand Panjabi. Bombay: Bharatiya Vidya
Bhavan, 1977. 4th ed. 299p. bibliog.
Vallabhbhai Patel, leader of the 'nationalist' wing of India's ruling Congress Party, was deputy prime minister in Nehru's cabinet. Tough-minded and stern, he exerted a moderating force on Nehru's socialist and internationalist idealism. It was he who charted the course that led to the integration of the several hundred quasi-autonomous princely states of British India into the Indian Union. Panjabi's biography is a straightforward narrative and, though lacking analytical rigour, it is the best available so far.

382 **The life and death of Mahatma Gandhi.**
Robert Payne. New York: Dutton, 1969. 703p. bibliog.
A sensitive, well-written, well-researched biography of India's most beloved political leader. Without detracting from Gandhi's enormous contributions to India and the world, Payne does not neglect to point out that Gandhi was a bad father, an impossible husband, and an idiosyncratic political leader. The account of Gandhi's final tragedy - India's partition and his assasination - is narrated movingly. For an equally good and objective biography, see *The life of Mahatma Gandhi* (New York: Harper, 1950. 558p. bibliog.) by Louis Fischer, who had the advantage of knowing Gandhi and Nehru personally.

383 **J. P.: his biography.**
Allan Scarfe, Wendy Scarfe. New Delhi: Orient Longman,
1975. 462p. bibliog.
Jayaprakash Narayan, the quixotic and charismatic Indian leader who was a founder of the Socialist Party and later converted to Gandhian non-violence, is the subject of this affectionate and well-researched biography by a Quaker couple. Once touted as Nehru's successor to the prime-ministership of India, Narayan chose to renounce partisan electoral politics, and devoted his life to a mixture of social reform and political agitation against government excesses. Written in 1975, the book naturally does not cover the period of Narayan's apotheosis in 1977-78 when he became the guiding philosopher of India's Janata Party in its triumph over Mrs. Gandhi's Congress.

384 **Sri Aurobindo: a biography and a history.**
K. R. Srinivasa Iyengar. Pondicherry, India: Sri Aurobindo
International Centre of Education, 1972. 3rd rev. enl. ed. 2
vols. bibliog.
A biography of Aurobindo Ghose, college professor, political revolutionary, and philosopher. The book describes Aurobindo's lonely years in England, his efforts to obtain an appointment to the Indian Civil Service, his employment in the

princely state of Baroda, his relationship with Tilak and other political revolution-
aries during 1902-10, and his activities as a poet-philosopher in Pondicherry between 1910 and 1950. Well written.

385 India's walking saint: the story of Vinoba Bhave.
Hallam Tennyson. New York: Doubleday, 1955. 224p.

An absorbing and human account of the life and socio-economic activities of
Gandhi's spiritual heir. In the early 1950s, Bhave caused a stir in Indian political
life by travelling on foot from village to village preaching non-violence and asking
large land-holders to voluntarily distribute their land to the landless. This sensitive biography is a valuable contribution to our understanding of Gandhian
'voluntarism' and its distrust of centralized forms of government.

386 Tilak and Gokhale: revolution and reform in the making of modern India.
Stanley Wolpert. Berkeley, California: University of
California Press, 1977. 370p. bibliog.

A study of the contributions of India's two chief nationalist leaders before
Gandhi's post-First World War emergence. Gokhale was a moderate who believed
in using constitutional methods to gain Indian independence. Tilak, on the other
hand, chose the confrontational path. Wolpert carefully examines the motives and
actions of both these leaders in an objective manner.

Political parties and elections

387 The Annual Register of Indian Political Parties.
New Delhi: Indian Institute of Applied Political Research,
1972/73-. annual.

This useful reference annual is a comprehensive record of organizational information and documents of all the major national political parties, and several regional
and communal parties. The strengths of these parties in the parliament and state
assemblies are provided in a tabular form. Invaluable.

388 Radical politics in South Asia.
Edited by Paul R. Brass, Marcus F. Franda. Cambridge,
Massachusetts: MIT, 1973. 449p. bibliog.

A comparative study of socialist and communist parties in six regions of India,
Bangladesh, and Ceylon that finally lays to rest the bogey of Moscow's meddling
in the affairs of Indian communist parties. The thesis of the book is that the
tactics of radical parties in South Asia change as a result of factional, ideological,
and personal disputes, and that external pressures, whether from Russia or elsewhere, have very little to do with the development of radical politics in contemporary India.

389 India votes: a source book on Indian elections.
Edited by R. Chandidas, Ward Morehouse. Bombay:
Popular, 1968-70. 2 vols.

A thorough study of the 1967 general elections in India. The importance of these volumes lies in providing a statistical data base on the performance of all political parties in both state and national elections, thereby making possible future comparative studies. The second volume has statistical information on the 1968-69 mid-term elections to state assemblies.

390 The major socialist parties in India: a study of leftist fragmentation.
Lewis P. Fickett, Jr. Syracuse, New York: Maxwell School of Citizenship and Public Affairs, Syracuse University, 1976. 185p. bibliog.

An excellent discussion of the progressive fragmentation of socialist parties, particularly the Praja Socialist Party and the Samyukta Socialist Party, especially during the elections of 1967. Fickett examines the better performance of the parties of the right and points out that if the socialists had been united, they would have become the principal opposition to the dominant Congress Party.

391 The Naxalite movement: a Maoist experiment.
Sankar Ghose. Calcutta: Firma KLM, 1975. 301p. bibliog.

A study of the Naxalite movement (named after the town where it originated) under the leadership of a communist faction wholly committed to the Chinese path and to armed insurrection. Ghose has written an admirable account of the ideology propounded by the Naxalite leader Charu Mazumdar, the armed insurrection against the government led by him in eastern India, principally Bengal and Assam, and his expulsion from the Communist Party of India-Marxist (CPI-M) in 1971 after the failure of the insurrection.

392 The Akalis: past and present.
Kailash Chander Gulati. New Delhi: Ashajanak, 1974. 259p. bibliog.

A well-documented survey of the Sikh communal party and its movement for autonomy in the Punjab. Though less analytical than Nayar (q.v.), Gulati provides more facts and details about Sikh politicians, and their factionalism. A useful update to Nayar.

393 Political parties in India.
Horst Hartmann. Meerut, India: Meenakshi, 1982. 4th ed. 355p. bibliog.

First published in 1971, *Political parties in India* is widely used as a textbook in India and abroad. The author analyses the political parties in terms of their organizational structures, party-building techniques, and the roles they play in Indian politics and elections. He emphasizes the positive aspects of the constitution in strengthening the political consensus and national integration. He believes that democracy is suited to Indian pluralism and can provide stable government. Summaries of various election statistics and manifestos of political parties are provided. The revised edition brings the coverage of political parties up to the 1980 elections. Excellent bibliography.

Politics and Government. Political parties and elections

394 **Jan Sangh and Swatantra: a profile of the rightist parties in India.**
M. A. Jhangiani.   Bombay: Manaktalas, 1967. 223p.
bibliog.

A detailed account of the genesis, structure, ideology, and performance of two parties of the right with shared attitudes of opposition to communism. Each party is treated separately and their differences on certain vital issues are carefully summarized. Jhangiani's book should be read in conjunction with Craig Baxter, *The Jana Sangh: a biography of an Indian political party* (Philadelphia: University of Pennsylvania Press, 1969. 352p. bibliog.), which provides an analysis of the Sangh performance in the 1967 election, and Howard Erdman, *The Swatantra Party and Indian conservatism* (London: Cambridge University Press, 1967. 356p. bibliog.), which cogently analyses Swatantra's anti-statism.

395 **The Congress Party of India: the dynamics of one-party democracy.**
Stanley A. Kochanek.   Princeton, New Jersey: Princeton University Press, 1968. 516p. bibliog.

Examines the relationship between and among the president and the working (executive) committee of the Congress Party, the prime minister, and the Cabinet. The author's view is that since independence India has been a one-party democracy. He regards the loss of hegemony by the Congress Party in 1967 as a minor episode. The analysis of the party's success in remaining a viable force under changing political conditions is penetrating. Neat periodization is the book's main asset.

396 **Communism in India.**
Gene D. Overstreet, Marshall Windmiller.   Berkeley, California: University of California Press, 1959. 603p. bibliog.

A thorough and painstaking study of the growth of communism in India. The discussion of the failure of the communist movement to come to terms with Gandhian nationalism is treated most refreshingly. Equally impressive is the discussion of communist drives in the first decade of India's independence, a period which saw the movement divide into two - those who worked through 'constitutional' means, and those who, as in Telangana, took extralegal, often violent, measures to sieze land from the landholders, establish a parallel government, and to develop a communist sanctuary on the 'soviet' model. There is also an excellent discussion of the Communist Party's relationship with the Comintern and Stalin. While the book has certain factual errors and at times wrongly identifies some people as communist, it is nevertheless the most thorough account of the communist movement in India until 1957. For the specialist.

397 **Indian communism: split within a split.**
Mohan Ram.   Delhi: Vikas, 1969. 292p. bibliog.

An excellent supplement to the work of Overstreet and Windmiller (q.v.). Ram reviews a period of twenty years and throws light on the decline, re-emergence, and prospects of Maoism in India. His main contention is that the split within the Communist Party of India is not directly related to the Sino-Soviet rift.

398 Party and democracy in India.
S. N. Sadasivan. New Delhi: Tata-McGraw Hill, 1977.
537p. bibliog.
History and the socio-economic basis of local, regional, and national political parties (up to 1977) is the theme of this book. Sadasivan examines the internal structure and functioning of parties and their role in the larger political process. Comprehensive sketches are provided of Indian political parties.

399 Communism in Indian politics.
Bhabani Sen Gupta. New Delhi: Young Asia, 1978. 471p.
bibliog.
This highly informative book provides an excellent review of the role of communism in Indian politics since 1964. The development of three rival communist parties is fully explored, and their attitude toward participation in India's parliamentary system, as in labour and peasant movements, is carefully examined. Sen Gupta's main contention is that communism is a legitimate political force in India.

400 CPI-M: promises, prospects, problems.
Bhabani Sen Gupta. New Delhi: Young Asia, 1979. 296p.
bibliog.
A follow-up to the author's *Communism in Indian politics* (q.v.), this book deals with the strides made by the independent Communist Party of India-Marxist. The author analyses the party's success in mobilizing peasants as well as workers and lower middle-class civil servants in West Bengal, Tripura, and Assam, and its lack of success in Kerala. A chapter on inter-communist unity assesses its prospects.

401 A history of the Praja Socialist Party.
Hari Kishore Singh. Lucknow, India: Narendra, 1959.
239p. bibliog.
The author traces the growth of the Praja Socialist Party (People's Socialist Party) and the marriages of convenience between and among assorted rival factions, each unwilling to compromise on political ideology. Singh concludes that the party has a bleak future because of intense personal rivalries.

402 Split in a predominant party: the Indian National Congress in 1969.
Mahendra Prasad Singh. New Delhi: Abhinav, 1981. 315p.
bibliog.
According to the author, Mrs. Indira Gandhi's decision to leave the Indian National Congress and form her own congress was the most momentous upheaval in the grand old party of Indian nationalism since the 1907 split between the extremists and the moderates. The author analyses the major factors underlying this split and the reasons for the failure of the parent Congress Party to remain a dominant force in Indian politics.

403 **Faction and front: party system in south India.**
James Walch.   New Delhi: Young Asia, 1976. 464p. maps.
bibliog.

This study examines the evolution and workings of the party system in three
south Indian states: Tamil Nadu, Kerala, and Andhra Pradesh. In Tamil Nadu a
two-party system has emerged, in Kerala, a system of competing multi-party
coalitions, and in Andhra Pradesh a system of one-party dominance. The author
examines the 'content of conflict' in each state in order to explain why their
politics have developed differently.

404 **Party building in a new nation: the Indian National Congress.**
Myron Weiner.   Chicago: University of Chicago Press,
1967. 509p. maps. bibliog.

An empirical work based on five distinct Congress Party branches in five different
states. The thesis of the book is that the party has been eminently successful in
mediating conflicting demands of modernization and of traditional society. The
book, unfortunately, lacks any case study from the 'Hindi heartland' of India.

State and local politics

405 **Government and politics of big cities: an Indian case study.**
Ali Ashraf.   Delhi: Concept, 1977. 201p. bibliog.

A comparative study of three major cities in India - Calcutta, Kanpur, and
Ahmedabad. For each city Ashraf analyses the composition of civic leadership by
caste and occupation; the history of its municipal government; the relationship
between elected officials and civil servants; and finally the performance of the
city government in providing municipal amenities. Ashraf finds that the ethic of
the businessmen who dominate Ahmedabad's civic life has given the city a
responsible administration, whereas the bureaucratic ethic that permeates municipal administration in Kanpur and Calcutta has let the citizens of these two cities
down. Quite naturally the author recommends that city governments in India
emulate Ahmedabad.

406 **Language, religion, and politics in north India.**
Paul R. Brass.   New York: Cambridge University Press,
1974. 467p. maps. bibliog.

Communalism and linguistic regionalism, the two chief obstacles to national integration, are examined in this study. There are three case studies: the Maithili
language movement in Bihar, the Muslim community's struggle for state recognition of Urdu in several states, and the Sikh autonomy movement.

407 **Opposition in a dominant party system: a study of the Jan Sangh, the Praja Socialist Party, and the Socialist Party in Uttar Pradesh.**
Angela Sutherland Burger. Berkeley, California: University of California Press, 1969. 306p. bibliog.
An analysis of opposition political parties in India's most populous state. The author focuses on the processes and problems associated with party-building in a state dominated by the ruling Congress Party. Burger asks two key questions: can any opposition party succeed when the dominant party is identified with India's independence; and secondly, what is the relationship between the goals of the dominant party and the activities of the opposition parties? An eminently readable yet profoundly scholarly work. Though written in 1969, the insights offered on opposition party functioning continue to be valid.

408 **West Bengal and the federalizing process in India.**
Marcus F. Franda. Princeton, New Jersey: Princeton University Press, 1968. 257p. bibliog.
Using case studies of the Damodar Valley Corporation (an integrated water, energy, and other resources development project on the lines of the American Tennessee Valley Authority), reorganization of states on linguistic lines, and land reforms, the author examines the political and social context of federal-state relations in India. The analysis takes account of party politics, group pressures, and mass behaviour.

409 **Agrarian crisis in India: the case of Bihar.**
F. Tomasson Jannuzi. Austin, Texas: University of Texas Press, 1974. 233p. maps. bibliog.
A careful analysis of the Congress Party's commitment to agricultural reforms and its failure to achieve them. Jannuzi finds that entrenched landlord interests in the Congress Party, an antiquated bureaucratic set-up and the unresolved conflict between economic efficiency and distributive social justice have all combined to impede genuine agrarian progress in Bihar.

410 **The politics of power: defections and state politics in India.**
Subhash C. Kashyap. Delhi: National, 1974. rev. ed. 709p. maps. bibliog.
A scholarly and pioneering analysis of the wave of political defections that swept seven Indian states in the wake of the unprecedented Congress Party electoral débacle in 1967. This is a useful study of a demoralising political practice that continues to shape state and national politics in India.

411 **Ethnicity and equality: the Shiva Sena party and preferential policies in Bombay.**
Mary Fainsod Katzenstein. Ithaca, New York: Cornell University Press, 1979. 237p. bibliog.
A book about the political movement in the city of Bombay to obtain preferential treatment in employment opportunities for the Maharashtrians. This study explores the conflict between meritocratic recruitment irrespective of ethnic and caste affiliation, and preferential employment based on ethnic and regional representation. Katzenstein makes no normative assessment of the policy of

97

preferential treatment but argues that such treatment is here to stay and need not be considered contrary to democratic principles.

412 Elections in India: its [sic] social basis.
Susheela Kaushik.   Calcutta: K. P. Bagchi, 1982. 238p. bibliog.

Taking the view that most Indian election studies are 'too microscopic, time bound, and territorially delimited', this neo-Marxist scholar tries to incorporate the dynamics of political economy in her analysis. Mrs. Kaushik presents a lucid picture of rural and urban Indian society. Her interpretations of such standbys in Indian electoral analysis as the 'wave' phenomenon, vote banks, and primordial voter identifications are refreshing.

413 State politics in India.
Edited by Iqbal Narain.   Meerut, India: Meenakshi, 1976. 2nd ed. 620p. bibliog.

A collection of twenty-five articles dealing with various aspects of state politics in India. Each state is analysed. The book's main focus is on the period 1967-71, though adequate attention is paid to the years before and after that period. Most of the articles deplore the emergence of coalition politics in the states and emphasize the negative consequences of this trend. Three essays by the editor provide the conceptual framework and a cogent summary. This is the best survey of state politics in India.

414 Minority politics in the Punjab.
Baldev Raj Nayar.   Princeton, New Jersey: Princeton University Press, 1966. 373p. maps. bibliog.

A study of state politics in the Punjab since Indian independence in 1947. Nayar analyses the Sikh demand for a separate state, the Hindu resistance to that demand, and the Congress Party's and government's pragmatic attitude toward the Sikh autonomy movement. A precise, well-researched, and ably written study.

415 Big city government in India: councilor, administrator and citizen in Delhi.
Philip Oldenburg.   Tucson, Arizona: University of Arizona Press, 1976. 400p. bibliog. (Association for Asian Studies, Monograph no. 31).

A pioneering study of metropolitan administration and politics. Oldenburg argues that elected and administrative officials in the Indian metropolitan system are concerned almost entirely with policy implementation and that policy determination takes place at the state or federal level. Based on interviews, newspaper, periodical accounts, and government records, the author examines the relationship between elected municipal councillors, other ward constituents, and city administrators.

416 **Elections and political development: the South Asian experience.**
Norman D. Palmer. London: Hurst, 1975. 340p. bibliog.
A valuable study, for the specialist, of the role of parliamentary and other legislative elections in India, Pakistan, Sri Lanka, and Nepal, based in part on a sampling of Indian voters' opinions. The author believes that, despite their shortcomings, elections have given political stability to India, but, writing in 1974, he expresses caution concerning the future.

417 **1977 elections in India.**
Sharda Paul. New Delhi: Associated, 1977. 236p.

418 **1980 elections in India.**
Sharda Paul. New Delhi: Associated, 1980. 336p.
The above two entries, organized in identical fashion, are divided into two parts. The first parts deal with the political background of events leading to the 1977 and 1980 elections, and the second parts contain election manifestos of major national and regional parties participating in these elections. The 1977 election saw the defeat of Mrs. Gandhi's Congress Party and the 1980 election her re-emergence following the Janata Party's failure to rule in a united fashion. Separate chapters provide election results from the first parliamentary elections up to 1977 and up to 1980.

419 **Jammu and Kashmir: triumph and tragedy of Indian federalism.**
Balraj Puri. Delhi: Sterling, 1981. 280p. bibliog.
A thorough survey of the causes and consequences of the special status enjoyed by the state of Jammu and Kashmir in India's federal structure. The author examines all those provisions of the Indian constitution that are not applicable to the state and pays special attention to the interplay of ideological, communal and emotional factors in the state's politics.

420 **Bharatiya Jana Sangh, organization and ideology: Delhi, a case study.**
Geeta Puri. New Delhi: Sterling, 1980. 292p. bibliog.
An analytical survey of the ideology, leadership pattern, and organizational style of the Bharatiya Jana Sangh's Delhi unit. The ambivalent relationship of the Sangh to the Rashtriya Swayamsevak Sangh (RSS), a well-disciplined Hindu socio-cultural organization, is ably analysed. Additional chapters discuss the Jana Sangh's role in the anti-Indira Gandhi protest movements of the early 1970s, and in the Janata Party coalition government in India between 1977 and 1979.

421 **Patterns of panchayati raj in India.**
Edited by G. Ram Reddy. Delhi: Macmillan, 1977. 213p. maps. bibliog.
Panchayati raj - the administration of rual units by elected local leaders - has long been considered an ageless institution of participatory democracy in the Indian countryside. Reddy's introductory chapter discusses the modernization of this institution and its relationship to state bureaucracy. Fifteen other essays analyse *panchayati raj* in the states. A useful survey.

Politics and Government. State and local politics

422 Regionalism in India: a case study of the Telangana issue.
G. R. S. Rao. New Delhi: Chand, 1975. 191p. bibliog.
A study of the violent movement for a separate Telangana state. The author examines the safeguards promised to the residents of Telangana in the state of Andhra in such matters as jobs, education, property, economic development, and political representation, and the state government's failure to honour them in their entirety. An excellent case-study of sub-nationalism in India.

423 The expansive elite: district politics and state policy making in India.
Donald B. Rosenthal. Berkeley, California: University of California Press, 1977. 337p. maps. bibliog.
A useful case-study of how rural local élites in two districts in Maharashtra influence the course of state and national politics and policy-making. The book is based on extensive interviews. An epilogue written during the Emergency in India (1975-77) shows how most of the features delineated earlier are of continuing significance.

424 The Congress Party in Rajasthan: political integration and institution-building in an Indian state.
Richard Sisson. Berkeley, California: University of California Press, 1971. 347p. bibliog.
A turgidly written but very valuable behavioural study of political integration and institution-building in the state of Rajasthan by the Congress Party. Social and political antecedents of Congress in the princely states of Rajputana, post-independence recruitment and caste and factional mobility are analysed in detail.

425 The coalition ministries in Punjab.
Manju Verma. Patiala, India: Sonu Sales, 1978. 164p. bibliog.
This book discusses and analyses the three coalition governments that ruled the Punjab from 1967 to 1970, and also includes a brief review of the Akali-Janata coalition of 1977. Based on newspaper accounts, it sheds light on the failure of coalition parties to provide stable government in the state.

426 Sons of the soil: migration and ethnic conflict in India.
Myron Weiner. Princeton, New Jersey: Princeton University Press, 1978. 383p. maps. bibliog.
This book examines a fundamental problem facing many multi-ethnic federal states of the third world: the right of free inter-state migration versus the rights of the local population. Three case studies, of Assam, of the Chota Nagpur region of Bihar, and of Hyderabad, are the context for a brilliant analysis of the rise of 'nativist' movements, the costs and benefits of free migration, and the impact of ethnic conflicts on national identity.

Structure of government

427 The president of India.
Bhaskar Chandra Das.   New Delhi: Chand, 1977. 499p.
bibliog.

This work examines the powers of the president of India as prescribed by the constitution and the role this office has assumed in actual practice. Das believes that in times of political crisis the president can be of pivotal importance and can act independently of the advice offered by the prime minister. The author indicates that India's federal parliamentary system has the possibility of evolving into a French-style presidential system.

428 The office of the governor: its constitutional image and reality.
N. S. Gehlot.   Allahabad, India: Chugh, 1977. 320p.
bibliog.

The governor's powers, such as dissolution of the state legislature and naming chief ministers, are limited as long as one party has a clear majority and provides checks to his powers. However, since 1967, the governor's role has assumed special importance due to the emergence of shaky coalition régimes or one-party cabinets based on razor-thin majorities. This well-organized book examines the governor's role in India's changing political environment. A series of case-studies and appendixes add to the book's value.

429 Cultures in conflict: the four faces of Indian bureaucracy.
Stanley J. Heginbotham.   New York: Columbia University Press, 1975. 236p. bibliog.

Based on field-study in the Arcot district in Tamil Nadu state, this book focuses on the functioning of bureaucracy and its role in promoting rural development. Heginbotham concludes that four factors - the Hindu concept of dharma (duty), the Gandhian ideal of *sarvodaya* (total reconstruction), the Mughal legacy of non-intervention in rural life, and the general apathy of the western-oriented bureaucratic élite - are basic, often conflicting, constraints in the lives of Indian civil servants. The result is an indecisive, procrastinating bureaucratic tradition in modern India.

430 District administration in India.
Sucha Singh Khera.   New Delhi: National, 1979. 2nd rev.
ed. 359p. bibliog.

Written by a distinguished former civil servant, this book is an exhaustive and insightful description and analysis of district administration. Law, revenue, economic development, social welfare, and other areas are all discussed with expertise in this well-written study.

431 State governments in India.
Shriram Maheshwari.   Delhi: Macmillan, 1979. 328p.
bibliog.

A basic survey of the structure, function, and administration of state governments in India. The author discusses the evolution of state governments, their place in

Politics and Government. Structure of government

the overall constitutional framework, the role of the governor, the state council of ministers, the secretariat, various departments, the Boards of Revenue, divisional, district, urban and rural administrations. While additional chapters examine centre-state relations and regionalism, there is very little discussion of the role that state legislatures play in state government.

432 Glimpses of the working parliament.
S. L. Shakdher. New Delhi: Metropolitan, 1977. 396p. bibliog.

A descriptive institutional study of the parliament of India. Shakdher deals with distinctive features of parliamentary procedure in India, the powers of the Speaker, parliamentary privileges, and parliament's relationship to the judicial and executive brances of the government. The narrative is enlivened by numerous illustrative incidents.

433 State and district administration in India.
J. D. Shukla. New Delhi: National, 1976. 387p.

A detailed descriptive text on state and district administration. This book supplements Khera's discursive account (q.v.) of districts and also deals exhaustively with the structure and staffing patterns of state administration.

Constitution and Legal System

434 The Indian constitution: cornerstone of a nation.
Granville Austin. Bombay: Oxford University Press, 1972.
Indian ed. 390p. bibliog.

A political history describing how the constitution of India was shaped between 1946 and 1949. The author investigates the interplay of ideals and personalities, past constitutional practices in British India and future aspirations, and the economic and social assumptions implicit in the document. The discussion of the constitution's Directive Principles is extremely lucid.

435 Introduction to the constitution of India.
Durga Das Basu. New Delhi: Prentice-Hall of India, 1982.
9th ed. 423p. bibliog.

A readable book for the non-specialist on the basic features of India's constitution as interpreted and reinterpreted by the Indian judiciary. All leading court decisions until June 1981 are included, together with all major amendments to the constitution.

436 The Indian Supreme Court and politics.
Upendra Baxi. Lucknow, India: Eastern, 1980. 272p.
bibliog.

In India, as in the United States, the resolution of key political questions has often been left to the Supreme Court, which has issued conflicting opinions based on constitutional provisions. This lively, opinionated but informed book explains why the court is using a loose 'constructionist' approach and is gradually moving to a populist direction.

437 **The Supreme Court of India and parliamentary sovereignty: a critique of its approach to the recent constitutional crisis.**
Rajeev Dhavan. Bombay: Sterling, 1976. 404p. bibliog.

Are there limitations on the powers of the Indian parliament to amend the constitution? For over twenty years the Indian Supreme Court has been struggling to define with precision the 'implied' limitations on the powers of parliament to amend the constitution. Dhavan examines the leading judicial decisions on this issue, culminating in the famous Kesavanand Case of 1973 which held that parliament was vested with the power to amend or even abrogate the fundamental rights guaranteed by the constitution.

438 **The Supreme Court of India: a socio-legal critique of its juristic techniques.**
Rajeev Dhavan. Bombay: Tripathi, 1977. 524p. bibliog.

A thorough, well-researched, analytical survey of Indian Supreme Court judges and their influence on the development of Indian jurisprudence. Dhavan examines the background of key Supreme Court judges to assess their judicial contributions. He identifies key issues - such as preventive detention, property rights, secularism and minority protection, obscenity, parliamentary sovereignty - and explores them in depth, utilizing Supreme Court cases and majority and dissenting opinions expressed in decisions.

439 **Indian constitutional law.**
Mahabir Prasad Jain. Bombay: Tripathi, 1978. 759p. bibliog.

A clear and exhaustive narrative description of the theory and workings of the Indian constitution. The book's value is enhanced by a brief account of the historical background of each topic and by careful comparisons with other constitutions. References are made to the latest case law.

440 **The Indian legal system.**
Edited by Joseph Minattur. Bombay: Tripathi, 1978. 683p. bibliog.

This survey, sponsored by the Indian Law Institute, New Delhi, is intended for foreign scholars. Contributions from Indian legal practioners and scholars examine the more important aspects of the Indian legal system. Particularly noteworthy are the essays on constitutional, civil, criminal, labour, family, and administrative law. Documentation is primarily from court cases decided by the state high courts and the Supreme Court of India.

441 **India's constitution.**
Moolamattom Varkey Pylee. New Delhi: Asia, 1979. 3rd rev. ed. 471p. maps. bibliog.

An up-to-date and comprehensive undergraduate-level text. Following a brief introduction, the book is divided into six sections that mirror the constitution itself: preamble, territory and citizenship, fundamental rights and directive principles, machinery of the Union and state governments, the federal system, and miscellaneous provisions. A postscript includes amendments to the constitution adopted in 1978.

442 The framing of India's constitution.

Edited by B. Shiva Rao. New Delhi: Indian Institute of
Public Administration, 1966-68. 5 vols. bibliog.

Four volumes of documents and a final volume detailing the legislative history of
India's constitution-making effort, edited by the brother of the constitutional
adviser to the Indian Constituent Assembly (1946-49). Shiva Rao begins with the
nationalist effort at constitution-making with the Home Rule Scheme of 1889. In
the documentary volumes he reproduces all major documents dealing, among
other things, with the transfer of power to India, the organization of the Constituent Assembly, and such crucial issues as fundamental rights and centre-state
relations. In the final volume the editor provides a lively narrative of the clashing
of views and interests that influenced the constitution-makers at various stages.

443 Politics of president's rule in India.

J. R. Siwach. Simla, India: Institute of Advanced Study,
1979. 533p. bibliog.

According to the Indian constitution, the president can assume executive responsi-
bility in a state if a ministry loses its mandate from the legislative assembly and
an alternative stable government cannot be formed. The political autonomy of the
president's rule and the use and abuse of the constitutional power to impose such
rule is the subject of this objective and methodical study.

Defence and Military Affairs

444 India's nuclear bomb.
Shyam Bhatia. Sahibabad, India: Vikas, 1979. 169p. bibliog.
The background of India's nuclear policy from independence through to India's 1974 nuclear explosion is sketched in broad outline by a prominent Indian journalist. It is argued that, although the nuclear weapons option was not ignored in earlier years, the 1964 Chinese nuclear explosion resulted in rising pressures within India for nuclear weapon development. Bhatia suggests that the Shastri-Gandhi decision for a test explosion was a way to accommodate demands for weapons without actually producing them.

445 The Indian army: its contribution to the development of a nation.
Stephen P. Cohen. Berkeley, California: University of California Press, 1971. 216p. bibliog.
A social and political history of the Indian army. Well documented and clearly written, with extensive quotes from records and interviews, the book describes how the British created in India one of the largest, best disciplined volunteer armies in modern times. Cohen carefully examines the disputes between Whitehall and Delhi, and between British rulers and Indian politicians on the role and character of the Indian armed forces. Unfortunately, the discussion of the period 1947-71 is extremely brief.

446 India's nuclear option: atomic policy and decision making.
Ashok Kapur. New York: Praeger, 1976. 295p. bibliog.
Based on speeches of Nehru, interviews with international officials, and a sound understanding of Indian bureaucratic politics, this book examines India's nuclear policy in an historical perspective. First a third-party mediator, later an actor in the east-west negotiations on nuclear proliferation, and finally an independent

106

nuclear power, India is seen as a careful and methodical planner in the realm of international nuclear diplomacy and strategy.

447 Matter of honour.
Philip Mason. New York: Holt, 1974. 580p. bibliog.

A critical study of the growth and development of the Indian army from its 18th-century beginnings to India's independence in 1947. Mason argues that there was a bond of honour between the Europeans and the Indians, and among the Indians of various castes and linguistic groups who served in the armed forces. The characters of such diverse military leaders as Field Marshals Lord Roberts of Kandahar, Sir Claude Auchinleck and Sir William Slim, who saw service both in India and elsewhere, are drawn with compassion and understanding. Eminently readable.

448 Military history of India.
Jadunath Sarkar. Bombay: Orient Longman, 1970. 179p. maps. bibliog.

A study of the development of military science, published posthumously first in 1960 and subsequently reprinted several times. Sarkar discusses great battles and campaigns from Alexander the Great's invasion of the Punjab in the 4th century BC through to the 18th-century Maratha campaigns against the tottering Mughal authority. The author argues that superior technology, organization, strategy and tactics, and an adequate economic base eventually proved more important than the number of soldiers employed.

Foreign Relations

449 India, Pakistan, and Bangladesh: search for a new relationship.
Mohammed Ayoob. New Delhi: Indian Council on World Affairs, 1975. 185p. bibliog.

This brief book focuses on the Indo-Pakistan War of 1971, the secession of Bangladesh from Pakistan, and the Simla Conference of 1972 between prime ministers Bhutto of Pakistan and Indira Gandhi of India concerning the normalization of relations between the two countries. Ayoob is critical of American foreign policy toward India, Bangladesh, and Pakistan, and feels that normalization of relations between and among these countries will not take place until the United States develops a more objective posture on the supply of arms to Pakistan.

450 Making of India's foreign policy: determinants, institutions, processes, and personalities.
Jayantanuja Bandyopadhyaya. Bombay: Allied, 1970. 286p. bibliog.

A useful and enlightening survey of India's foreign policy. The book's thesis is that India's foreign policy is determined not only by its national interests and the state of the world, but also by the personal style of political leaders in power. Analytical rather than descriptive, it is an excellent brief analysis of the underpinnings of India's foreign policy.

451 Foreign aid to India.
Brojendra Nath Banerjee. Delhi: Agam Prakashan, 1977. 378p. bibliog.

This book examines the foreign and economic policy goals of the United States - and tangentially of the Soviet Union - in extending economic aid to India, paying special attention to the supply of food grains. The author argues that, although US aid has been helpful, it has done little to make India stand on its feet. The Soviet Union, on the other hand, has made a serious effort to make India self-reliant. Considerable statistical information is included.

452 **India, Pakistan, and the great powers.**
William J. Barnds. New York: Praeger, 1972. 388p. maps.
bibliog.

An exhaustive survey of the role of the major world powers on the Indian subcontinent. While critical of excessive United States involvement, the book nevertheless makes a strong case for continued American participation in the subcontinent's economic development and defence. Written by a former US government intelligence analyst, the book is balanced, well documented, and sensitive to Indian national aspirations. Unfortunately, the Indo-Pakistan conflict receives inadequate attention.

453 **India: emergent power?**
Stephen P. Cohen, Richard L. Park. New York: Crane,
Russak, 1978. 95p.

This essay by two prominent American political scientists argues that India's substantial economic, technological, and military infrastructure has established it as a world power. Subcontinental disputes have diminished in intensity precisely because other regional nations, particularly Pakistan, have recognized this fact. Although disputes with neighbours remain unresolved, India seems to the authors to be well equipped to deal effectively with them. The authors recommend that the US should not threaten India's regional supremacy. A well-written essay.

454 **India's economic relations with the U.S.S.R. and eastern
Europe, 1953 to 1969.**
Asha Laxman Datar. London: Cambridge University Press,
1972. 278p. bibliog.

This work assesses the costs and benefits to India of its 'aid and trade' relations with the USSR and eastern Europe. Its broad purpose is to examine the results of economic co-operation between mixed and communist economies. The author concludes that India's gains have been less than expected and predicts that India will continue to rely mostly on the west for some time to come. Scholarly and well documented.

455 **Soviet policy toward India: ideology and strategy.**
Robert H. Donaldson. Cambridge, Massachusetts: Harvard
University Press, 1974. 338p. bibliog.

Based mainly on Russian sources, this is a careful examination of the nature of Soviet policy towards India. Donaldson carefully analyses Soviet attempts to modify Marxist-Leninist foreign policy doctrines to suit changing patterns of Soviet interest in India. For an update, see the author's *The Soviet-Indian alignment: quest for influence* (Denver, Colorado: Graduate School of International Studies, University of Denver, 1979. 70p. bibliog.).

456 **Kashmir: a study in India-Pakistan relations.**
Sisir Gupta. Bombay: Asia, 1966. 511p. maps. bibliog.

A carefully documented, definitive analysis of Indo-Pakistani relations *vis-à-vis* Kashmir from 1946 to 1965. With minute details, Gupta examines the background of the 1947-48 hostilities in Kashmir, the main UN resolutions on Kashmir, and Indian legal claims to the territory. The volume ends with a plea for the restoration of amicable relations between the two neighbouring states on the basis of legitimization of the present cease-fire line into a permanent boundary. This book should be supplemented with Lars Blinkenberg, *India-Pakistan: the history of unresolved conflicts* (Copenhagen: Munksgaard, 1972. 440p. maps. bibliog.).

457 A diplomatic history of modern India.
Charles H. Heimsath, Surjit Mansingh. Bombay: Allied, 1971. 559p. maps. bibliog.

A straightforward historical narrative of Indian diplomacy. The book is rich in detail and is amply documented from government sources. It should be read together with the more analytical work of Bandyopadhyaya (q.v.) in order to provide a balanced basis for the study of India's foreign policy.

458 Soviet-Indian relations: issues and influence.
Robert C. Horn. New York: Praeger, 1982. 231p. map. bibliog.

Based on joint communiqués issued by Indian and Soviet leaders, and the press commentaries on them, Horn examines how leaders of these two countries have influenced each other's policies and perceptions. He finds that each nation 'will successfully influence the other on occasion, but, generally, such influence will likely remain limited'. He concludes that the popularly held view that India is a Soviet ally is a myth.

459 International Studies.
Delhi: Vikas, 1959- . quarterly.

Contains scholarly articles on international law, international organization, and international relations, with emphasis on India's policies and its role in international affairs. A good book review section. Carries an annual bibliography of Indian publications on India in world affairs.

460 Indian foreign policy: the Nehru years.
Edited by B. R. Nanda. Honolulu, Hawaii: University Press of Hawaii, 1976. 279p. bibliog.

The foreign policy performance of India's first prime minister is evaluated by prominent Indian academics, journalists, and diplomats in this collection of lectures delivered at the Nehru Memorial Museum and Library, New Delhi. The volume is organized thematically and regionally. India's policies of disarmament and non-alignment, relations with Pakistan, the Muslim world, superpowers, China, and Southeast Asia are discussed. An introduction by the museum's director ably synthesizes all the contributions. Well worth reading.

461 American geopolitics and India.
Baldev Raj Nayar. New Delhi: Manohar Book Service, 1976. 246p. bibliog.

An examination of Indo-US relations. The author believes that the United States has neither made India one of its satellites nor reached accommodation with it. Instead, it has been the aim of US policy to 'contain' India as a regional power. Well written and ably argued.

462 India's foreign policy: studies on continuity and change.
Edited by Bimal Prasad. New Delhi: Vikas, 1979. 540p.
bibliog.

Contains revised versions of papers originally presented by Indian scholars at a conference in Delhi in 1978. Almost all authors argue that there has been far more continuity than change in India's foreign policy, notwithstanding the Janata interregnum of 1977-78 which temporarily eclipsed Mrs. Gandhi. There are several overviews of India's foreign policy which reflect the general consensus that politico-economic constraints tend to inhibit any drastic alteration of India's foreign policy. Other essays deal with India's relations with her neighbours - Pakistan, Sri Lanka, and China, with superpowers, with Arab oil-producing countries, and with other third world countries. There are papers on India's attitude towards such global issues as disarmament, non-alignment, and nuclear policy. An excellent collection of essays.

463 The fourth round: Indo-Pak war 1984.
Ravi Rikhye. New Delhi: ABC Publishing House, 1982. 253p.

Written along the lines of John Hackett's *The Third World War*, this book takes an apocalyptic view of the future. In Rikhye's scenario, a pre-emptive Indian strike against the Pakistani nuclear establishment triggers a war between the two neighbours that is longer, more costly, and more brutal than any of the earlier ones. At the war's end Pakistan is entrenched in 2,000 square kilometres of Indian territory while Indian forces occupy 18,000 square kilometres of Pakistan. Civilian casualities are enormous and there is widespread economic disruption resulting from the thirty-six day conflict. If not entirely realistic, this is a useful stimulus to strategic thinking.

464 The fulcrum of Asia: relations among China, India, Pakistan and the U.S.S.R.
Bhabani Sen Gupta. New York: Pegasus, 1970. 383p. bibliog.

A careful survey of changing alignments between and among four major powers in southern Asia: one of them an established superpower, another an emerging world power, and the other two neo-nationist regional states. The author feels that relations between India and Pakistan are not likely to run a smooth course until a détente between Russia and China is achieved.

465 Foreign aid to India: an economic study.
R. K. Sharma. New Delhi: Marwah, 1977. 175p. bibliog.

A critical assessment of the considerable foreign aid of all kinds (public and private, bilateral and multilateral, eastern bloc and western) that India has received since 1951. It exhaustively describes the amounts, terms, and conditions of all such assistance. The author concludes that the terms and conditions have tended to be so harsh as to diminish the real worth of this substantial assistance. A solid work of description and analysis but lacking any larger theoretical perspective.

466 Indo-Soviet relations: economic analysis.
R. K. Sharma. New Delhi: Allied, 1980. 112p. bibliog.

A flattering but competent account of Indo-Soviet economic relations since 1947. The author argues that India's début as an exporter of capital goods is largely attributable to Soviet economic assistance, and opines that Soviet trade and aid, with its novel repayment features, has involved neither political nor economic exploitation.

467 The Indian Ocean: big power presence and local response.
K. Rajendra Singh. New Delhi: Manohar, 1977. 336p. bibliog.

One of the most thorough and comprehensive accounts yet published on the politics of the Indian Ocean. Data about superpower naval strength and strategies, resources and raw material potentials of the region, and the interests of littoral and extra-regional states in these resources are especially valuable.

468 India and the Soviet Union: the Nehru era.
Arthur Benjamin Stein. Chicago: University of Chicago Press, 1969. 320p. bibliog.

A balanced and scholarly work which analyses Indo-Soviet relations during the period 1947-64. After providing the historical background of early Bolshevik interest in India, the author devotes three chapters to Stalin's policy toward India. The remaining six chapters discuss the rapid growth of the warm relationship between India and Russia since 1962 when China militarily humiliated India and siezed control of most of the Himalayan border territory in dispute between the two countries. Both Indian and Russian sources have been utilized.

469 Indo-German economic relations.
J. K. Tandon. Delhi: National, 1978. 241p. bibliog.

A careful and balanced examination of Indo-German cultural and economic relations. The author examines the role and contribution of German aid in the development of India's industrial base and higher education. He also offers some suggestions for improving and enlarging these relations.

470 India's aid diplomacy in the third world.
Dewan C. Vohra. New Delhi: Vikas, 1980. 331p. bibliog.

As a newly industrializing country, India is both a recipient and a donor of foreign aid. It has aided over 100 'southern' nation-states, specializing in areas often neglected by the major powers and in which its own experience as a developing nation is of immediate relevance. A thorough work of description and pragmatic analysis.

471 The Chinese calculus of deterrence: India and Indochina.
Allen Suess Whiting. Ann Arbor, Michigan: University of Michigan Press, 1975. 299p. maps. bibliog.

An excellent study of Chinese crisis behaviour, this work includes a section on Chinese efforts to deter, by a variety of means, Indian reoccupation of the border areas in the western Himalayas, neighbouring Kashmir, disputed by India and China and forcibly siezed by the latter in 1962. Final chapters speculating on possible future Chinese behaviour argue that it is likely to be unpredictable - once Peking acquires a second strike capability against likely adversaries.

472 Himalayan frontiers: a political review of British, Chinese, Indian and Russian rivalries.
Dorothy Woodman.   New York: Praeger, 1970. 423p. maps. bibliog.

An exhaustive analysis of the influence of the Himalayas on the Indian subcontinent and on the Sino-Indian conflict. Woodman argues that the Sino-Indian conflict, involving dispute over where the exact boundary between India and China in the Himalayas should lie and which resulted in the Sino-Indian War of 1962, is the legacy of European rivalries in Asia in the 19th and early 20th centuries, when Britain arbitrarily drew the boundary between India and China, the latter being too powerless to protest. She analyses Sino-Pakistani *rapprochement* in the light of Sino-Indian and Indo-Pakistani conflicts and concludes that India has been living in a state of suspended hostility with its neighbours for a generation. Extensively documented, it contains numerous maps and twenty appendixes of hard-to-trace documents.

Economy

General

473 The Indian economy: poverty and development.
Pramit Chaudhuri. New Delhi: Vikas, 1979. 279p. bibliog.
An introductory text for anyone with a basic knowledge of economics. Focusing on internal problems and relationships, this book does full justice to the complexity of India's problems. Like many others (e.g. Frankel, Mellor, Minhas, q.v.), Chaudhuri observes that the Indian economy developed steadily until 1967 after which structural constraints led to stagnation. The author soundly criticizes the vagueness of planning goals in Indian politics. Short and readable.

474 Commerce.
Bombay: Commerce Ltd., 1910- . weekly.
India's oldest weekly dealing with economic and financial affairs. Usual features include a special article on some aspects of the economy, analysis and interpretation of governmental statistical data, an in-depth survey of a particular industry, and company news. Special airmail edition for foreign subscribers.

475 Economic and Political Weekly.
Bombay: Sameeksha Trust, 1966- . weekly.
Similar in format to the *Economist* of London, this influential weekly reviews economic and political affairs with emphasis on India. Both Indian and foreign scholars and journalists contribute. Occasional special issues. Most articles are urbane and scholarly in tone.

476 Far Eastern Economic Review.
Hong Kong: Far Eastern Economic Review, 1946- . weekly.
The liveliest and most extensive weekly coverage of Asian economic and political affairs. The review's editorial outlook is liberal and Keynesian. International trade and aid, foreign investments, and the activities of transnational corporations receive special attention. Indispensable for keeping abreast of Asian affairs and India's role in them.

477 **The Indian economy: its nature and problems.**
Alak Ghosh. Calcutta: World, 1979. 22nd ed. 689p.
bibliog.
This comprehensive work of description and analysis is widely used as a college
text in India. The book has eight parts: nature of the Indian economy in the
pre-planning period; planning and the Indian economy; natural resources and
national income; population and agriculture; industry and labour; public finance;
banking and currency; and trade, exchange and transport. Each part includes
statistical tables.

478 **ICSSR Journal of Abstracts and Reviews: economics.**
New Delhi: Indian Council of Social Science Research,
1972- . quarterly.
The Indian Council of Social Science Research started this quarterly abstracting
service in 1972. Items are classified according to the American Economic Association's nomenclature. Abstracts of selected articles from over forty Indian economic journals are given. Each issue includes a few book reviews.

479 **India: a political economy of stagnation.**
Prem Shankar Jha. London: Oxford University Press, 1980.
300p. bibliog.
The author attempts to review the 'economic decline' in India and explains it in
terms of economic policies which have not been well thought out. Jha lays the
blame for the Indian economy's failure to perform on the shoulders of the 'intermediate' class of the self-employed in the trade, manufacturing and business
sectors who profit from a régime of shortages. This powerful indictment covers
almost all the perennial controversies about Indian economic policies.

480 **India: an uncommitted society.**
J. C. Kapur. New Delhi: Vikas, 1981. 289p. bibliog.
The author, an engineer and social philosopher, argues that the western free-
market consumer-oriented societies cannot be a model for India because they
emphasize production and consumption to the detriment of employment and environmental health. Kapur also rejects the Soviet model because it is coercive. He
sees India's future as a new model of an ecologically sound, integrated society
utilizing solar and biomass energy for its development.

481 **India: a rising middle power.**
Edited by John W. Mellor. Boulder, Colorado: Westview,
1979. 374p. bibliog.
Developed from papers and comments presented by US-based scholars at a 1977
conference in New York, the focus of this volume is contemporary India playing
an increasingly significant role in the world arena. The domestic roots of India's
waxing international, political, and economic strengths, and strains in its relationship with the United States and other foreign powers, are described and analysed
in twenty papers of uniformly high quality.

482 **Monthly Commentary on Indian Economic Conditions.**
New Delhi: Indian Institute of Public Opinion, 1959- .
monthly.
Scholarly articles on the Indian economy. Excellent analysis and interpretation of
official statistical data. Special supplements deal 'with the particular industries or
phases of the economy'. Occasional notes on corporations or companies.

483 **Economics of the black market.**
S. K. Ray. Boulder, Colorado: Westview, 1981. 250p.
bibliog.
This book examines the structure and functioning of India's huge underground
economy and its effect on India's economic development, political integrity, and
financial stability. According to Ray, price behaviour and inflation in India have
been affected by the 'black' market as well as by fraud and misfeasance by
bureaucrats. A concluding chapter suggests some remedies to eradicate the black
economy.

484 **India's economic problems: an analytical approach.**
Edited by J. S. Uppal. New York: St. Martin's, 1979. 2nd
ed. 409p. bibliog.
Intended for a general audience, this collection of articles deals with national
economy, human resources, agriculture, industry, Gandhian economics, labour,
economic policy, black money, and a variety of other topics. Most of the essays
are excellent and do not require in-depth knowledge of India's economy.

Economic history

485 **Famines in India: a study in some aspects of the economic
history of India, 1860-1965.**
B. M. Bhatia. London: Asia, 1967. 2nd ed. 367p. bibliog.
This book narrates the famines and scarcities that have occurred in India since
1860 and examines their causes. The author finds that the economic distortions of
colonialism were the main cause of these calamities. Economic dislocations
increased the size of the underclass, and government efforts to remedy the situation were too little and ameliorative measures always too late. The book includes
a chapter on the unprecedented 1943 famine in Bengal. Written from a nationalist point of view.

486 **Cambridge Economic History of India.**
Cambridge, England: Cambridge University Press, 1982. 2
vols. bibliog.
The first volume, edited by Tapan Raychaudhuri and Irfan Habib, covers the
period ca. 1200-1750 when Islamic dynasties dominated the Indian subcontinent.
The authors argue that during this period all economic changes reflected a gradual evolution and the continuation of traditional economic norms. The second
volume, edited by Dharma Kumar and Meghnad Desai, covers the period ca.

1757-1970, and discusses changes in Indian economic life introduced as a result of India's commercial trade and economic ties with Europe. Two concluding chapters discuss Indian economic policies during the first two decades of independence.

487 Economy and society: essays in Indian economic and social history.

Edited by K. N. Chaudhuri, Clive J. Dewey. Delhi: Oxford University Press, 1979. 358p. bibliog.

The essays in this work contain the recent research of a number of younger Indian and western scholars and span Indian economic and social history from the 17th to the 20th centuries. The book is divided into four parts: agrarian structure and agricultural development; trade and finance; industry and labour; and towns. The essays are highly specialized and comprise a good introduction to recent advances in Indian historiography.

488 Changing India.

Sankar Ghose. Bombay: Allied, 1978. 298p.

A wide-ranging critique of Indian planning and economic transformation during the last three decades, by an Indian economist sympathetic to the Marxist tradition but not bound by it. The book's strength lies in an objective assessment of competing theories and strategies relating to Indian socio-economic and political development. An extremely readable book.

489 Indian capitalist class: a historical study.

V. I. Pavlov. New Delhi: People's Publishing House, 1964. 408p. bibliog.

The textbook of Indian Marxists, this classical Marxist-Leninist analysis examines two key issues: the role of trading and moneylending régimes during the Mughal and British periods, and the origin and development of the Indian bourgeoisie especially as a result of British capitalism. Separate chapters are devoted to the development of the Gujarati, Marwari, Marathi, and Bengali bourgeoisies. The author challenges the conventional wisdom that the Indian middle class developed largely as a service élite to meet British imperial needs rather than as an autonomous economic class.

490 Industrialisation in India.

Rajat K. Ray. New Delhi: Oxford University Press, 1979. 384p. bibliog.

The story of the growth of corporate enterprise and its failure to transform India's agricultural economy into a predominantly industrial one. The author points out that during 1913-38 Indian industrial growth was much above the world average, while that of the 'small' sector was pitiable. According to Ray it was the failure of the 'small' sector to achieve high growth rates before independence in 1947 that caused Indian industrialization on the whole to lag behind.

Economy. Economic history

491 The economic history of India, 1857-1956.
Edited by V. B. Singh. Bombay: Allied, 1970. 830p.
bibliog.
This collection of twenty-nine articles by twenty-five leading scholars attempts to
identify and interpret major trends in the Indian economy since the Indian Revolt
of 1857. Especially noteworthy are articles on natural resources, demography,
agriculture and irrigation, land reforms, cotton and jute industry, railways,
currency and banking, and industrial workers. Written from the Indian nationalist
point of view which holds that the British hindered India's economic development.

492 Economic growth in China and India, 1952-1970: a comparative appraisal.
Subramanian Swamy. Chicago: University of Chicago
Press, 1973. 84p. bibliog.
A careful and well-documented statistical analysis of the economic growth rate in
India and China. The author concludes that the overall growth rates in both the
agricultural and industrial sectors have been approximately the same in both
India and China. He points out that the lack of accurate statistical data from
China renders precise comparisons impossible, and that a large part of China's
seemingly rapid growth in some sectors is attributable to the lower base from
which it started.

493 Land and labour in India.
Daniel Thorner, Alice Thorner. New York: Asia, 1974.
227p. bibliog.
Although the articles in this pioneering book were written between 1952 and
1960, they are of continuing relevance to the contemporary scene. The first section deals with the rural power structure; the second examines rural development
from the mid-18th century to the 1960's; and the final section is a penetrating
critique of the methodology used in Indian census and sample surveys. Thorner's
influential and recently reissued *The agrarian prospect in India* (Columbia, Missouri: South Asia Books, 1976) argues that agrarian forces emerging since 1950
have produced a 'capitalist revolution in socialist India'.

494 The shaping of modern India.
Daniel Thorner. New Delhi: Allied, 1980. 404p. bibliog.
This book by one of the most penetrating western social and economic historians
of modern India contains an extract from Thorner's unpublished 1948 interpretive
essay on the British period in Indian history. In addition the book includes a
selection of articles and other writings that spans the subsequent quarter-century
of the author's career. The twenty essays presented in the volume includes his
critique of the theories of Marx and Chayanov, of the studies of H. H. Mann, S.
L. F. D. Nyle, and Henry Maine, and his own bold thesis on the emergence of
capitalist agriculture in India. Thorner's work is of supreme value because it
combines a depth of first-hand knowledge of India with a first-rate grasp of the
relevant social science theory. Indispensable.

Economic and social indicators

495 Economic Survey.
Department of Economic Affairs, Ministry of Finance. New Delhi, 1963- . annual.
This annual review is the most comprehensive description of the functioning of the Indian economy. A brief topical review of the economy as a whole pinpoints major achievements and shortfalls. Chapters on agriculture, industry, prices, price policy, budgets and fiscal policy, banking, and foreign trade are followed by a brief perceptive chapter outlining the tasks for the year ahead. The second part of the survey has cumulative statistical tables on production, money supply, finance, employment, balance of payments, foreign trade, and other relevant topics. Latest issue covers 1981-82.

496 Levels of living in India: an inter-state profile.
B. N. Ganguli, Devendra B. Gupta. New Delhi: Chand, 1976. 273p. bibliog.
A comparative study of fifteen states of the Indian Union and the standards of living prevailing in them in 1955, 1960, and 1965. Components of level of living include nutrition, housing, medical care, education, clothing, leisure, economic security, and environment, as suggested by various United Nations studies. In one section of the book the authors examine the interrelationship between the components of living on the one hand, and several economic, demographic and social variables on the other.

497 India: a statistical outline.
Indian Oxygen Ltd. Calcutta: Oxford & IBH, 1976. 5th rev. ed. biennial.
A handy guide to information on such topics as national income and wealth, demographic conditions, agricultural and industrial production, foreign trade and external assistance, vital statistics on health, education, communications, general elections, labour and industrial disputes, and irrigation and power.

498 National Account Statistics.
New Delhi: Central Statistical Organization, 1956- . annual.
Provides annual estimates of income at both current and constant prices. The latest issue (January 1979) provides data for the period 1970/71-1976/77 in six parts: national product; factor incomes; consumption expenditure; public sector transactions; net domestic product, savings, and capital formation; and consolidated accounts of the nation.

499 Statistical Abstract, India.
New Delhi: Central Statistical Organisation, 1949- . annual.
This annual abstract contains the latest available data on economic and social development. The data covers periods of five to ten years, with brief explanatory notes preceding each section. For further information and research, primary sources are cited under each table. Title varies: *Statistical Abstract of the Indian Union*.

Economy. Planning and development

500 Statistical Outline of India, 1982.
Bombay: Tata Services, 1953- . presently annual. 15th ed.,
1982, 215p.
This handy pocket-book presents a statistical profile of India's economy. Almost all the data are in tabular form. A separate section compares leading Indian economic and social indicators with those of other principal countries, both developing and developed.

501 Statistical Pocket Book - India.
New Delhi: Central Statistical Organization, 1956- . annual.
This latest volume relates to 1977, and presents a factual account of social and economic trends in the country based on principal statistical series on various sectors of the economy. National aggregates are given on a five-yearly basis.

Planning and development

502 Indian economic development and policy: essays in honour of Professor V. L. D'Souza.
Edited by P. R. Brahmananda, D. M. Nanjundappa, B. K.
Narayan. New Delhi: Vikas, 1979. 352p. bibliog.
Twenty-one essays from both senior, well-established scholars like C. N. Vakil and D. T. Lakdawala, and young scholars belonging to the 'Mysore' school of Indian economics. These essays cover such diverse topics as development, taxation, income differentials, inflation, foreign economic assistance, agricultural growth, irrigation projects, and the socio-economic development of backward classes and regions.

503 Planning process in Indian polity.
V. D. Divekar. Bombay: Popular, 1978. 398p. bibliog.
This book covers the planning process in India and its relationship with India's political forces and socio-economic institutions. An opening chapter describing the structure and functioning of the Planning Commission is followed by others dealing with the influence of parliamentary democracy, federal political structure, the single party dominant system obtaining before 1967, organized interest groups, external assistance, and the role of the general public in the planning process. More descriptive than analytical.

504 India's political economy, 1947-1977: the gradual revolution.
Francine R. Frankel. Princeton, New Jersey: Princeton
University Press, 1978. 600p. maps. bibliog.
This book grapples with the dilemmas and contradictions inherent in India's development goal of rapid improvement in the living conditions of the poorest without the chaos of revolution. Frankel argues that India's strategy of 'accomodative politics and radical social change' has resulted in both growing socio-political conflict and sluggish economic growth. The evidence presented suggests that without a direct attack on the propertied castes and classes, economic deve-

lopment and social change will continue at their current unsatisfactory rate.
Perhaps the best analysis of India's post-independence political economy.

505 Reflections on economic development and social change: essays in honour of Professor V. K. R. V. Rao.
Edited by C. H. Hanumantha Rao, Puran Chandra
Joshi. Bombay: Allied, 1979. 486p. bibliog.

These essays in honour of an Indian economist, founder-director of Delhi's Institute of Economic Growth and former education minister in the government of
India, bring together the contributions of an international group of eminent scholars who share Rao's wide-ranging interest in economic development and social
change. The twenty-four papers in this volume are divided into five parts: rethink-
ing on development; economic structure and policy; the demographic dimension;
development as a social process; and perspectives in social sciences. A separate
thirteen-page section provides a complete bibliography of Professor Rao's own
publications.

506 The new economics of growth: a strategy for India and the developing world.
John W. Mellor. Ithaca, New York: Cornell University
Press, 1976. 335p. bibliog.

An analysis of current economic conditions and development strategies by an
agricultural economist who argues in favour of labour rather than capital-
intensive enterprises. Mellor holds that, in India and almost all other developing
countries, economic development must be based on increased agricultural production and high employment rates. Admitting that this would be a radical departure
from current planning strategies, Mellor maintains that such changes are the only
way to accelerate India's sluggish development. Well worth reading.

507 Planning and the poor.
Bagicha Singh Minhas. New Delhi: Chand, 1974. 141p.
bibliog.

The author, a former economist with the Indian Planning Commission, argues
that radical land reforms are the only way to solve the problem of continuing
mass poverty. Convincing empirical data are presented to show that structural
unemployment and underemployment have increased in recent decades and that
new industries have not been able to provide employment to both skilled and
unskilled workers.

508 India's second revolution: the dimensions of development.
Lawrence A. Veit. New York: McGraw-Hill, 1976. 402p.
bibliog.

A highly critical evaluation of India's goal of establishing a pattern of mixed
economy, written by an American unsympathetic to that goal. The author attributes the growing gap between rich and poor to centralized planning, and argues
that denationalization of key industries and opening the economy to massive
foreign investments would accelerate economic development and lessen economic
inequality. Veit maintains that the key element in United States assistance is
humanitarianism while in Soviet foreign aid it is political self-interest. Though the
general theses of the book are debatable, it is technically sound.

Finance and Banking

509 **Substitution, exchange rates, and economic development.**
Vinay Bharat Ram. Delhi: Oxford University Press, 1982.
193p. bibliog.
An analysis of the conditions for technological development in the third world, using India as a case-study. The author argues that foreign exchange shortages are a blessing because they stimulate import substitution, and hence economic development and technological progress.

510 **Union state financial relations and finance commissions.**
Sudha Bhatnagar. Allahabad, India: Chugh, 1979. 355p.
bibliog.
A comprehensive and analytical study of fiscal relations between the federal and state governments in India and the role of various finance commissions in articulating these relations. Bhatnagar examines the relative powers and jurisdictions of the states and the Union government, the Planning Commission, and the finance commissions. She recommends the establishment of a permanent finance commission along the lines of the Planning Commission.

511 **The changing structure of industrial finance in India.**
Lakshmi Chandra Gupta. Oxford, England: Clarendon,
1969. 182p. bibliog.
An integrated analysis of the structure of Indian industrial finance during the formative stage of India's contemporary economic development. The author examines the significance of commercial banks, the government-owned life insurance company, government-sponsored mutual funds, and a variety of intermediate developmental financial institutions. A separate section deals with overwhelming public interest in purchasing new capital securities offered in the stock market.

512 Monetary planning for India.

Suraj B. Gupta. Delhi: Oxford University Press, 1981. 1st paperback ed. 240p. bibliog.

A discussion of the aims of monetary planning and controls. Based on an empirical examination of the practices of Indian monetary institutions, the book examines the demand for money in India, the income velocity of money, credits to commercial banks by the Reserve Bank of India, and the relationship of development banks to India's central bank. Written for the specialist.

513 National savings movement in India.

Gokaran Nath Mehrotra. Delhi: Atma Ram, 1978. 444p. bibliog.

A descriptive study of the government effort to stimulate 'small' savings and their utilization in the Indian development effort. The author discusses national and state savings organizations, the Post Office savings scheme, and other thrift organizations. In addition he provides basic facts and other statistical data about various savings schemes, time deposits, annuities and bonds, and the rate of interest on each of them.

514 Monetary politics in India.

Sid Mittra. Bombay: Vora, 1972. 249p. bibliog.

A careful and lively study of the relations between India's central bank - the Reserve Bank of India - and the Union government, especially the finance ministry, between 1935 and 1969. Mittra analyses the areas of harmony and conflict during the tenure of seven governors of the bank, two of whom resigned, another two of whom turned out to be 'harmonizers' of bank-government relations, and three of whom turned out to be vigorous defenders of the bank's independence.

515 Reserve Bank of India Bulletin.

Bombay: Reserve Bank of India, 1947- . monthly.

The most authoritative source on Indian banking and finance. In general each issue contains a monthly review of finance and the economy, seasonal trends in prices, national debt, current statistics, and one or two articles. Some issues are accompanied with supplements. Provides cumulative index decennially.

516 Inflation in India.

S. L. N. Simha. Bombay: Vora, for the Institute for Financial Management and Research, Madras, 1974. 378p. bibliog.

Twenty-two papers analysing the problem of inflation in the Indian economy and making suggestions to combat it. These papers fall between two widely differing schools of thought: one holds that monetary expansion was the root cause of inflation, the other considers such expansion irrelevant to inflation. Several articles deal with the economics of 'black' money, or income concealed from the government, and its role in generating both inflation and stagnation in the economy.

Finance and Banking

517 **The Indian financial system.**
V. K. Subramanian. New Delhi: Abhinav, 1979. 233p.
bibliog.

A descriptive account of the Indian financial system. The book covers such key issues as the fiscal provisions of the constitution, state and federal financial administrations, legislative control over finances, the role of the planning and finance commissions, the taxation system, public debt, the Reserve Bank of India and the banking system, foreign borrowing, and rural credit. There are numerous statistical tables and lists of financial and industrial institutions.

518 **War against inflation: the story of the falling rupee: 1943-77.**
Chandulal Nagindas Vakil. Delhi: Macmillan, 1979. 338p.
bibliog.

A scathing analysis of Indian inflation. The author, a long-time critic of India's five-year-plans based on the Mahalanobis model which recommended the development of heavy industries through deficit financing, argues that India's hyperinflation has been caused by erroneous planning and compounded by such political events as the India-Pakistan-Bangladesh war of 1971-72. Vakil presents his own wage goods model, which emphasizes production of consumer supplies and growing structural employment as the cure for India's hyperinflation.

Trade and Commerce

519 **The development impact of barter in developing countries: the case of India.**
Ranadev Banerji. Paris: OECD, 1978. 205p. bibliog.
Using India as a case-study, this book examines the circumstances in which a country is induced to adopt a policy of bilateral barter trade agreements. In addition, Banerji examines the impact of such bilateral trade on India's internal economy, export and import-substituting industries, and internal price movements. Using input-output analysis, the author also makes a comparative analysis of employment generation in the Indian economy through exports on a bilateral and multilateral basis.

520 **Exports of manufactures from India: an appraisal of the emerging pattern.**
Ranadev Banerji. Tübingen, GFR: J.C.B. Mohr, 1975.
347p. bibliog. (Kieler Studien, Institut für Weltwirtschaft an der Universität Kiel).
An exhaustive and analytical survey of the emergence of India as an exporter of manufactured goods. Banerji examines the growth pattern of these exports, their capital and labour intensities, India's share in world exports, and the employment implications of India's export activities. The study is rigorously statistical.

521 **Foreign trade regimes and economic development: India.**
Jagdish N. Bhagwati, T. N. Srinivasan. New York:
Columbia University Press, 1975. 261p. map. bibliog.
This study examines the interaction between India's foreign trade and domestic policies and objectives. The pre-1966 import substitution policies are compared unfavourably with liberalized trade policies following the 1966 currency devaluation. The authors argue that the earlier restrictive foreign exchange allocation and industrial licensing policies, together with import controls and restricted exports, encouraged wasteful resource allocation and blunted inter-firm competition.

Trade and Commerce

522 India's export performance: some policy implications.
K. S. Dhindsa. New Delhi: Intellectual Publishing House, 1981. 243p. bibliog.

An analysis of poor Indian performance in the export of such traditional commodities as tea, cotton textiles, and jute manufactures between 1950 and 1980. The author argues that the primary causes of the poor performance are not external demand factors, but rather internal supply problems and the relative profitability of domestic sales.

523 Indo-Soviet economic cooperation and trade relations.
A. Granovsky, V. Koptevsky, L. Raitsin. New Delhi: Sumeet, 1977. 54p.

Basic facts and figures on economic, trade, scientific, and technical co-operation between India and the Soviet Union, 1953-77. Soviet assistance in developing agriculture, the iron and steel industries, heavy electricals, pharmaceuticals, power projects, engineering institutions, machine tools, and oil exploration and development are described, together with the share of Soviet-assisted projects in different economic categories.

524 The benefits and costs of import substitution in India: a microeconomic study.
Anne O. Krueger. Minneapolis, Minnesota: University of Minnesota Press, 1975. 140p. bibliog.

A study of Indian policies of import substitution in the automobile and ancillary industries before 1970. Krueger finds that these policies have indeed led to the growth of the industry in India. However, she concludes that this growth cannot be sustained, largely because under protectionism these firms have become high cost and inefficient. Her suggestion that India embark upon policies that promote exports has now become the official Indian policy.

525 India's exports and export policies in the 1960s.
Deepak Nayyar. New York: Cambridge University Press, 1976. 392p. bibliog.

A valuable analysis of India's export performance and policies in the 1960s. The author empirically examines eleven traditional as well as non-traditional items that together constitute 60 per cent of India's total export earnings. The author believes that India's relatively poor export performance is primarily due to internal factors: rising domestic demand, inappropriate export promotion policies, and substantial inflow of foreign remittances from Indians overseas.

526 India's foreign trade: its nature and problems.
H. C. Sainy. New Delhi: National, 1979. 317p. bibliog.

A descriptive study of foreign trade policy and practices, and their national and local impacts. The internal problems of export industries, export promotion, trade diversion schemes, export finances and insurance, bilateral and multilateral treaty arrangements, regional trade groups and state trading are discussed in detail. The author argues for the need to expand non-traditional exports, especially to third-world nations.

527 **Aid to collaboration: a study in Indo-U.S. economic relations.**
P. G. Salvi. Bombay: Popular, 1978. 173p. bibliog.

A careful analysis of the past performance of Indo-US trade, which accounts for 25 per cent of Indian imports and 13 per cent of exports. Salvi summarizes basic facts of US economic assistance to India, Indo-American joint ventures, and Indo-US trade. He concludes by arguing that the Generalized Scheme of Preferences which came into effect in 1976 promises a significant market for India's exports of non-traditional goods to the United States.

528 **India's economic ties with the non-aligned countries.**
Gurdip Singh. New Delhi: Sumeet, 1978. 168p. bibliog.

A short survey of India's economic ties with the non-aligned free market economies of Asia, Africa, and Latin America, and with developing communist countries such as Cuba and Vietnam that have centrally planned economies. Based on newspaper accounts, the book provides basic facts and figures on India's export trade to the non-aligned nations rather than a careful aggregate and disaggregate economic analysis of Indian export performance.

529 **India's trade with South East Asia: a study.**
K. Romani Kumar Singh. Allahabad, India: Chugh, 1978. 160p. bibliog.

An examination of the extent, problems, and prospects of India's growing trade with Southeast Asian nations. The author gives a country-by-country survey of Indian trade. Other chapters deal with traditional and non-traditional export items, selected Indian imports, and India's bilateral joint venture industrial and consultancy projects in Southeast Asia. Problems and difficulties inherent in developing a regional common market are touched upon.

530 **Multinationals and Indian export.**
K. K. Subrahmanian, P. Mohanan Pillai. New Delhi: Allied, 1979. 115p. bibliog.

This study examines the implication of relaxing controls on foreign collaboration in order to stimulate exports. An empirical analysis is made of engineering, pharmaceutical, and chemical goods produced in the export-processing zones by Indo-foreign joint ventures. The author concludes that the net benefit derived from such arrangements is marginal and continued courtship of foreign multinational companies can lead to a position of perpetual economic dependence.

Industry

531 Public sector steel industry in India.
G. C. Agrawal. Allahabad, India: Chaitanya, 1976. 258p. bibliog.

This study analyses Indian investments in the steel industry and the industry's strategic importance to the nation's economic development. The author makes an in-depth analysis of the steel plants at Rourkela, Bhilai, and Durgapur, controlled by Hindustan Steel, a unit of the Steel Authority of India, and Bokaro, controlled by a separate unit of the authority. The analysis is two-fold: management practices and product expansion and diversification.

532 The development of capitalistic enterprise in India.
Daniel Houston Buchanan. New York: Augustus M. Kelley, 1971. reprint of 1934 ed. 497p. bibliog.

Written almost fifty years ago and reprinted twice, this book remains a monumental achievement. It examines the growth of plantation industries, coal mining, cotton and jute manufacturing, and other industrial units, first under the aegis of British managing agency houses, and then under Indian patronage until the 1930s. There are additional chapters on capital, banking, labour, wages, and heavy industries. Buchanan concludes by saying that India would have accomplished more if native economic power also had the control of administrative machinery, a view also held by Indian nationalists.

533 Business India.
Bombay: Advani, 1978- . fortnightly.

Issued every two weeks Business India is similar in content and style to the popular US weekly Business Week. Articles on business, industry, finance, and economic and fiscal policies are written from the corporate, free-enterprise perspective. Special sections provide macro-statistical economic data.

534 **The Bokaro steel plant: a study of Soviet economic assistance.**
Padma Desai. New York: American Elsevier, 1972. 108p.
A chronological and analytical account of the interaction of three elements in the planning and execution of the controversial Bokaro steel plant: the need for foreign assistance, the availability of Indian design capabilities, and the government's steel policy objectives. Desai gives a full account of initial American interest and subsequent withdrawal from the Bokaro project, and later Soviet readiness to help India in building this plant.

535 **Monopoly capital and public policy.**
S. K. Goyal. Bombay: Allied, 1979. 146p. bibliog.
A thorough study of the trends in Indian business concentration during the period 1937-76. The author points out that while the government of independent India made pronouncements against concentration of economic power in private hands, it often encouraged such concentration through liberal bank loans to large private-sector companies. Goyal presents a case study of India's two leading business houses - the Tatas and the Birlas - to sustain his thesis. An admirable work.

536 **Kothari's Economic and Industrial Guide to India.**
Madras: Kothari, 1936- . biennial.
This biennial guide continues Kothari's *Economic Guide and Investor's Handbook of India*. It gives detailed information about major companies which are classified according to their broad industrial categories. Provides information on taxation, import-export regulations, foreign aid, national economic plans, national and per capita income, agriculture, and other economic and social indicators. Useful for foreign investors.

537 **Regional variations in industrial development.**
D. T. Lakdawala, Yoginder K. Alagh, Atul Sarma. Bombay: Popular, for the Sardar Patel Institute of Economic and Social Research, Ahmedabad, 1974. 333p. bibliog.
Within the Indian federal economic and political structure, the region is an important planning unit. The authors discuss in detail the industrial base of each economic region in India and the changes that took place in them between 1960 and 1965. The study also explores the dichotomy between optimal and efficient allocation of resources on the one hand, and balanced regional development on the other. Based on substantial statistical data, this study concludes by saying that Indian planners have struck a good balance between efficiency and inter-regional equality.

538 **Performance of Indian public enterprises, macro report: a research study sponsored jointly by International Development Research Centre, Ottawa, Canada, and government of India.**
New Delhi: Standing Conference of Public Enterprises, 1978. 262p. bibliog.
A study of state-owned enterprises in India: their organization and management structure, their achievements in generating employment and production, and their role in creating an economic infrastructure. The book systematically describes the

public enterprise sector and identifies some of its specific objectives. One of the principal strengths of this volume is that it includes a complete listing of state-controlled enterprises in India.

539 Foreign collaboration in Indian industry: second survey report, 1974.
Reserve Bank of India.   Bombay, 1975. 185p. bibliog.

An examination of foreign participation in Indian industry. The survey covers all private and public companies with foreign capital participation or technical collaboration agreements. It provides statistics on equity participation, repatriation of assets and dividends, research and development investments, royalty rates, and restrictive clauses. While no conclusions are specifically drawn, there is an implicit recognition of the beneficial effects of foreign collaboration in Indian economic development.

540 Politics of multinationals: a pattern in neocolonialism.
Mahander Kumar Saini.   New Delhi: Gitanjali, 1981. 342p. bibliog.

A neo-Marxist analysis. The author argues that joint ventures, foreign subsidiaries, financial and technical collaboration, and consultancy services are devices enabling capitalist multinationals to maintain control over the productive processes in India and other third-world nations. In addition, Saini argues, such multinationals strengthen local capitalists and use them to exert pressures on the government, thereby seeking a retreat from the socialist and egalitarian goals of the society.

541 Role of industrial estates in a developing economy.
R. L. Sanghvi.   Bombay: Multi-Tech, 1979. 285p. bibliog.

Since 1978 the small-scale sector has been assigned a key role in the Indian developmental process in order to generate employment and to achieve spatial dispersion of industrial activity. The author finds that urban industrial estates have been more successful than rural ones and that industrial units within such estates have proved economically more viable than those outside such confines, and argues that spatial dispersion must be achieved through 'cluster industrialisation'.

542 Foreign collaboration: its significance in India's industrial progress.
Prem Kumar Srivastava.   Agra, India: Shiva Lal Agarwala, 1975. 245p. bibliog.

This balanced account gives a history of foreign collaboration in industry in post-independence India. The author analyses specific types of collaborative agreements and assesses the contribution of foreign collaboration to the country's industrial development. He concludes that such collaboration, though not without problems, has encouraged Indian entrepreneurship and industrial expansion.

543 **Private foreign investment and economic development: a case study of petroleum in India.**
R. Vedavalli. New York: Cambridge University Press, 1976. 222p. bibliog.

A case-study of the economic effects of direct foreign private investment in the Indian petroleum industry between 1948 and 1973. The book analyses in detail the causes of the gradual strengthening of state control over the Indian oil industry, and carefully examines government taxation, pricing, and refinery nationalization policies.

544 **Enterprise and economic change: 50 years of FICCI.**
H. Venkatasubbiah. New Delhi: Vikas, 1977. 176p. bibliog.

A study of the role of Indian industrialists, organized as the Federation of Indian Chambers of Commerce and Industry (FICCI), in critical economic and political issues between 1927 and 1976. The author points out that FICCI responses were often developed not by Indian capitalists but rather by their 'managers' such as T. T. Krishnamachari and G. L. Mehta, who later played a significant role in India's planning as Union ministers. Venkatasubbiah's painstaking study clearly shows that the Indian government has had a positive bias towards free enterprise and 'bigness' but has steadfastly opposed monopolies.

Agriculture and Food

545 **Agricultural development in China and India.**
Kalyani Bandyopadhyaya. New Delhi: Wiley-Eastern,
1976. 204p. bibliog.
A comparative study of Indian and Chinese agrarian structure, land reforms,
agricultural institutions, and food grain production. The author finds that between
1952 and 1973 agricultural production in India achieved a higher growth rate
than in China in spite of the larger volume of inputs in Chinese farms.

546 **Poverty, agriculture, and economic growth.**
B. M. Bhatia. New Delhi: Vikas, 1977. 260p. bibliog.
A survey of the role of the agricultural sector in the economic development
process. The author argues that tenurial reforms need to be supplemented by
adequate availability of capital, credit, and agricultural inputs as well as by
reform of agricultural taxation policies.

547 **India's rural development: an assessment of alternatives.**
Marcus Franda. Bloomington, Indiana: Indiana University
Press, 1979. 288p. bibliog.
A balanced description and analysis of Indian rural and agricultural policies
during the past thirty years. Franda reports on problems and accomplishments in
small-scale rural industries, co-operatives, village democratic organizations, volun-
tary community development, and caste-class relations. The author favours gradu-
alism, voluntarism, and pragmatic social planning to achieve growth, equity, and
efficiency in India's rural sector.

548 **Alternatives in agricultural development: report.**
ICSSR Working Group. New Delhi: Allied, 1980. 136p.
bibliog.
This report, commissioned by the Indian Council of Social Science Research,
evaluates the performance of Indian agriculture since 1950. The study proposes
an alternate strategy for agricultural development based on an increased role for
co-operative institutions and severe limitations on the private property rights of
large landholders.

132

549 Land reform in India: trends and perspectives.
Puran Chandra Joshi. Bombay: Allied, 1975. 181p. bibliog.
A far-reaching essay that poses all the major theoretical and empirical issues associated with the study of land reforms in India. Joshi examines such issues as the ideological parameters of land reform movements, the relationship of land legislation to agrarian social structure, and the implementation of land reforms by political leaders and public administrators. The author concludes by saying that during the last thirty years all land legislation has benefitted the middle and upper peasantry and perpetuated inequalities in India's rural economy.

550 Agricultural problems of India.
C. B. Mamoria. Allahabad, India: Kitab Mahal, 1979. 9th ed. 1,064p. bibliog.
A comprehensive text covering geographical, environmental, agronomic, sociological, fiscal, administrative, and political aspects of Indian agriculture. Mamoria includes sections on animal husbandry, dairying, and fisheries. A valuable introduction to the major problems and accomplishments of Indian agriculture.

551 Agriculture and social structure in Tamil Nadu: past origins, present transformations, and future prospects.
Joan P. Mencher. Durham, North Carolina: Academic Press, 1978. 314p. bibliog.
Based on detailed village studies over an eight-year period in a growing district, this book synthesizes statistics, archival materials, interviews, and secondary sources to create a broad-based analysis of India's rural problems. The author argues that rural inequalities have been reinforced by present developmental strategies and are the basic impediment to increasing agricultural productivity.

552 In defence of the irrational peasant.
Kusum Nair. Chicago: University of Chicago Press, 1979. 154p. bibliog.
A spirited challenge to neo-classical agricultural economics. Nair compares Punjab's progress with Bihar's stagnant agriculture and argues that socio-cultural patterns rather than purely economic factors are the main determinant of difference.

553 Studies in the development of capitalism in India.
Ashok Rudra (and others). Lahore: Vanguard: 1978. 459p. bibliog.
A collection of essays examining the debate among neo-Marxist scholars about whether the predominant mode of production in Indian agriculture is semi-feudal or capitalist. Among the more important essays are those by Ashok Rudra, Daniel Thorner, Usha Patnaik, Paresh Chattopadhyay and Dalip Swamy. The book is useful for its detailed and empirical consideration of the problem of class relations in the Indian countryside.

554 **Food trends and prospects in India.**
Fred Hugo Sanderson, Shyamal Roy. Washington, DC:
Brookings Institution, 1979. 162p.

An analysis of the policies and institutions that influence food grain production
and distribution in India. The first part examines long-term trends of food grain
production and employs statistical analysis to separate the effects of weather and
technology on this production. The second part projects India's food requirements
to the year 2000 and examines how increased demand could be met from domestic production. The authors believe that India has the capability of feeding over a
billion people at a vastly improved standard of living.

555 **The green revolution in India: a perspective.**
Bandhudas Sen. New York: Wiley/Halsted Press, 1974.
118p. bibliog.

A careful appraisal of the changes wrought in Indian agriculture by the introduction of high-yield seeds, fertilizers, and other inputs. Brief chapters analyse the
growth of food grain output in various regions of India. The author concludes by
saying that the green revolution has been limited geographically, but in the areas
where it has taken place, its impact is both positive and pervasive. Sen's assessment is more optimistic than Francine Frankel's in her *India's green revolution:
economic gains and political costs* (Princeton, New Jersey: Princeton University
Press, 1971. 232p. bibliog.).

556 **Amul: an experiment in rural economic development.**
S. P. Singh, Paul L. Kelly. Delhi: Macmillan, 1981. 180p.
bibliog.

The story of one of India's most successful large-scale dairy co-operatives. By
eliminating exploitative middle-men, dairy farmers near Bombay have been able
not only to improve their lot but to extend the scope of the co-operative's activities both geographically and economically.

Transport and Communications

557 **Transport in modern India.**
K. P. Bhatnagar (and others). Kanpur, India: Kishore
Publishing House, 1974. 9th rev. ed. 749p. bibliog.
A detailed description of the transport system in India. The authors examine the
relevance of various economic theories of transport to Indian conditions. Railways,
roads, inland water transport, rural transport, shipping, and air transport are
exhaustively covered, with emphasis on financing, rate structures, and administration of these systems. To be used as a college text.

558 **Road transport industry: a review.**
National Council of Applied Economic Research. New
Delhi, 1979. 99p. bibliog.
An examination of the impact of government policy, rules, and regulations on the
road transport industry. The study also examines the internal organizational structure of the industry and the policies affecting the financing of roads and road
transport. The authors find that roads in India are inadequately developed, that
check points have created bottle-necks to modernization, that there is inefficient
use of both capital and energy sources, and that both the employees of the truck
industry and low-level representatives of government agencies engage in widespread corrupt practices.

559 **Distance and development: transport and communications in
India.**
Wilfred Owen. Washington, DC: Brookings Institution,
1968. 170p. bibliog. (Transport Research Program).
A study of the role of transport and communications in the social and economic
development of India. Owen argues that a well-organized system of transport and
communications is necessary to build the nation, to exploit natural resources, and
to develop agriculture and industries. He examines the problems of inter-city and
rural transportation networks, as well as the role of telecommunications in the

India of the 1960s, and makes eleven specific recommendations in the concluding chapter.

560 Railways of the Raj.
Michael Satow, Desmond Ray.   New York: New York University Press, 1980. 120p. bibliog.

An album of prints, paintings, and photographs assembled and interpreted by two railroad buffs. Both the text and the illustrations vividly recreate the era when major urban centres built lavish railroad stations with their pavilions, waiting and dining rooms, and noteworthy architecture. The descriptions of Bombay's Victoria Terminus, the model railroad of the Maharaja of Gwalior, and the night-soil trolleys of Jodhpur are, indeed, fascinating.

561 Railways of India.
J. N. Westwood.   Newton Abbot, England: David & Charles, 1974. 192p. maps. bibliog.

Intended for the general reader, this book provides a brief survey of the development and operations of railroads in India from their mid-19th century beginnings to the early 1970s. Three long descriptive chapters dealing with the period 1850-70, 1870-1947, and 1947-72 are followed by a survey of infastructure and rolling stock. Brief appendixes include information on major types of locomotives, nine zonal railway maps, and many photographs.

Energy

562 India: the energy sector.
Patrick David Henderson. London: Oxford University Press, for the World Bank, 1975. 191p. maps. bibliog.

Henderson, a World Bank specialist, presents a careful and balanced study of India's energy sources and their utilization. He provides a thorough review of India's coal, petroleum, hydro-electric, thermal, nuclear, and biomass resources. Some chapters deal with the development of fuel and power industries, energy shortages, and policies for the future.

563 Oil: rich man, poor man.
Sucha Singh Khera. New Delhi: National, 1979. 240p. bibliog.

Written by a distinguished former Indian civil servant, this survey discusses the historical roots of India's drive for independent control of its petroleum industry. The impact of the 1973 Arab-Israeli war on international oil prices in general and on India's import bill in particular are carefully examined. The role of Indian state-run oil companies with technical support from the Soviet Union and other eastern bloc nations, particularly Rumania, is analysed.

564 Energy and economic development in India.
R. K. Pachauri. New York: Praeger, 1977. 187p. bibliog.

This book attempts to present a total picture of the role of India's energy sector in the nation's economic development. Demand, resources, and alternative technologies as well as the power sector are discussed. The author argues that greater conservation efforts need to be made and believes that coal, solar and other alternatives to petroleum need to be vigorously pursued.

565 Summary data on India's animal energy resources.
N. S. Ramaswamy. Bangalore, India: Indian Institute of Management, 1978. 110p. bibliog.

Animal energy resources remain the largest component of India's energy supply. This short book examines their role in Indian economic development and recommends a coherent policy for the development of biogas, especially for agriculture and rural development.

566 India's water wealth: its assessment, uses, and projections.
K. L. Rao. New Delhi: Orient Longman, 1979. rev. ed. 267p. maps. bibliog.

This book, by a former minister in the Indian government, is divided into three parts. The first deals with water resources of India, the second with water uses, and the third with growing water demand. In his coverage of irrigation, hydro-electric power, flood control, and navigational projects the author admits that India has not yet made rapid strides in the harnessing of river waters for economic development.

567 Power development in India: the financial aspects.
K. Venkataraman. New Delhi: Wiley-Eastern, 1972. 166p. bibliog.

Financial aspects of India's state-run but federally financed power sector are reviewed in this book. Venkataraman provides comprehensive information on the institutional set-up, the role of foreign aid, and state-federal relations in power generation and electrical equipment production. He argues that there is considerable scope for both cost reduction and revenue optimization to enable various electricity boards to undertake rapid development of additional power resources.

Labour and
Employment

568 Gheraos and industrial relations.
Arjun P. Aggarwal. Bombay: N. M. Tripathi, 1968. 186p.
bibliog.
Gherao is a peculiarly Indian labour agitational form in which employees surround their supervisors, often depriving them of food and other amenities, and continue their lock-in until their grievances are settled. Based on extensive interviews, the author assesses the pros and cons of *gherao*, and analyses the phenomenon in the context of Indian development and industrial relations.

569 Indian and American labor legislation and practices: a comparative study.
Arjun P. Aggarwal, Brijen K. Gupta. London: Asia, 1967.
329p. bibliog.
A pioneering study of the influence of American labour legislation and court decisions on the development of labour laws and arbitration practices in India. The authors argue that Indian courts have in significant instances misinterpreted American judicial decisions.

570 Agricultural labour unions.
K. C. Alexander. Hyderabad, India: National Institute of
Rural Development, 1978. 50p. bibliog.
A study of agrarian labour unions in three south Indian states. The author suggests that unionization efforts have benefitted from new agricultural technologies which have sharpened class conflicts in rural areas. The impact of unions on farmer-labour relations and on agricultural productivity is also examined.

Labour and Employment

571 **Industrial relations systems in India: a study of vital issues.**
Sahab Dayal. New Delhi: Sterling, 1980. 268p. bibliog.

Prices and wages, labour dispute settlement machinery, labour unrest and strikes, and government pay commissions are the vital issues discussed in this book. The author finds the government's policies to be incoherent and inconsistent, and he suggests how these policies could be revised to achieve better industrial relations.

572 **South Indian factory workers: their life and their world.**
Mark Holmström. New Delhi: Allied, 1979. 158p. bibliog.

Four factories in the organized sector of Bangalore form the backdrop to this book. The author probes the attitude of workers towards life, fellow workers, caste and linguistic consciousness, trade unionism, job satisfaction, and economic security. The book's strength lies in presenting shades of variation in attitudes rather than a broadly generalized mean.

573 **Indian Labour Yearbook.**
New Delhi: Labour Bureau, Ministry of Labour, 1946- . annual.

This official annual presents a comprehensive picture of the latest developments in the field of labour. Included are data on employment, wages, prices, living standards, labour administration, industrial disputes, agricultural labourers, and Indian workers overseas. A bibliography of official publications dealing with labour and several topical appendixes provide additional useful information. The most recent edition covers 1978.

574 **Surplus labour and the city: a study of Bombay.**
Heather Joshi, Vijay Joshi. Delhi: Oxford University Press, 1976. 189p. bibliog.

Using the city of Bombay as a case-study, the authors demonstrate that the employment problem in India is an expression of economic dualism: a small highly productive, well-paying, modern organized sector and an enormously large unorganized, low-paying, traditional sector. The authors recommend limitations on capital intensity in the organized sector and promotion of technology and training in the unorganized sector to lessen the disparity between the two and increase employment in each.

575 **Indian trade unions: a survey.**
V. B. Karnik. Bombay: Popular, 1978. 3rd ed. 431p. bibliog.

A broad survey of the trade union movement in India since the end of the First World War. Historical in scope, it describes and analyses the role of the Marxian, Gandhian, and other assorted socialists in the development, unity and diversity, and politicization of the Indian trade unions. There are several statistical tables and short biographical sketches of labour leaders.

576 **Trade union movement in Indian railways.**
Mahesh Kumar Mast. Meerutt, India: Meenakshi, 1969. 210p. bibliog.

The Indian railways are the single largest public-sector undertaking. The railway workers' unions have been pioneers in both the Indian nationalist and trade union movements. This study examines the history, evolution, and organization of railway unions, industrial relations, and dispute settlement machinery since Indian independence.

577 Employment, technology and development.
Amartya Sen.   Oxford, England: Clarendon, 1975. 193p. bibliog.

This book examines the issue of technological choice as it impinges on employment in developing countries, with special emphasis on India. Written from the perspective of political and economic feasibility, this well-balanced study emphasizes the role of political and social institutions in increasing employment opportunities.

578 Unemployment problem in India.
Edited by L. M. Singhvi, Phul Chand, R. S. Kapuria.   New Delhi: National, for the Institute of Constitutional and Parliamentary Studies, New Delhi, 1977. 365p. bibliog.

Ten articles by leading politicians, labour economists, and journalists on the problem of unemployment in India. The authors discuss such key issues as structural unemployment in the Indian economy, marginal employment in the rural sector, and the feasibility of full employment in India. The analysis, though grim, sees light at the end of the tunnel.

579 Labour welfare in India.
K. N. Vaid.   New Delhi: Shri Ram Centre for Industrial Relations, 1970. 392p. bibliog.

This comprehensive treatment discusses the theory of labour welfare in India. It traces the evolution of policy, summarizes labour welfare legislation, and examines social welfare programmes for the working class. The history and role of government in fostering welfare legislation and the response of employers, unions, and industrial co-operatives is carefully explored.

580 Trade unions in India: concepts, cases and case law.
Pramod Verma, Surya Mookherjee.   New Delhi: Oxford University Press, 1982. 408p. bibliog.

A dynamic overview of contemporary Indian trade unionism. Eight case-studies are presented to evaluate major issues in Indian industrial and labour relations. A separate section examines ten leading court cases dealing with labour law and the impact of judicial rulings on Indian labour legislation.

581 Factbook on manpower: population and labour force.
Y. S. Yegnaraman.   New Delhi: Institute of Applied Manpower Research, 1979. 3rd ed. 379p. bibliog.

Statistical tables, diagrams, and charts on Indian manpower based on census data and other government documents. The work-force is distributed into several categories. A separate section deals with employment and underemployment.

Science and Technology

General

582 **International transfer of technology to India.**
V. N. Balasubramanyam. New York: Praeger, 1973. 144p.
bibliog.
A study of Indo-foreign technical collaboration agreements. The author examines in depth twenty such agreements and concludes that those joint ventures in which there was significant foreign equity participation succeeded better in transferring locally adaptable technologies than those agreements that were based on royalty payments. A pioneering study.

583 **Economic growth and technological change in India.**
Bepin Behari. Delhi: Vikas, 1974. 274p. bibliog.
A study of the relationship between economic growth and technological change. Written from the Gandhian perspective, the book argues that the first priority of planners should be to develop a technological system that is easily adaptable to Indian conditions, particularly its rural clientele.

584 **Science and technology in India.**
Edited by Vadilal Dagli. New Delhi: Chand, 1982. 338p.
bibliog.
Twenty-seven essays on the role of science and technology in India's development. Several deal with Indian research and development efforts in such key sectors as electronics, fuel and power, metallurgy, information systems, and the chemical industry. Others deal with the development of technologies that are appropriate for Indian agriculture and small rural industries. A group of essays examine such national and broad issues as the relationship of science to economic development, manpower for research, institutional management, and Indian science policy.

585 **Directory of scientific reseach institutions in India.**
Delhi: Indian National Scientific Documentation Centre,
1969. 1,120p.

Even though somewhat dated, this is the most exhaustive listing of India's scientific research institutions. Each entry provides the name of the institute, its address, director's name, year of establishment, budget, library holdings, history of the institute, objectives and activities, and serial publications. There are also separate name, subject, and periodicals indexes. A revised edition is forthcoming.

586 **The political economy of science and technology in north-south relations: assessment of U.S.-Indian science and technology relations.**
Ward Morehouse, Brijen K. Gupta, Anil
Deolalikar. Springfield, Virginia: National Technical
Information Service, 1980. 252p. bibliog.

A definitive economic study of the transfer of science and technology from the United States to India, presenting comprehensive data on Indo-US science and technology relations. Four key sectors - drugs, agricultural implements, technical and managerial education, and hydro-power development - are examined in detail and assessment is made of the US contribution to them as well as the growing Indian capability to assume total control of future growth in these sectors.

587 **Science in India: institution building and the organizational system for research and development.**
Ward Morehouse. Bombay: Popular, 1971. 144p. bibliog.

A pioneering study of science in India in two major sections. The first looks at the organizational system of Indian science and the efforts of the Indian government to build intellectually self-sustaining scientific research institutions. The second provides basic data on major scientific and technological research societies, institutes, universities, and other organizations engaged in the advancement of scientific learning.

588 **Triveni: science, democracy and socialism.**
A. Rahman. Simla, India: Indian Institute for Advanced
Study, 1977. 111p. bibliog.

A definitive statement of his views by the founder of science policy studies in India. Rahman, a biochemist influenced by J. D. Bernal, argues that Indian scientists must on the one hand develop alternative technologies which are appropriate to Indian conditions, and on the other participate in building a nation committed to socialism and secularism.

589 **Science and Culture.**
Calcutta: Indian Science News Association, 1935- . monthly.

Though this journal is increasingly publishing articles in the sciences, it carries a large number of articles on the impact of science on society, research planning in India, and analyses of investments in science for social welfare.

590 **Science, technology and development: essays in honour of Professor A. Rahman.**
Edited by K. D. Sharma, M. A. Qureshi. New Delhi: Sterling, 1978. 478p. bibliog.
Twenty-six essays in honour of the director of the Centre for the Study of Science Technology and Development, written by eight Indian and eighteen foreign scientists. These essays range from science policy and development to science and society, technology assessment, and research management. Perhaps the most fruitful are the essays dealing with science in India, China, Japan, and Egypt.

History of science

591 **A concise history of science in India.**
D. M. Bose (chief editor). New Delhi: Indian National Science Academy, 1971. 689p. maps. bibliog.
A collection of articles, including a survey of sources and an overview by the editors, dealing with Indian contributions to various branches of mathematics and the physical and biological sciences. There are chapters on astronomy, mathematics, medicine, chemistry, agriculture, botany, zoology, and the physical world as well as a brief discussion of western science in India during the 19th century. This valuable survey is enhanced by a chronological table, a detailed bibliography, and excellent drawings, charts and photographs.

592 **History of Hindu mathematics: a source book. Volume 1: Numerical notation and arithmetic. Volume 2: Algebra.**
Bibhutibhusan Datta, Avadesh Narayan Singh. New York: Asia, 1962. reprint. 2 vols. in 1. bibliog.
A comprehensive, topically arranged account of the growth and development of Indian mathematics from ancient times through the 17th century. In addition to a detailed discussion of Hindu invention of the decimal place value system of numerical notation, the authors discuss original Hindu contributions in the fields of arithmetic and algebra. Translations of the relevant texts and, whenever necessary, explanations of them are provided for each topic. Originally published 1935-38.

593 **The classical doctrine of Indian medicine: its origins and its Greek parallels.**
Jean Filliozat, translated by Dev Raj Chanana. Delhi: Munshiram Manoharlal, 1964. 298p. bibliog.
A classic in its field, written by a distinguished French Indologist trained in medicine. The volume discusses popular legends about the Indian system of medicine known as *ayurveda*, traditions of medicine and surgery established by Caraka and Susruta, and the doctrines prevailing in contemporary indigenous medical practice. A separate chapter is devoted to a comparative study of the 'doctrine of wind' as adumbrated in Greece and India. The last chapter examines Indo-Greek contacts in the field of medicine.

594 **History of chemistry in ancient and medieval India**
incorporating the *History of Hindu chemistry* **by Acharya**
Prafula Chandra Ray.
Edited by P. Ray.   Calcutta: Indian Chemical Society,
1956. 494p. bibliog.

A chronological history of the development of chemistry in India from its alchemic roots, based on an earlier two-volume work by Prafula Chandra Ray which is copiously extracted. Indian skills in the art of making glazed pottery, in the extraction and working of metals, in the preparation of caustic alkalies, oxides, sulphides of metals, and dyes are outlined. The author attributes the decline of the scientific spirit of India to the development of the caste system which separated theoretical speculation from practical experimentation.

Education

595 Turmoil and transition: higher education and student politics in India.
Edited by Philip G. Altbach. New York: Basic Books, 1969. 227p. bibliog.

Six brilliant essays examining student unrest in Indian universities, which has become chronic in recent decades. Altbach's principal essay argues that this unrest is caused by increased educational opportunities, on the one hand, and shrinking job opportunities on the other. The essay by Edward Shils argues that this unrest is caused by hostility against authority which has been endemic in Indian universities for several decades. There are three case-studies in the collection: Di Bona's on unrest in Allahabad University, Shaw's on such unrest at Osmania, and Singh's dealing with Ranchi.

596 The university in transition: an Indian case study.
Philip G. Altbach. Cambridge, Massachusetts: Schenkman, 1972. 136p. bibliog.

A study of the transformation of the University of Bombay from an élitist institution with 20,000 students in 1950 to a mass education system with 77,000 students in 1967. Altbach finds that despite the decline of educational standards, including the knowledge of English, and the growth of student and faculty unrest, the university remains a viable academic institution.

597 The Indian academic profession: crisis and change in the teaching community.
Edited by Suma Chitnis, Philip G. Altbach. Delhi: Macmillan, 1979. 192p. bibliog.

A critical study of the hard times being endured by India's nearly 175,000 college and university teachers. Four of the volume's seven essays deal with the University of Bombay teachers and examine such issues as their personality make-up, constraints to their professionalization, and their relationship to academic organization. Other essays deal with teachers in engineering institutions, teachers and unionism, and modernization of their roles.

598 **U. S. educated engineering faculty in India.**
Thomas Eisemon. Bombay: Tata Institute of Social
Sciences, 1974. 129p. bibliog.

A careful, rigorously quantitative study based on 115 US-educated and 52
Indian-trained engineering teachers. It points out that foreign-trained teachers are
both more productive in scholarship and more dissatisfied with their working
conditions than are locally trained teachers. Equally significant is Eisemon's conclusion that US-educated faculty were equally productive whether they taught at
prestigious institutes of technology or regional engineering colleges with lesser
resources.

599 **Institution building in India: a study of international
collaboration in management education.**
Thomas M. Hill, W. Warren Haynes, Howard Baumgartel,
Samuel Paul. Boston, Massachusetts: Harvard University,
Graduate School of Business Administration, 1973. 381p.
bibliog.

A study of the US contribution to the development of institutes of management
in India, principally at Ahmedabad and Calcutta, and to a lesser extent to the
development of the Administrative Staff College at Hyderabad. The authors conclude that the strategic planning process in these institutions was ill-managed, and
foreign models of institution-building were incorporated without due regard to
local factors.

600 **Students' history of education in India, 1800-1965.**
Syed Nurullah, J. P. Naik. Calcutta: Macmillan, 1971. rev.
ed. 447p. bibliog.

A college-level survey text of the history of education in India since the establishment of British-sponsored schools in Calcutta in the late 18th century. The book
includes information and statistics on primary, secondary, and tertiary education
and discusses various education reform movements, both government inspired and
publicly generated. The authors also provide their own views on how Indian
education should be reformed for the rest of the century.

601 **Partners with India: building agricultural universities.**
Hadley Read (and others). Urbana-Champaign, Illinois:
University of Illinois, 1974. 159p. bibliog.

In 1948, India resolved to build a chain of agricultural universities on the lines of
US land grant institutions. Read's book analyses the role of American institutions
in establishing these universities, their growth, their expenditures, and future outlook. One of the authors' main concerns is the exceptionally high cost of training
students in these institutions and the limited opportunities for them in the job
market.

Education

602 **The assistance of four nations in the establishment of the Indian institutes of technology, 1945-1970.**
Kim Patrick Sebaly. Ann Arbor, Michigan: University of Michigan, School of Education, 1972. 180p. bibliog. (Comparative Education Dissertation Series, no. 24).
In 1945, the government of India decided to establish several institutions of engineering modelled after the Massachusetts Institute of Technology. The first of these at Khargpur was established with UNESCO assistance, a second in Bombay with Russian assistance, a third in Madras with German assistance, a fourth in Kanpur with US assistance, and a fifth in New Delhi with British assistance. Sebaly's book discusses the role of these foreign agencies in the establishment of these institutions, and inter-institutional variations in their academic organization.

603 **The higher learning in India.**
Edited by Amrik Singh, Philip G. Altbach. Delhi: Vikas, 1974. 451p. bibliog.
Twenty-two essays devoted principally to seven issues: the enormous size of India's population, unemployment of college graduates, decline in prestige of the academic profession, the examination system, language and education, and education as a commodity. Additional essays on the 'brain drain', academic financing, student activism, and women in higher education complete the broad survey. There is an extensive bibliography.

604 **University and college finances: seminar papers.**
Edited by Amrik Singh, G. D. Sharma. New Delhi: Association of Indian Universities, 1981. 246p. bibliog.
Indian higher education is principally financed by both state and federal governments, and to a lesser extent by private donations and student fees. Seventeen essays in this volume examine union-state relations in financing higher education and the need for alternative methods of financing, provide case-studies from the states of Karnataka, Bombay, Rajasthan, and Baroda and the Union territory of Delhi, and assess limitations of each mode.

605 **Universities Handbook: India.**
New Delhi: Association of Indian Universities, 1927- . biennial.
This handbook provides information about ninety universities, nine institutions 'deemed to be universities', and nine institutions of national importance. Founding dates, names of officers, deans of faculties, courses of studies, degree requirements, and degrees awarded are given, as well as lists of constituent and affiliated colleges. The index contains references to subjects and courses at degree level. Doctoral degree programmes are listed at the end of the index. Latest edition is 1981-82.

Literature

Classical literature in English translation

606 Bhartrihari: poems.
Bhartrihari, translated by Barbara Stöler Miller. New
York: Columbia University Press, 1967. 156p. bibliog.
Bhartrihari composed three volumes of lyrical poetry in the 5th century: one
devoted to love, another to indifference to sensual pleasures, and the third to wise
conduct. Every stanza stands as a poem in itself and expresses one idea com-
pletely. Mrs. Miller's translation is exquisite.

607 The ten princes: Dandin's *Dash-kumara-charitra*.
Dandin, translated by Arthur W. Ryder. Chicago:
University of Chicago Press, 1980. reprint of 1927 ed. 240p.
A delightful picaresque novel of the Gupta period, ably translated and originally
published in 1927. It depicts the low life of courtesans, unfaithful wives, hypocritical priests, unscrupulous ascetics, rakes, fervent lovers, and sinful gods. Dandin's
moral point is that none of us can reach perfection: duty, profit, and love are
always in conflict, and one of these three must be sacrificed to attain the other
two.

608 *Shilappadikaram*: the ankle bracelet.
Illango-Adigal, translated by Alain Daniélou. London:
Allen & Unwin, 1967. 211p.
An ancient Tamil tragic verse-epic of the 3rd century. The story has two con-
trasting characters: a devoted wife with natural beauty and a woman of pleasure
with contrived virtues. Much technical material is included on stringed instruments, music and drama, and major forms of dance.

609 **Love song of the dark lord: Jayadeva's** *Gitagovinda.*
Jayadeva, edited and translated by Barbara Stöler
Miller. New York: Columbia University Press, 1977. 225p.
(Unesco Collection of Representative Works, Indian Series).
Perhaps the most lyrical and sensuous poem in the entire Sanskrit literature, this describes the estrangement of Radha from her divine lover, Lord Krishna. Written by a Bengali court poet of the 12th century, the poem is an allegory of the human soul oscillating between erotic and divine love and finally transcending them both. Mrs. Miller's introduction explains the poem's structure and its symbolism in an excellent fashion.

610 **The cloud messenger:** *Meghaduta.*
Kalidasa, translated by Franklin Edgerton, Eleanor
Edgerton. Ann Arbor, Michigan: University of Michigan
Press, 1964. 96p.
A poem of rare beauty by India's greatest dramatist, combining the theme of love with the unity and variety inherent in India's geographical landscape. An exiled lover sends his message of longing to his wife through the monsoon clouds, and the passage of these clouds over various parts of India provides the poet with the opportunity to describe India's mountains, streams, and valleys, her cities and villages, her seasons, and her people and their aspirations. The translation captures the poem's spirit, though not entirely its lyrical quality.

611 **Great Sanskrit plays in new English transcreations.**
Edited and translated by P. Lal. New York: New
Directions, 1964. 396p. bibliog.
Six classical plays - Sudraka's *Toy cart*, Vishakadatta's *Signet ring*, Bhasa's *Dream*, Bhavabhuti's *Latter story of Rama*, Harsha's *Ratnavali*, and Kalidasa's *Shakuntala* - have been 'transcreated' in modern idiom. An introductory essay and a concluding bibliography provide excellent information on Indian drama as a literary form.

612 **The interior landscape: love poems from a classical Tamil anthology.**
Translated by A. K. Ramanujan. Bloomington, Indiana:
Indiana University Press, 1967. 128p.
Imaginative and accurate phrase-by-phrase translations of several Tamil classical poems of the first three centuries AD. All the poems celebrate love and represent generalized human types set in idealized landscapes. A concluding essay summarizes Tamil poetics.

613 **The** *Panchatantra.*
Translated by Arthur W. Ryder. Chicago: University of
Chicago Press, 1964. 470p.
India's great treasury of animal fables dating back to the 2nd century BC, with over 200 different versions in at least 50 languages outside India. The translation is exquisite. Example: 'Scholarship is less than sense. Seek intelligence'.

614 **The sacred** *Kural* **or the** *Tamil Veda.*
Tiruvalluvar, edited and translated by H. A.
Popley. Calcutta: YMCA Publishing House, 1958. 2nd ed.
157p.

A 5th-century Tamil epic. It is a long didactic poem divided into three parts, each dealing with the three major ends of existence: man with himself (righteous conduct), man with society (material gains), and man with woman (pleasure and companionship).

615 **The** *Ramayana.*
Valmiki, translated by Hari Prasad Shastri. London:
Shanti Sadan, 1952-59. 3 vols.

The standard complete prose translation of India's second-longest and most popular epic, with detailed glossaries of Sanskrit proper names and epithets. For abridged versions, see *The Ramayana of Valmiki: condensed from Sanskrit and transcreated into English* by P. Lal (New Delhi: Vikas, 1981. 341p.), and *The Ramayana of R. K. Narayan: a shortened modern prose version of the Indian epic suggested by the Tamil version of Kamban* (New York: Penguin, 1977. 171p.), both of which cover the central life story of the exemplary Rama, his marriage, exile, the abdication of his wife, her later recovery, and the triumphant return to his kingdom.

616 **Tales of ancient India.**
Translated by Johannes Adrianus Bernardus van
Buitenen. Chicago: University of Chicago Press, 1969.
260p.

A selection of stories from *Brihat kathasaritsagara* and *Brihat kathasloka-samgraha*, originally composed in the 8th or 9th century and ascribed respectively to Somadeva and Budhasvamin. Van Buitenen has chosen several secular stories, especially those dealing with the mystery of woman in her infinite variety. Excellent translations.

617 **Two plays of ancient India:** *The little clay cart, The minister's seal.*
Translated by Johannes Adrianus Bernardus van
Buitenen. New York: Columbia University Press, 1968.
278p.

Two plays of the Gupta period. *The Little clay cart,* by Sudraka, is a 'rambunctious comedy of manners' and *The minister's seal,* by Vishakadatta, is a 'taut political drama'. In both plays urban characters such as gamblers, spies, courtesans, ministers, learned thieves, hypocritical monks, and rebel princes are carefully delineated. An introductory essay discusses several aspects of the Indian world-view and the role of drama in explaining it.

618 *Sankalpa suryodayam*: **a Sanskrit allegorical drama in ten acts.**
Venkatanatha, translated by M. R. Rajagopala Iyengar. Madras: Vedanta Desika Research Society, 1977. 383p.

This 14th-century allegorical play expounds Ramanuja's Vedantic philosophy Visishta-advaita. Human beings, says the author, can escape the cycle of birth, death, and rebirth through meditation, communion with god, and finding grace. The translation is satisfactory, and is preceded by two essays dealing with Ramanuja's philosophy and its influence on the play.

619 **Sanskrit poetry from Vidyakara's treasury.**
Compiled by Vidyakara, translated by Daniel H. H. Ingalls. Cambridge, Massachusetts: Belknap Press of Harvard University Press, 1968. 346p. bibliog.

During India's mediaeval period, several Sanskrit anthologies were compiled to preserve selections from the works of earlier minor poets. Vidyakara's *Subhasita ratna kosh*, edited in the 12th century, is one of the most distinquished. Ingalls has arranged stanzas of different poets under fifty different themes such as adolescence, young women, blossoming of love, sunset, and moon. A judicious selection.

620 **Love songs of Vidyapati.**
Vidyapati Thakura, translated by Deben Bhattacharya, edited by W. G. Archer. Ann Arbor, Michigan: University Microfilms, 1979. reprint of 1970 ed. 148p. bibliog.

Vidyapati, like Jayadeva, is one of the most lyrical poets of India. These poems, written in the 14th century, stress that erotic love is a divine obligation. Archer and Bhattacharya have included thirty-one art plates from mediaeval Indian paintings which illustrate the theme of these poems.

621 **The *Mahabharata* of Krishna Dwaipayana Vyasa.**
Vyasa, translated by Kisari Mohan Ganguli. Calcutta: Oriental, 1962. 12 vols.

A complete and faithful translation of India's longest epic. Originally published between 1884 and 1896 by Pratap Chandra Roy, these volumes have been listed inaccurately in earlier bibliographies as having been translated by Roy. A new complete translation was undertaken by J. A. B. van Buitenen (*The Mahabharata*, University of Chicago Press, 1973-), but only three volumes were completed before the translator's death. For abridged versions, see *The Mahabharata of Vyasa: condensed from Sanskrit and transcreated into English* by P. Lal (New Delhi: Vikas, 1980. 3rd ed. 400p. bibliog.) and *The Mahabharata: an English version based on selected verses* by Chakravarthi V. Narasimhan (New York: Columbia University Press, 1965. 254p.).

Regional literature in English translation

622 **Boatman of the Padma.**
Manik Bandyopadhyay, translated from the Bengali by
Hirendranath Mukherji. New Delhi: National Book Trust,
1977. 2nd ed. 144p.

Originally published in 1936, *Boatman* remains one of the truly great novels of
Bengal. Written by a Marxist with keen Freudian insights, the story deals with
the oppressed life of a boatman whose fortunes depend on the flow of the river
and the water level in it, phenomena often in conflict with the desires of other
villagers.

623 *Pather panchali*: **song of the road.**
Bibhutibhushan Banerji, translated by T. W. Clark, Tarpada
Mukherji. Bloomington, Indiana: Indiana University Press,
1975. 316p.

The odyssey of a Bengali Brahman boy through childhood, youth, marriage, and
despair, and the encounter of tradition with modernity are superbly told. The
novel has achieved additional acclaim via Satyajit Ray's rendering in film: *The
Apu trilogy.*

624 **Contemporary Indian short stories.**
Edited by Bhabani Bhattacharya. New Delhi: Sahitya
Akademi, 1967-69. 2 vols.

Thirty-seven stories from sixteen Indian languages, including some written originally in English, make up these volumes. Brief notes on authors are also provided.

625 **The whispering earth.**
Kota Shivarama Karanth, translated from the Kannada by
A. N. Murthy Rao. Delhi: Vikas, 1974. 206p.

A novel of village India where life is harsh and stark, ravaged by nature's
capriciousness. Karanth writes about three generations of a Brahman family in
which women, though subservient to men, have both courage and compassion to
overcome the pain inflicted by nature as well as by vagabond husbands.

626 **The village had no walls.**
Vyankatesh Digambar Madgulkar, translated from the
Marathi by Ram Deshmukh. New York: Asia, 1967. 172p.

A distinguished short novel, originally entitled *Bangarwadi,* of a Marathi she-
pherd's village and the way it functions, as seen through the eyes of a school teacher.

627 The Vikas book of modern Indian love stories.
Edited by Pritish Nandi. New Delhi: Vikas, 1979. 212p.

Twenty-five stories from as many writers, with nineteen translated from various Indian languages, and devoted to intriguing facets of relationships between the opposite sexes. The translations are uniformly good. Included in the anthology are several distinguished writers such as Mulk Raj Anand, Amrita Pritam, Krishan Chander, Khushwant Singh, Vijay Tendulkar, Sasthi Brata, Manik Bandyopadhyay and Kamala Das.

628 Modern Hindi short stories.
Translated and edited by Gordon C. Roadarmel. Berkeley, California: University of California Press, 1974. 211p.

Fifteen stories from as many writers, ably translated. Many depict middle-class city dwellers bound by tradition yet caught in a changing world. The prevalent theme is alienation: the emotional and physical settings are distinctly north Indian.

629 Chemmeen.
Thakazhi Sivasankara Pillai, translated by Narayan Menon. Westwood, Connecticut: Greenwood, 1979. 228p.

One of the finest contemporary Indian novels. Set in Kerala, the theme is forbidden intercommunal love in a fishing village. The novel received the Sahitya Akademi's Award, and has been published in more than twenty Indian languages and at least twelve western languages.

630 The gift of a cow: a translation of the Hindi novel *Godaan*.
Dhanpat Rai Srivastava, translated by Gordon C. Roadarmel. Bloomington, Indiana: Indiana University Press, 1968. 442p.

A magnificient translation of a powerful novel about rural India. Srivastava (*pseud*. Premchand) depicts the oppression of the Indian peasantry by moneylenders and priests, and the all-pervasive spirit of resignation that permeates Hindu life. The author, torn between Gandhism and socialism, offers no solution.

Indo-Anglian literature

631 Ocean of the night.
Ahmed Ali. Delhi: Hind Pocket Books, 1972. 165p.

Set in early 20th-century Lucknow, a citadel of both cosmopolitan and feudal Islamic culture.

632 Twilight in Delhi.
Ahmed Ali. New Delhi: Sterling, 1973. 2nd ed. 290p.

Life and death in an aristocratic Muslim family of Delhi in the early 20th century. The novel boldly captures the highly stylized, culturally polished, and patriarchal life of a family who, though urban and urbane, still live with most Mughal feudal values intact.

633 **Coolie.**
Mulk Raj Anand. New Delhi: Arnold Heinemann, 1980. 320p.

The foremost Indian novelist of the 1930s and 1940s, Anand chose the disadvantaged and the unprivileged as his central characters. In *Coolie* we encounter a hill-boy who works at various menial jobs and dies of tuberculosis as a young rickshaw-puller in imperial Simla.

634 **Two leaves and a bud.**
Mulk Raj Anand. Delhi: Hind Pocket Books, 1972. 203p.

In this novel, Anand portrays a Punjabi worker destined to toil and murder in an Assam tea plantation. This novel of protest represents a sharp indictment of British imperial rule in India.

635 **He who rides a tiger.**
Bhabani Bhattacharya. New Delhi: Arnold Heinemann, 1977. 245p.

Superstitions, urban vices, and caste tyranny by the rich are the themes of this poignant Indian novel, set during the Bengal famine of 1943. A village blacksmith fakes a miracle, becomes a holy man, secures wealth from his former oppressors and is detected as a fraud, but is still loved by his own low-caste people.

636 **Cry, the peacock.**
Anita Desai. New Delhi: Orient Paperbacks, 1980. 218p.

Though Anita Desai has written several novels since this and the following entry were published in the 1960s, they have not been as successful. In *Cry*, Mrs. Desai portrays the breakdown of a wife who cannot cope with her husband's cold detachment.

637 **Voices in the city.**
Anita Desai. Delhi: Hind Pocket Books, 1968. 257p.

In *Voices*, Desai's theme is the inability of a woman to cope with the cruelties of a marriage in a Hindu joint-family.

638 **All about H. Hatterr.**
Govindas Vishnoodas Desani. New York: Farrar, Straus, 1970. rev. ed. 287p.

Hailed by T. S. Eliot and others as a literary sensation, this novel's strength lies in the beauty of its language and a Joycean construction. A Eurasian ('I am fifty-fifty of the species') turns up on the shores of India, seeks the wisdom of its seven sages, and develops a comprehensive philosophy of life which is then told in this 'autobiography'.

639 **The naked triangle.**
Balwant Gargi. New York: Advent Books, 1981. 168p.

A brutally frank autobiographical novel by one of India's leading dramatists and stage directors. The novel deals with three triangles: the triangle with a wife and a mistress; the triangle when the mistress finds a new lover; and the triangle when the betrayed wife seeks love elsewhere. A controversial novel of passion and compassion, elegantly written.

640 **Heat and dust.**
Ruth Prawer Jhabvala. New York: Harper, 1983. 181p.

Perhaps the best-known novel of a European expatriate in India, this won the Booker Prize in 1975 and inspired the film of the same name. Set in central India, it is the story of an Englishwoman who deserts her husband for inter-racial romantic love and the resulting agony. This episode is subsequently re-evaluated fifty years later by the woman's stepdaughter with a deeper understanding of what really happened to her stepmother.

641 **Nectar in a sieve.**
Kamala Markandaya. New York: John Day, 1955. 255p.

The great 'sob-story' of India, this masterfully portrays the tragic assault upon a traditional village by modern technology and industry. Rukmini, the heroine, is Mother India, whose virtues, stoic courage, and boundless capacity to endure suffering are characteristic of village India.

642 **Azadi.**
Chaman Nahal. Boston, Massachusetts: Houghton Mifflin, 1975. 372p. map.

An unexceptional middle-class family suddenly faces both freedom and disaster during India's independence and partition in 1947. The author handles with sensitivity the explosive theme of religious conflict and intercommunal love. Both male and female characters are equally well drawn.

643 **The bachelor of arts.**
R. K. Narayan. Chicago: University of Chicago Press, 1980. 264p.

Narayan is perhaps the least didactic or political Indian novelist. *The bachelor of arts* is an amusing story of a college student, his desire to become a hermit, the recovery of love in an arranged marriage, and the powerful influence of a mother-in-law on a young bride.

644 **The vendor of sweets.**
R. K. Narayan. London: Heinemann, 1980. 192p.

In *The vendor of sweets* we meet a foreign-educated Indian and his American sweetheart and learn of their efforts to invent a story-writing machine in order to evade taxes. Both this and the preceding novel treat simple ironies of Indian life.

645 Kanthapura.

Raja Rao. New York: New Directions, 1967. 244p.

Raja Rao is India's foremost philosophical novelist writing in English. The reassertion of Indian traditions, the recovery of Hinduism, and the exploration of spiritual depths by an intellectual hero form the substance of both this and the novel below. In *Kanthapura* Rao examines the impact of Gandhi on Indian spiritual life.

646 The serpent and the rope.

Raja Rao. Westport Connecticut: Greenwood, 1975. 407p.

In *The serpent and the rope*, a major work of fiction in English, a young intellectual recovers his basic Hindu values, and finds them totally universal.

647 Midnight's children.

Salman Rushdie. New York: Knopf, 1981. 445p.

An extraordinary novel of rare beauty that encapsulates the reality of modern India. The first thirty-one years of Indian independence (1947-78) are seen through the eyes of two persons, born in the first hour of India's independence, 15 August 1947, in a Bombay nursing home, and switched: one destined to an aristocratic Muslim home, and the other to a street-singer's family. Expected to be the nation's hope, the children grow up as mortal enemies, and watch their country's loss of innocence. A *tour de force*.

648 Train to Pakistan (Mano Majra).

Khushwant Singh. New York: Grove Press, 1981. 181p.

A pitiless indictment of cruelty by all communal groups during the fateful days of India's partition. This is the only novel to capture the parameters of the Hindu-Muslim-Sikh holocaust of 1947.

649 Song of Anasuya: a novel.

Uma Vasudev. New Delhi: Vikas, 1978. 174p.

The first novel by a distinguished political analyst, *Song of Anasuya* tells of the torment and rapture of a man who, after years of loveless sex, finds himself involved with two women. The characters of the tormented hero and his two women, one involved platonically and the other erotically, are drawn with subtle sensitivity. Well written.

Literary biographies and memoirs

650 Autobiography of an unknown Indian.

Nirad Chaudhuri. Berkeley, California: University of California Press, 1968. 506p.

Boyhood experiences and intellectual growth of a distinguished Bengali author. Autobiographical information is used to make some startling comments about India, its history and nationalism, and its culture. For instance, Chaudhuri dismisses as superannuated folly the notion that the Hindu civilization can be revived.

651 Rabindranath Tagore: a biography.
Krishna Kripalani. Calcutta: Visva-Bharati, 1980. 491p. bibliog.

A fine, well-balanced biography of India's Nobel Laureate in literature. Kripalani covers many facets of Tagore's life: his educational philosophy, his involvement in Indian politics, his search for a synthesis of east and west, and his loneliness both as a child and as India's senior statesman in his old age.

652 Munshi Premchand: a literary biography.
Gopal Madan. New York: Asia, 1964. 462p.

A first-rate biography of north India's foremost Hindi-Urdu story-teller, who achieved most of his recognition after his death. Madan carefully analyses Premchand's writings and places them squarely in the context of his middle-class 'white-collar' background.

653 Daddyji.
Ved Mehta. New York: Oxford University Press, 1979. 195p.

A brilliant portrait of a north Indian family in the 1930s. The central character is the author's physician father, a product of education in India and in Britain, and uncomfortable in both cultures. The ambivalent impact of the west on India's cultural tradition is clearly indicated by the book's title - an English word with an Indian suffix.

654 Raja Rao.
C. D. Narasimhaiah. New Delhi: Arnold Heinemann, 1973. 170p. bibliog.

A distinguished literary biography of the author of *The serpent and the rope* and *Kanthapura* (q.v.), two magnificient novels written in English in the 20th century.

655 My days: a memoir.
R. K. Narayan. London: Chatto & Windus, 1975. 186p.

This autobiography of India's foremost story-teller is more a recollection of his boyhood than a full-length account of his life. Narayan keeps his adult life private, but he does provide information about his excursions into the occult. Well worth reading.

Literary history and criticism, literary journals

656 A new history of Sanskrit literature.
Krishna Chaitanya. New Delhi: Manohar, 1977. 2nd ed.
490p. bibliog.

This is the best short but comprehensive history of Sanskrit literature, which includes a discussion of epic poetry (*Ramayana* and *Mahabharata*) and also of epic legends (*Puranas*, Buddhist and Jain legends), often exluded in traditional histories. For a more detailed history, Winternitz (q.v.) remains unsurpassed.

657 The literatures of India.
Edward C. Dimock, Jr. (and others). Chicago: University of Chicago Press, 1978. 265p. bibliog.

Initiated by the Asian literature programme of the Asia Society of New York, this volume approaches the problems of Indian literatures primarily from a critical point of view. Van Buitenen analyses India's epics, classical dramas, and the story literature. Ramanujan and Gerow critically review Indian poetics, and Dimock and Roadarmel examine Bengali and Hindi prose fiction. Though the editors, by their own account, have not been entirely successful in identifying common variables and influences in the entire corpus of Indian literatures - classical and modern, national and regional -these essays constitute a serious attempt to define unity and variety in them.

658 A survey of Malayalam literature.
K. M. George. Bombay: Asia, 1968. 354p. bibliog.

A good survey of Malayalam literature of southwest India, based on lectures delivered at the University of Chicago in 1964. The author carefully examines the role of the oral tradition of Kerala, the Tamil tradition of south India, and the classical Sanskrit tradition in the development of a distinct Malayalam literature. Separate chapters deal with such topics as early prose; traditional poetry; modern poetry; the novel, short story, and drama; and other prose writings. Several short stories and poems, translated into English, have been included and enhance the value of this work.

659 A history of Indian literature.
Edited by Jan Gonda. Wiesbaden, GFR: Harrasssowitz, 1975 - . in progress.

Under the editorship of Gonda, a distinguished European Indologist, a comprehensive survey of the history of Indian classical, mediaeval, and modern literatures has been undertaken. The following are the titles of each volume of the set. *Hindi literature in the twentieth century*, Hans Peter Theodor Gaeffke (188p. bibliog.); *Kashmiri literature*, Braj B. Kachru (114p. bibliog.); *Hindi literature of the nineteenth and early twentieth centuries*, Ronald Stuart McGregor (60p. bibliog.); *Assamese literature*, Satyendra Nath Sarma (76p. bibliog.); *Classical Urdu literature from the beginning to Iqbal*, Annemarie Schimmel (139p. bibliog.); *Islamic literatures of India*, Annemarie Schimmel (60p. bibliog.); *Sindhi literature*, Annemarie Schimmel (41p. bibliog.); *Classical Marathi literature from the beginning to A.D. 1818*, Shankar Gopal Tulpule (160p. bibliog); *Bengali literature*, Dusan Zbavitel (188p. bibliog.); *Tamil literature*, Kamil Veith

Literature. Literary history and criticism, literary journals

Zvelebil (316p. bibliog.). All these volumes are significant improvements on the volumes on regional literatures of India published by the Sahitya Akademi. Additional volumes on Gujarati literature (by Mallison), Kannada literature (by Nayak), Maithili literature (by Misra), Malayalam literature (by Asher), Marathi literature (by Sontheimer), Oriya literature (by Bolton), Punjabi literature (by Singh), and Telugu literature (by Mahadeva Sastri) are in preparation.

660 Indian Literature.
New Delhi: Sahitya Akademi, 1957- . quarterly.
This publication of India's national academy of letters provides English translations of poems and short stories and topical articles on Indian writers and regional literatures. Occasionally special issues on selected authors are included.

661 History of Gujarati literature.
Mansukhlal M. Jhaveri. New Delhi: Sahitya Akademi, 1978. 260p. bibliog.
A short, satisfactory history of major Gujarati writers since 1500. However, the volume lacks literary criticism - the author's approach is to list authors serially, discuss major influences on them, and mention their principal publications.

662 Contemporary Indian literature and society.
Edited by Motilal W. Jotwani. New Delhi: Heritage, 1979. 251p.
Sixteen essays by as many literary critics on the literary output of sixteen principal classical and modern Indian languages. The authors deal with developments in various Indian literatures during the last thirty years, and how they have contributed to raising Indian national consciousness. Two appendixes list winners of prestigious Sahitya Akademi and Bharatiya Jnanpith awards and their prize-winning publications.

663 Journal of South Asian Literature.
East Lansing, Michigan: Asian Studies Center, Michigan State University, 1963- . quarterly.
The only journal in the west devoted primarily to the literatures of South Asia. While north Indian literature is emphasized generally, there are occasional pieces on other regional literatures. Literary criticism, literary history, translations into English, and good book reviews are the standard fare. Between 1963 and 1972, it was known as *Mahfil: a quarterly magazine of South Asian literature.*

664 Prakrit languages and their contribution to Indian culture.
Sumitra Mangesh Katre. Poona, India: Deccan College, 1964. 2nd ed. 95p.
Katre's volume deals with a group of languages generally categorized as Middle Indo-Aryan and used widely in India between 600 BC and 1100 AD. The author has written a topical rather than a chronological history of the Prakrit languages. He emphasizes their linguistic features and their contribution to other Indo-Aryan languages, literatures, and arts and sciences. Well balanced.

665 The influence of the west on Punjabi literature.
Mohindar Pal Kohli. Ludhiana, India: Lyall Book Depot, 1969. 258p. bibliog.

An excellent work of literary criticism, this book deals with major Punjabi writers since 1850. The author contends that under western influence traditional Punjabi literature underwent a significant metamorphosis resembling the impact of the Renaissance on European literary output. Separate chapters deal with poets, dramatists, novelists, storytellers, and literary critics.

666 History of Oriya literature.
Mayadhar Mansinha. New Delhi: Sahitya Akademi, 1962. 203p. bibliog.

Oriya, like Bengali and Assamese, is a member of the eastern group of Indo-Aryan languages. It is a language remarkably free of the dialectic variations which are so common in other Indian languages. Approximately half of the book deals with Oriya literature from the 13th to 18th centuries and the remaining half with the last two centuries. Well balanced and readable.

667 History of Kannada literature.
Ranganath Shrinivas Mugali. New Delhi: Sahitya Akademi, 1975. 143p. bibliog.

A short history of the Kannada literature of south India, written for the non-specialist. Sections on early and mediaeval Kannada literary history are succinct and without controversy. In his discussion of modern writers the author tends to be factual, and does not take into account the role of socio-economic forces in moulding modern Indian literatures. Good introductory text.

668 History of Telugu literature.
Gidugu Venkata Sitapati. New Delhi: Sahitya Akademi, 1968. 314p. bibliog.

A short history of the Telugu literature of south India written for the non-specialist. Like other Sahitya Akademi volumes this one suffers from a lack of any critical evaluation of the major Telugu writers and their publications, but it does provide a succinct synopsis of the major periods, trends, and authors of Telugu literature.

669 Indian writing in English.
K. R. Srinivasa Iyengar. London: Asia, 1973. 2nd ed., rev. and enl. 761p. bibliog.

A comprehensive review of Indian writing in English from its beginnings in the early 19th century to the achievements of contemporary authors like Mulk Raj Anand, Raja Rao, and Bhabhani Bhattacharya. The author believes that Indian writing in English has distinct, identifiable literary qualities and that it cannot be considered a part of English literature. The book combines literary history with literary criticism. Excellent.

670 **A history of Indian literature.**
M. Winternitz, vols. 1 and 2 translated by S. Ketkar, vol. 3
translated by Subhadra Jha. Calcutta: University of
Calcutta, vols. 1 and 2, 1959-63. 2 vols. bibliog.; Delhi:
Motilal Banarsidass, vol. 3 (in 2 parts), 1963. 2 vols. bibliog.

Winternitz's history remains unsurpassed both in its scope and scholarship. The
first volume deals with early Vedic literature and the great epics; the second with
Buddhist and Jain legends; the third with ornate poetry, dramas, and other technical literatures. The first two volumes were translated during Winternitz's lifetime under his supervision. S. N. Dasgupta and S. K. Dey produced a *History of
Sanskrit literature, volume 1* (University of Calcutta, 1977. 2nd ed. 833p.
bibliog.), based in part on Winternitz's third volume and put together when the
University of Calcutta decided to defer the translation of this volume. Subhadra
Jha has now completed the translation of Winternitz's last volume. The second
part of the Dasgupta volume was not published due to his untimely demise. On
kavya (ornate poetry and poetic dramas) the Dasgupta-Dey history is superior to
the appropriate section in the third volume of Winternitz.

The Arts

General

671 **5000 years of the art of India.**
Mario Bussagli, Calembus Sivaramamurti. New York:
Abrams, 1978. reprint of 1971 ed. 335p. plates.
A lavishly illustrated, aesthetically satisfying volume on the figural art of India
from the Harappan culture (1500 BC) to the supreme Indo-Muslim synthesis in
the 17th century. The authors argue that the art of non-Muslim India is one of
the world's most consistent in its themes even though it adapted foreign influences, and that it showed comparative disinterest in inanimate objects. Islamic
intervention in Indian art was rather traumatic because it challenged basic Indian
aesthetic assumptions rooted in the Hindu-Buddhist ethos; however, early Islamic
art in India was the basis for a rich Indo-Islamic synthesis under the Rajputs and
the later Mughals.

672 **History of Indian and Indonesian art.**
Anand Kentish Coomaraswamy. New York: International
Publications Service, 1972. reprint. 295p. maps. bibliog.
This well-illustrated standard work, written by a pioneer historian of Indian art
and originally published over fifty years ago (1927), covers the entire range of
Indian and Indonesian sculpture, painting, bronzes, terracottas, and architecture
from pre-Mauryan times to the mediaeval period. The term 'Indonesian' is used
to include the areas of Asia which experienced the penetration of Indian art. The
Mughal school of painting and architecture is omitted.

673 **A concise history of Indian art.**
Roy C. Craven. London: Thames & Hudson, 1976. 252p.
bibliog.
A noted American museum director and professor of art history reviews, for
non-specialists, the whole of the art of India from the 3rd millenium BC Harappan finds through to the 18th-century miniature painting schools. By means of
the illustrations, which appear on almost every page of the book, and the text

which interprets them, the author guides the reader through the main periods, major forms, and some outstanding examples of Indian art. An excellent survey for students and generalists.

674 Lalit Kala Contemporary.
New Delhi: Lalit Kala Akademi, 1962- . semi-annual.

This lavishly illustrated journal, published by India's National Academy of Fine Arts, is devoted exclusively to modern Indian art. Individual issues are mainly thematic and include articles, statements, and reviews by artists, critics and art historians.

675 Iconographic dictionary of the Indian religions: Hinduism, Buddhism, Jainism.
Gosta Liebert.   Leiden, the Netherlands: Brill, 1976. 377p.
(Studies in South Asian Culture, vol. 5).

Iconographic terms for Professor Liebert's dictionary are primarily drawn from Sanskrit, but some from Pali and other modern Indian languages are also included on a selective basis. Geographic scope of the dictionary is South Asia. It is intended primarily for those who do not possess knowledge of Sanskrit or other Indian languages and yet have an interest in Indian iconography, art history, or history of South Asian religion. A very useful listing of over 2,500 Sanskrit terms, classified under several subject headings, is given in the appendixes to facilitate the use of the dictionary.

676 Marg: a magazine of the arts.
Bombay: Marg Publications, 1946- . quarterly.

Edited and published by Mulk Raj Anand, a well-known Indian literary figure, this quarterly is devoted to the arts and crafts of South Asia. Well illustrated, each issue is devoted to a single art form.

677 Folk origins of Indian art.
Curt Maury.   New York: Columbia University Press, 1969. 245p. bibliog.

A survey of the religious imagery of village India and its role in shaping traditional Hindu iconography. The author utilizes anthropological, mythological, and linguistic evidence from the villages of central and south India. He demonstrates the tenacity of pre-Aryan gods and godesses in the formation of both Vaisnavite and Saivite iconography. Basic for an understanding of the origins of Hindu art.

678 An approach to Indian art.
Niharranjan Ray.   Chandigarh, India: Publications Bureau, Punjab University, 1974. 299p. bibliog.

Inspired by Coomaraswamy's pioneering work, as well as by the studies of Kramrisch, Zimmer and others, Ray argues for a humanistic, social, and aesthetic approach instead of the religious, symbolical, and intellectual perspectives that have dominated the field. Ray views Indian art objects as possessing aesthetic values that are of intrinsic and immediate appeal to the human mind and senses rather than as simply illustrations.

679 **The art and architecture of India: Buddhist, Hindu, Jain.**
Benjamin Rowland. Baltimore, Maryland: Penguin Books,
1967. 3rd ed., rev. 314p. map. bibliog.

An authoritative, lucid, and beautifully illustrated history of the Buddhist, Hindu,
and Jain art of India, the most satisfying single volume on the subject. It is a
connected narrative, not unduly burdened by archaeological and iconographical
details. The author includes the impact of Greco-Roman art on the art of India
and surveys the influence of Indian art in Turkestan, Tibet, Nepal, Sri Lanka,
Burma, Cambodia, and Java.

680 **Classical Indian dance in literature and the arts.**
Kapila Vatsyayan. New Delhi: Sangeet Natak Akademi,
1977. 2nd ed. 431p. bibliog.

This very detailed, scholarly work on the place of dance in classical Sanskrit
literature and traditional sculpture is both analytical and evaluative. It deals also
with the subject of aesthetics as relevant to Indian dance and with the general
theory and technique of Indian classical dance. The photographs of sculptural
representation give a comprehensive picture of the dance as found in ornamental
stone imagery and in iconography. A smaller and simpler treatment of Indian
dance is the author's *Classical Indian dance* (Thompson, Connecticut: InterCul-
ture Associates [c. 1975]. 153p. photos.).

681 **The art of Indian Asia: its mythology and transformations.**
Heinrich Robert Zimmer, completed and compiled by Joseph
Campbell. Princeton, New Jersey: Princeton University
Press, 1968. 2nd ed., rev. 2 vols. bibliog.

A valuable and insightful philosophical analysis of India's visual arts. The first
volume is a historical outline of the transformations of Indian visual images
through successive internal and external aesthetic stimuli. The second contains
over 600 high-quality photographs of the most well know images. Zimmer's opinions of Near Eastern influences on the evolution of Indian art are now rejected
by most scholars.

682 **Myths and symbols in Indian art and civilization.**
Heinrich Zimmer, edited by Joseph Campbell. Princeton,
New Jersey: Princeton University Press, 1972. 248p.

A brilliant introduction to the Indian mythological tradition and its influence on
the development of Indian thought and aesthetics. Zimmer utilizes his vast knowledge of the Sanskrit literary tradition to convey the significance of Indian myths
and symbols and their representation in Indian art.

Painting

683 Indian paintings from the Punjab hills: a survey and history of the Pahari miniature painting.

William G. Archer.   London: Sotheby Parke-Bernet, 1973. 2 vols.

A catalogue of all Punjab hill paintings held principally in the Victoria and Albert Museum, London. There are over 900 small, clear monochromes in this volume, with descriptions of twenty-one major schools of the region, grouped by periods. A crowing achievement by a distinguished art historian and critic.

684 The life of Krishna in Indian art.

Priyatosh Banerjee.   New Delhi: National Museum, 1980. 348p.+plates. bibliog.

In the Indian pantheon, God-incarnate Krishna's universalism in religion and the arts is pre-eminent. Banerjee's book is a definitive contribution to both biography and art history. It includes illustrations and biographical data compiled from Indian art collections in western Europe, the United States, India, and Southeast Asia. Reproductions from the *Razm nama*, a 16th-century illustrated manuscript in the royal library at Jaipur combining fine Arabic calligraphy with the Indo-Persian painting style, are utilized to show the Indo-Muslim synthesis in art. A book of rare beauty.

685 A history of Indian painting.

Krishna Chaitanya.   New Delhi: Abhinava, 1976- . 3 vols. bibliog.

The first volume covers the mural tradition of India from its prehistoric beginnings to the development of the classical style of Ajanta and its extension beyond India. The second volume treats the influence of early spread-out murals on the development of miniatures during the Pala period in Bengal (ca. 800-1150), their maturity under the Mughals (ca. 1500-1650), and their re-emergence in south India in the 17th and 18th centuries. In the third volume, Chaitanya, one of India's most versatile scholars, deals with the genesis of the Rajasthani school of miniature art and its climax in the Kishangarh style. Further volumes are expected.

686 Modern Indian painting.

P. R. Ramachandra Rao.   Madras: Rachna, 1953. 100p.+plates.

687 Contemporary Indian art.

P. R. Ramachandra Rao.   Delhi: UBS Distributors, 1976. 60p.+plates.

In the above two books the author, a well-known Indian journalist and art critic, traces the evolution of modern Indian art from Abanindranath Tagore and the Bengal school (approximately 1900) into the 1960s. The first book is concerned exclusively with painting and artists up to the early 1950s. He divides the painting of the period into various schools such as the Shantiniketan school, the western school, and regional groups. The art of this period is seen to be very miscellaneous and the author is not selective, though the large number of illustrations help us to understand the general range. Short notes are given on the major painters, many of whom later developed their styles and became nationally and internationally famous. The second volume is a continuation of the earlier work, but deals also with sculpture and graphics. Artists are arranged chronologically. Short critical and biographical notes follow a general introduction. Much of the emphasis is on artists who have come into prominence since India's independence, among them Amrita Sher-Gil, Jamini Roy, M. F. Hussain, and Avinash Chandra. A conspicuous shortcoming is the lack of dates for most of the paintings. Considering the amount of work in progress in all of India, the selection of works must be regarded as limited.

688 South Indian paintings.
Calambur Sivaramamurti. New Delhi: National Museum, 1968. 174p. bibliog.

This definitive, detailed work by the long-time director of the National Museum, New Delhi, presents a history of the regional styles and periods of development of south Indian painting from the time of the 1st century BC Sathvahana dynasty to the modern school. The mural paintings of the Pallava, Chalukya, and Chola dynasties are particularly emphasized, the author providing a rich background of iconographic identifications. He also draws interesting parallels between art motifs and literary motifs derived from Sanskrit literature or inscriptions, between Ajanta wall paintings and Amaravati carvings, between Badami murals and the Mamallapuram carvings. The plates might have been better handled to enable the student to understand the grandeur of the paintings as well as their details.

689 Women painters of Mithila.
Yves Véquaud, translated from the 1976 French ed. by George Robinson. London: Thames & Hudson, 1977. 112p.+plates.

The ritual paintings created by the women, and only the women, of matriarchal Mithila, a region of eastern India, are the subject of this strikingly handsome book. The author deals comprehensively with the Mithila style which, though not as sophisticated as the Rajput-Mughal style, is nevertheless both unique and full of vitality. The main motif of these paintings is marriage on both the earthly and spiritual planes.

690 A flower from every meadow: Indian paintings from American collections.
Stuart C. Welch. New York: Asia Society, 1973. 142p. bibliog.

This exhibition catalogue of the Asia House Gallery is a history of Indian painting from the 15th century to the early 20th century. The text discusses the content and style of Mughal, Rajput, Ahmednagar, Bijapur, and Golconda paintings and also paintings done under British patronage. The superb reproductions include gods and men, animals and nature.

Architecture and sculpture

691 A dictionary of Hindu architecture.
Prasanna Kumar Acharya. New Delhi: Oriental Books
Reprint Corp., 1982. 861p.

This is a dictionary of all architectural forms used in the classical *Mansara*, the standard work on Hindu architecture, with explanations in English and illustrative quotations from cognate literature (especially *silpasastras*, treatises defining rules for craftsmen) where available for the purpose. The term architecture has been used broadly to include all sorts of buildings, roads and allied civil works, household chattels, sculpture and other images. There are approximatley 3,000 entries with extensive quotations. Words have not been arranged in the English alphabetical order but according to the Sanskrit alphabetical scheme. In transliteration the author has generally followed the style of the Archaelogical Survey of India. First published in 1927.

692 An introduction to modern Indian sculpture.
Jaya Appasamy. New Delhi: Indian Council for Cultural
Relations, 1970. 100p. bibliog.

Jaya Appasamy, artist and art critic, is editor of contemporary art publications at the Lalit Kala Akademi, the national academy of art. This concise account of the story of modern Indian sculpture from about 1900 to 1970 covers British-influenced monumental art, the beginnings of modern sculpture at about 1935, and the later regional schools. All the important sculptors are included as well as some of the promising younger talents.

693 Indian architecture.
Percy Brown. Bombay: Taraporevala, 1976. 7th rep. ed. 2
vols. maps. bibliog.

These two volumes provide an objective historical study of the religious and civil architecture of India from the earliest recorded times to about the middle of the 19th century. The coverage is comprehensive not only with regard to the monuments found all over the country, but also with regard to the various forms and styles in which they are conveniently grouped. The volumes, however, suffer from poor layout, printing and illustrative material except for the excellent sketches and drawings which help to explain architectural features and problems.

694 Indian sculpture: masterpieces of Indian, Khmer and Cham art.
W. Forman, B. Forman, text by M. M. Deneck. London:
Hamlyn, 1970. rev. ed. 35p. + 264 plates. bibliog.

A beautifully photographed collection of representative Indian sculptures from the 1st century BC to the Madurai style of the 17th century. By including representative works from Cambodia, Thailand, and Laos, the author provides graphic and convincing evidence of Hindu and Buddhist influences on the development of art in Southeast Asia.

695 **Masterpieces of Indian temples.**
Rustam Jehangir Mehta. Bombay: Taraporevala, 1974.
67p. + 100 plates.
A judicious selection of key architectural styles of Indian temples, photographed in black and white. Each plate is explained in detail and a long introductory essay places the plates in the perspective of various periods and styles. In selecting temples for this study, Mehta has paid careful attention to all major national and provincial styles.

696 **Buddhist monuments.**
Debala Mitra. Calcutta: Sahitya Samsad, 1971. 307p.
maps. bibliog.
An exhaustive, authoritative, elegantly produced account of the Buddhist sites and monuments of India. Laymen and specialists alike will find this work a most important reference source for the study of Indian Buddhist art, archaeology, and iconography. All the sites and monuments of India, Pakistan, and the Nepalese-Terai are described in detail and are arranged regionally.

Decorative arts and crafts

697 **Decorative designs and craftsmanship of India: with over 10,001 designs and motifs from the crafts of India.**
Enakshi Bhvnani. Bombay: Taraporevala, 1969. 109p.
A handsomely illustrated book of designs and motifs found in fabrics, carpets, ceramics, pottery, wood carving, lacquerware, jewellery, and many other crafts and decorative arts. A brief chapter discusses the symbolism in various traditional designs, and another examines how old modes of decoration have provided inspiration for modern designs. An excellent reference book.

698 **Decorative designs on stone and wood in India.**
Enakshi Bhavnani, line-drawings from original sources by
Percy B. Bhathenna. Bombay: Taraporevala, 1978. 67p. + 56
plates. bibliog.
A skilful study of traditional ornamental designs and motifs popular in Indian architecture, both Hindu and Islamic. The book discusses how wood and stone have been the basic materials for embellishment, combining the skills of both the wood-carver and the stone-cutter in mosaics, murals, and frescoes. In the descriptive text Bhavnani has explored the delicacy of motifs and themes; the harmony of colour, texture, and contours; and the symbolic imagery found in Indian architecture and sculpture.

699 **Masterpieces of Indian jewelry.**
Jamila Brijbhusan. Bombay: Taraporevala, 1979. 54p. + 88
plates. bibliog.
A fascinating study of Indian jewellery, its history, and techniques from ancient times to the present, together with local names of ornaments worn on various

parts of the body. In her introduction, the author discusses the astrological significance of precious metals, stones, and gems and their relationship to various
castes. The incorporation of Hindu views on the significance of the jewellery of
Mughal emperors and princes, the encrustation of jade with floral patterns, and
the art of enamelling are all described in detail. A valuable book.

700 Handicrafts of India.
Kamaladevi Chattopadhyaya. New Delhi: Indian Council
for Cultural Relations, 1975. 146p. map.
Written by one of the leading experts on the traditional handicrafts of India, this
book provides a perceptive introduction to the following crafts: earthenware,
woodwork, stoneware, textiles, metalware, jewellery, ivory, basketry and mat
weaving, horn and *shola* (a type of carving) work, toys and dolls, leatherwork,
glasswork, folk painting, and theatre crafts. The book is comprehensive in coverage and the information given about each craft is accurate and concise.

701 Indian carpets and floor coverings.
Kamaladevi Chattopadhyaya. New Delhi: All India
Handicrafts Board, 1974. 68p. plates. bibliog.
This elegant little volume contains interesting material on an ancient craft,
accompanied by several fine colour plates. The scholarship is unpretentious and
combined with a fine aesthetic sense. For the beginner.

702 Costumes of India and Pakistan: a historical cultural study.
Shiv Nath Dar. Bombay: Taraporevala, 1969. 244p.
bibliog.
A thoroughly documented study of South Asian sartorial styles from ancient
times to the present. Considerable attention is given to regional and communal
variations in dress. A section of the book describes various dresses customarily
associated with different musical ragas. An able survey for reference shelves.

703 Metalcraftsmen of India.
Meera Mukherjee. Calcutta: Anthropological Survey of
India, 1978. 461p.
A study of the traditional techniques employed by artisans in the preparation of
brass, bell-metal, and bronzeware. The book is divided into three sections: the
first deals with metalcraftsmen, their castes and their position in society; the
second describes how the author located and interviewed artisans in different
parts of India; the third gives information on the techniques used by these artisans. Unfortunately three significant centres of metal craftsmanship - Assam,
Gujarat, and Maharashtra - could not be included in the study. A thoroughly
reliable and exhaustive study of the areas covered.

704 Textiles and ornaments of India, a selection of designs.
Museum of Modern Art, New York, text by Pupul Jayakar,
John Irwin. New York: Arno, 1972. 95p. bibliog.
This brief book devoted to textile and ornamental artistry contains an essay by
John Irwin on Indian textiles in historical perspective and another by Pupul
Jayakar on fabrics in Indian life. Superb examples of shawls, saris, embroideries,
rugs, enamels, copper and brass vessels, metal filigree, ornaments, and toys are

included. The illustrations, many in colour, have been chosen with care, and the value of the book is enhanced by an excellent bibliography by Irwin. For a general audience.

Performing arts

705 A panorama of theatre in India.
Som Benegal. Bombay: Popular, 1968. 132p. bibliog.
This attractive little book is a suitable introduction to the Indian theatre from Sanskrit times through the contemporary theatre movement. Written by the editor of a theatre arts journal who has directed many plays in India, the book is unpretentious and the style lively.

706 Dance in India.
Faubion Bowers. New York: AMS Press, 1967. reprint of 1953 ed. 175p.
The chapters in Faubion Bower's book that describe Bharata Natyam, Kathakali, and Manipuri dance are highly communicative and dependable, those on Kathak and folk-dances rather pedestrian. The photographs are few, mediocre, and not very helpful. Despite its weaknesses, this is one of the best books available on Indian dance and is an excellent introductory guide. It was written at a time when the revival of Indian dance was just starting, which explains why the book contains next to nothing on the Kuchipudi, Odissi, Kutiyattam, Chhau, and Yakshagana forms.

707 Classical and folk dances of India.
Bombay: Marg Publications, 1963. 372p. bibliog.
A comprehensive survey of Indian dances and their modern exponents, written by scholars, art critics, and some of India's great dancers. The volume deals with six principal forms: Bharata Natyam, Kathakali, Kathak, Orissi, Manipuri, and folk-dances from sixteen different regions of India. For each school of dance, its origin, characteristics, content, music, costume, techniques, and major contemporary exponents are described with appropriate illustrations. A mine of information as well as a book of great beauty.

708 Folk theater of India.
Balwant Gargi. Seattle, Washington: University of Washington Press, 1966. 217p.
Despite its occasional glaring inaccuracies in factual detail, this is an excellent entertaining study of the popular theatre of India. The emphasis is on regional variations: the author has chosen seven theatrical forms from north and central India and two from south India. They include Jatra, Nautanki, Bhavai, Tamasha, Ramlila, Raslila, Therukoothu, Yakshagana, and Chhau (it is questionable whether Gargi is correct in characterizing the Chhau of northeast India as a form of theatre). Easily the best illustrated book on Indian theatre, it combines art and literature to describe the staging, costumes, make-up, ritual, and pageantry associated with these folk performances.

709 **Theatre in India.**
Balwant Gargi. New York: Theatre Arts Books, 1962.
145p. bibliog.
Written in a lively style, Gargi's book has long been one of the only general surveys of Indian theatre. It is now quite dated, but it is still important for its perceptive examination of the origins and development of modern Indian theatre, with which Gargi has been intimately involved as a teacher, producer, and playwright - half the book and most of the illustrations are lavished on this topic. The major weakness of the study is its whirlwind coverage of Sanskrit drama.

710 **At play with Krishna: pilgrimage dramas from Brindavan.**
John Stratton Hawley, in association with Shrivatsa Goswami. Princeton, New Jersey: Princeton University Press, 1981. 339p. bibliog.
A unified view of the myth of Lord Krishna in its living dramatic form. Hawley has chosen four texts from the Raslila genre of north Indian folk theatre, translated them, and linked them to reconstruct Krishna's life. An introductory essay deals with Brindavan as a pilgrimage centre.

711 **Kathakali: an introduction to the dance-drama of Kerala.**
Clifford R. Jones, Betty True Jones. San Francisco: American Society for Eastern Arts, 1970. 115p.
The coverage of this excellent documentary introduction to the Kathakali dance-drama of Kerala ranges from the making of a Kathakali dancer to the presentation of a full play. Costumes, make-up, dance and musical accompaniment, the use of tala and raga, acting techniques, and the drama itself are all included. The book is lavishly illustrated and possesses a running commentary that makes the art come alive for the reader.

712 **The theatric universe: a study of the *Natyasastra*.**
Pramod Kale. Bombay: Popular, 1974. 196p. bibliog.
The *Natyasastra*, dating from the 3rd century and attributed to Bharata, stands as the foundation of all modern speculation on the manner in which ancient Sanskrit plays were probably performed. Kale provides a sensible and enlightening interpretation of its meaning. His work should be used to expand and enrich the general factual information that may be gleaned from other sources. He unfortunately chose to exclude music and dance from his discussion, two essential ingredients necessary to a complete understanding of classical theatre practices.

713 **Tradition of Indian classical dance.**
Mohan Khokar. London: Peter Owen, 1980. 168p.
An elegantly produced volume by an acknowledged expert. 160 pages of text complemented by 51 photographs cover history and aesthetics, as well as all genres and styles of Indian classical dance. Twenty-five distinct modes of classical dance, regionally grouped, are clearly and logically presented. A welcome, if somewhat slender, addition to the meagre critical literature on Indian dance.

714 **The Indian drama: the Sanskrit drama.**
Sten Konow, translated from the German by S. N. Ghosal. Calcutta: General Printers and Publishers, 1969. 213p. bibliog.

Originally published in 1915, this is a critical and provocative study of the origin and development of classical Indian drama by a distinguished German Indologist and linguist. Konow argues that Sanskrit drama grew out of the pantomime shows common in early India on the one hand, and the tradition of reciting stanzas from the epics in assemblies on the other. The dramatist, he argues, combined the two. The author analyses the structure of Indian dramas and provides critical commentary on major Sanskrit and Prakrit dramatists through the 15th century.

715 **Indian theatre.**
Adya Rangacharya. New Delhi: National Book Trust, 1971. 163p.

A succinct and readable survey of the development of Indian theatre from classical times to the present. Rangacharya argues that although classical Sanskrit drama declined after the 10th century, it was replaced by regional folk dramas with their own lively traditions, and Indian drama did not go through a dark age as is popularly assumed. The author is at his best in describing and analysing Indian theatrical traditions of the 19th and 20th centuries.

716 **Sangeet Natak.**
New Delhi: Sangeet Natak Akademi, 1965- . quarterly.

Published by India's National Academy of Music, Dance, and Drama, this quarterly carries articles on the classical forms of the performing arts. Occasionally includes illustrations and book reviews.

717 **Traditions of Indian folk dance.**
Kapila Vatsyayan. New Delhi: Indian Book Company, 1976. 280p. bibliog.

A close look at regional folk-dances of India. Vatsyayan classifies Indian folk dances in seven categories: hunt dances, dances of fertility rites and magic, functional-occupational dances of the peasants, dances that re-enact scenes from the epics, dances reflecting seasons and seasonal festivals of India, devotional dances, and dance-dramas found both in urban and rural India. Likewise, the author divides India into eight distinct cultural regions. The result is a book of great depth and full of insight, eminently readable.

Music

718 Ustad Allauddin Khan and his music.
Jotin Bhattacharya. Ahmedabad, India: B. S. Shah
Prakashan, 1979. 242p.

Written by a distinguished musicologist, cultural organizer, and disciple of a great
sarod maestro, this work is a valuable study of a man who modernized Indian
classical music and taught his son-in-law Ravi Shankar and his son Ali Akbar
Khan, two of the greatest sitar players of India. The book has a chapter on the
origin of the *sarod*, a stringed instrument, and several other chapters on Allaud-
din Khan's variations on major north Indian ragas.

719 Musical instruments of India.
B. Chaitanya Deva. Calcutta: Firma KLM, 1978. 306p.
bibliog.

An exhaustive treatment of the subject. Art, literature, archaeology, ancient and
modern literary references, and the musical traditions of neighbouring countries
are combined to present comprehensive accounts of various instruments. Pre-
Aryan, Aryan, Central and West Asian, Persian, and Arab musicological influence on the shaping of Indian instruments are carefully discussed, and the east-
ward and westward spread of Indian music described. Over 200 photographs
enhance the value of the book.

720 The opera in south India.
S. A. K. Durga. Delhi: B. R. Publishing Corp., 1979. 152p.
bibliog.

Simple and lucidly written and supplemented with copious photographs. The
author traces the history of south Indian opera from its 10th-century origins
through its 18th-century classical era, and concludes with an intelligent discussion
of its 20th-century decline.

721 The ragas of north India.
Walter Kaufmann. New York: Da Capo Press, 1983.
reprint of 1968 ed. 640p. bibliog.

722 The ragas of south India: a catalogue of scalar material.
Walter Kaufmann. Bloomington, Indiana: Indiana
University Press, 1976. 732p. bibliog.

In the above two entries the author analyses hundreds of ragas of north and south
India and gives their details in western notation, making these books necessities
for serious students of Indian music. The introduction to the first volume gives a
concise explanation of the Indian musical system, with time-theory included.
Ragamala paintings are used as illustrations. These are excellent reference
volumes for libraries.

723 **Discovering Indian music.**
Raghava R. Menon. Bombay: Somaiya Publications, 1974.
87p. bibliog.

724 **The sound of Indian music: a journey into raga.**
Raghava Menon. New Delhi: Indian Book Co., 1976. 85p.
bibliog.
The first of the above two books is preferable for the non-specialist and the beginner. It contains much information on the Indian scale, voice patterns, and the raga (musical mode), and it has a long section on how to teach yourself Indian music. The text of the second work gives good information on theory and performance styles. Both volumes have bibliographical and discographical notes.

725 **My music, my life.**
Ravi Shankar. New York: Simon & Schuster, 1969. 160p.
map.
This autobiographical account by India's best-known and universally acclaimed musician discusses his musical heritage and provides basic information about the history, theory, and instruments of Indian music. The description of his childhood in Benares and his utter devotion to his music teacher are delightful. A manual for sitar explains both the melodic and rhythmic systems for playing the instrument. The introduction by Yehudi Menuhin provides an excellent appreciation of sitar-playing as a performing art.

Photography

726 **The last empire: photography in British India, 1855-1911.**
Text by Clark Worswick, Ainslie T. Embree. London:
Fraser, 1976. 149p. bibliog.
In the summer of 1976 the Asia House of New York and the American Federation of Arts organized a travelling exhibition of about 150 photographs selected from British and American collections. This book includes all the photographs in the exhibition together with a concise essay by Worswick on the history of British photography in India and another by Ainslie Embree on the political and social conditions of India in the Victorian and Edwardian eras.

727 **Princely India: photography by Raja Deen Dayal.**
Edited by Clark Worswick. New York: Knopf, 1980. 151p.
bibliog.
Clark Worswick has selected and reproduced 123 photographs from the huge collection by Raja Deen Dayal, a court photographer for the Nizam of Hyderabad in the late 19th century. Topics covered by the photographs include upper-class British and Indian society, military operations, religious ceremonies, and royal hunts.

175

Folk Culture and Traditions

Folklore

728 The riddle of Indian life, lore, and literature.
Durga Bhagwat. Bombay: Popular, 1965. 135p. bibliog.
An exhaustive and useful study of Indian riddles. Bhagwat discusses twenty-one Indian synonyms of the word 'riddle', and points out that the custom of using riddles to illustrate a point is very ancient in India and is an integral part of both the faith and the wit of the people.

729 The *Katha sarit sagara*: or ocean of the streams of story.
Somadeva Bhatta, translated from the 11th-century original Sanskrit by C. H. Tawney. Delhi: Munshiram Manoharlal, 1968. 2nd ed. 2 vols.
The earliest and largest collection of stories extant in the world, and the source of many tales in *The thousand nights and a night* and by Boccacio, Chaucer, La Fontaine, and others in the west. Somadeva's introduction gives an account of the work's contents, an outline of various chapters, and the origin of the tales.

730 The thief of love: Bengali tales from court and village.
Translated by Edward C. Dimock, Jr. Chicago: University of Chicago Press, 1975. 305p.
Two sections of this volume contain the major portion of a Bengali myth of the goddess Manasa and other humorous folk-tales of Bengal. Manasa, the snake-goddess, not only strikes and kills randomly but is also strangely merciful and compassionate. The people of the folk-tale are equally ambivalent in their character: both weak and proud. A lucid and readable volume, with several helpful introductory sections.

731 **When the world was young: folk tales from India's hills and forests.**
Verrier Elwin, with illustrations by Amina Jayal. New Delhi: Publications Division, Ministry of Information and Broadcasting, 1970. 82p. (National Trust Book).
Verrier Elwin devoted his adult life to the study of Indian folk traditions and tribal life, publishing over 2,500 folk-tales. In this representative volume, Elwin has included thirty-eight tales dealing with the cycle of life from birth to death.

732 **A bibliography of Indian folklore and related subjects.**
Sankar Sen Gupta, Shyam Parmar. Calcutta: Indian Publications, 1967. 196p. (Indian Folklore Series, no. 11).
About 5,000 entries, mostly articles, in the English language on various aspects of Indian folklore. The book is divided into seventeen sections, including: general folklore; prose narratives; folk music, dance, and drama; art, crafts, and architecture; proverbs, parables, and epigrams; totems, taboos, and superstitions; and material culture.

733 **Folklore and folklife: an objective study in Indian perspective.**
Sankar Sen Gupta. Calcutta: Indian Publications, 1975. 192p. bibliog.
An argument for recognizing folklore as an academic discipline in Indian university curricula. Sen Gupta reviews the history of the discipline in the west; assesses the contribution of major scholars in the field; analyses the work of Indian and foreign students in collecting Indian folklore and folk art; and provides his own perspective on folk arts and crafts, talismans and folk cures, and folk-music of India.

734 **Ancient Indian magic and folklore: an introduction.**
Margaret Stutley. Boulder, Colorado: Great Eastern, 1980. 190p. bibliog.
Based mainly on the *Atharvaveda*, a classical magico-religious text compiled about 1400 BC, the book describes charms relating to women, priests, demons and sorcerers as well as charms for prosperity, harmony, healing, longevity and war. Stutley argues that the wearing of lucky charms and talismans; the belief in lucky and unlucky days, birds, and animals; and the fear of demonic possession or curses are common in both European and Indian folklore.

735 **Studies in Indian folk traditions.**
Ved Prakash Vatuk. New Delhi: Manohar, 1979. 221p. bibliog.
Nine essays analysing the content and significance of various folklore genres. Almost all the essays deal with north Indian folk literature and art. Vatuk covers several areas such as opera, riddles, hymns, songs, private sayings, and the character of the stepmother in Indian folk traditions.

Festivals

736 **Festivals in India.**
K. Gnanambal. Calcutta: Anthropological Survey of India, 1969. 105p. bibliog.

A delightful little book which describes the major festivals of India celebrated by various religious as well as provincial communities. For a more detailed description see Brijendra Nath Sharma and for the origin of principal Hindu and Buddhist festivals V. Raghavan, both listed below.

737 **Festivals, sports and pastimes of India.**
V. Raghavan. Ahmedabad, India: B. J. Institute of Learning and Research, 1979. 287p. bibliog.

A textual study of the origin of major Hindu and Buddhist festivals of India. The author has drawn his information from Vedic, epic, Buddhist and Jain religious literature as well as from such secular literature as Dandin's plays. A separate chapter enumerates festivals and pastimes in seasonal order. Highly technical.

738 **Festivals of India.**
Brijendra Nath Sharma. New Delhi: Abhinav, 1978. 156p. bibliog.

This well-illustrated book provides a panoramic view of Indian festivals of all faiths. Its first part describes 44 festivals of ancient India and the second part has information on 185 modern festivals. Dr. Sharma has also included the principal sites of these festivals such as Sivaratri at Varanasi, Holi at Mathura, Baisakhi at Amritsar, Id uz-Zuha at Delhi and Lucknow, Christmas at Goa, and Parsee Navroz at Bombay. Each description has a brief history of the festival and its approximate date according to the local calendar.

Social customs and superstitions

739 **Keys of power: a study of Indian ritual and belief.**
John Abbott. Secaucus, New Jersey: University Books, 1974. reprint. 560p. bibliog.

Written by an Indian civil servant in 1932, this is a careful study of the belief in a universal supernatural cosmic power underlying Hindu and Muslim rituals. The author has collected and recorded axioms and rules of conduct for changing bad luck into good fortune. The cosmic powers of such objects as special stones, metals, trees, agricultural products, and salt, and elements like water and fire are discussed. In addition the roles in popular belief of the evil eye, numbers, curses and oaths, and certain colours are noted.

Folk Culture and Traditions. Social customs and superstitions

740 **Hindu omens.**
C. D. Bijalwan. New Delhi: Sanskriti, with Arnold
Heinemann, 1977. 176p. bibliog.
A large part of this book is a translation from *Shakunauti*, an 18th-century
compilation of omens, and from *Basantarajashakunodaya*, a pre-12th-century
text. Twelve chapters include omens based on animals, throbbing limbs, and
sneezing; augurs related to prominent religious characters; and omens based upon
astrological indications. The author includes traditional amulets used by the
superstitious to ward off bad omens.

741 **Hindu manners, customs and ceremonies.**
Jean Antoine Dubois, translated by Henry K.
Beauchamp. Oxford, England: Clarendon, 1968. 3rd ed.
741p. bibliog.
Though written with the bias of a Catholic priest toward Hindu heathens, this is
perhaps the most informative book on early 19th-century socio-religious customs.
Dubois himself observed most of these customs in south India but his information
on north India is from other informants. Practices such as suttee (burning of the
widows) have now been banned, but Dubois provides an eyewitness account of
many of them.

742 **Hindu predictive astrology.**
Gopesh Kumar Ojha. Bombay: Taraporevala, 1972. 347p.
bibliog.
In no country of the world is astrology as popular and yet taken as seriously as in
India. Even the exact time of the transfer of British power to Indians in 1947 was
determined astrologically. Ojha's beautifully written book is an authoritative
introduction to this occult science. The author rejects the unequal house division
system now being popularized by some south Indian astrologers.

743 **Cults, customs and superstitions of India.**
John Campbell Oman. New York: AMS, 1975. reprint of
1908 ed. 336p. bibliog.
A reprint of the original 1908 edition, this book contains material that has, in
part, been updated by other scholars. Oman reports in detail on fairs and festivals, domestic relations, witchcraft, superstitions, and fortune telling. The book's
strength lies in its reporting Hindu customs at the turn of the century, long
before reform movements began making their mark on Indian life.

744 **Hindu religion, customs, and manners.**
Paul Thomas. Bombay: Taraporevala, 1975. 6th ed. 144p.
bibliog.
A profusely illustrated compendium of Hindu myths, beliefs, philosophical and
religious cults, social customs and practices, superstitions, costumes, festivals, erotics, music and dance. Updates the information provided by Dubois (q.v.).

Cookery

745 Twenty-two authentic banquets from India.
Compiled by Robert Christie. New York: Dover, 1975. 156p.

The menus and recipes for each banquet, arranged by local region and by religious origin, are presented in this short book. Overall there are recipes for over 200 dishes. A list of equivalents and substitutions for ingredients not readily available in the west is also given.

746 An invitation to Indian cooking.
Madhur Jaffrey. New York: Knopf, 1978. 285p.

Written by a leading radio, television, and film personality of India especially for foreigners, this book provides recipes for a wide variety of north Indian dishes, vegetarian and non-vegetarian: appetizers, breads, salads, soups, entrées, pilafs (rice dishes), relishes, and desserts. Included in the book is information on how to obtain spices and other supplies and how to use modern electrical appliances in place of traditional Indian utensils and heating media.

747 The Hindu hearth and home.
Ravindra S. Khare. New Delhi: Vikas, 1976. 315p. bibliog.

An ethnographic account of contemporary ways of handling food in north India. Khare examines Hindu culinary and gastronomic traditions as practiced in everyday life and on ceremonial occasions. A concluding chapter examines how the theory and practice of commensality has changed in the recent past.

748 Cooking of India.
Santha Rama Rao, with the editors of Time-Life Books. Alexandria, Virginia: Time-Life, 1981. 208p.

A lavishly illustrated cookery book with recipes for dishes from all parts of India, written by a distinguished novelist and playwright. Though the recipes retain their authentic character, the use of 'hot' spices has been modified to suit western taste.

749 Cooking delights of the Maharajahs.
Digvijaya Singh. Bombay: Vakils, 1982. 192p.

Written by the former ruler of a princely state in Madhya Pradesh, this book contains 164 recipes for dishes, ranging from snacks through entrées to desserts, that once supposedly graced the tables of India's princely rulers. Many of the recipes - especially those dealing with game - are not found in other Indian cookery books. Attractively designed with many photographs.

Sports

750 Patrons, players and the crowd: the phenomenon of Indian cricket.
Richard Cashman.   New Delhi: Orient Longman, 1980. 194p. bibliog.

An excellent socio-economic survey of cricket in India. The first three chapters deal with the promotion of cricket, first by British officials in India, later by India's princes, and now by industrial houses and government agencies. Subsequent chapters deal with 'Test' players, the crowd, and cricket commentators and writers. Several statistical appendixes describe the socio-economic characteristics of both the patrons and the players.

751 Reaching for excellence: the glory and decay of sports in India.
Melville DeMellow.   New Delhi: Kalayani, 1979. 200p.

A judicious indictment of the dimishing of standards of excellence in Indian sports, by one of India's foremost sports commentators. DeMellow points out that in spite of the proliferation of sports academies and sports organizations, and increased government funding, sports in India have shown a marked decline in recent years.

752 Indian hockey: extra time or sudden death?
Sunil Gujral.   New Delhi: Vikas, 1978. 128p.

Believed to be the oldest stick-and-ball game, field hockey has the distinction of being the national game of India, and the Indian team has been a dominant force in Olympic competition. Gujral's book highlights Indian achievements and the sport's recent decline in India.

753 Indian cricket: a complete history.
N. S. Rangaswami.   New Delhi: Abhinav, 1976. 146p.

A short history of the origin and development of cricket as an Indian sport. The book deals with the development of cricket teams along communal lines; zonal and national tournaments; tours by Indian teams abroad; and pioneers of Indian cricket such as Duleep, Deodhar and Irani. There are several statistical appendixes. For latest information, consult the *Indian Cricket Field Annual* (1962/63-) which contains a who's-who in Indian cricket.

754 Kabaddi: native Indian sport.
C. V. Rao. Patiala, India: National Institute of Sports, 1971. 72p.

A game of tag between two teams of seven persons each, played on a court 13x10 metres divided into two halves (one for each team), and composed of two twenty-minute innings. The game of kabaddi is essentially of Indian origin, and is one of the most popular of India's outdoor sports. In the west it was first exhibited, but not included, in the 1936 Olympics, and in India it has been included in annual sports competitions since 1950. Rao's short book traces the growth of this sport, its popularity in India, Pakistan, Ceylon, Burma, Nepal and Malaysia, and recent efforts to standardise its rules.

Mass Media

Film and radio

755 **Indian film.**
Erik Barnouw, S. Krishnaswamy. New York: Oxford
University Press, 1980. 2nd ed. 327p. bibliog.
This is a magisterial history and analysis of Indian cinema from its 1896 origins
to contemporary times. The book explains the extraordinary apotheosis of Indian
film stars in a land with a penchant for deification. The interplay between cinema
and politics is examined, as is the twin role of India's film makers as reinforcers
and destroyers of tradition. Government censorship policy is also discussed. All of
this is interspersed with a first-rate critical evaluation of India's greatest films
and film makers, including the post-Satyajit Ray generation. Exhaustively
researched and lucidly written.

756 **75 years of Indian cinema.**
Firoze Rangoonwalla. New Delhi: India Book Company,
1975. 168p.
A short, succinct, and readable history of the Indian film industry from its
beginnings in 1896 to 1975. The book discusses all of the noteworthy phases and
landmarks in the emergence, evolution, and development of the Indian cinema.
The author laments that the majority of Indian cinema has not as yet achieved
genuine maturity as either an art form or a vehicle for national integration and
social change.

757 **Indian cinema today: an analysis.**
Kobita Sarkar. New Delhi: Sterling Publishers, 1975. 167p.
The book explores the vast gap between the commercial and artistic films produced in India. The commercial market is dominated by the Hindi film with its
inevitable happy ending, frequent songs and dances, unrealistic costume and backgrounds, and idealization of the values of the mediaeval village. The author
analyses the culture and impact of these films using as reference specific films
and particular scenes therein. The discussion of regional films, experimental
movies, and the film society movement is brief. The author concludes that the

183

possibility for films combining high artistic standards and mass appeal remains remote in India.

758 Portrait of a director: Satyajit Ray.
Marie Seton. London: Dobson, 1978. reprint of 1971 ed. 350p.

A profusely illustrated critical study of one of the most distinguished Indian film directors. The author provides substantial information on Ray's contribution as a writer, composer, and film director. Ray's own writings, some of which have been reproduced as appendixes to the text - including his article on the French film director Jean Renoir - have been used to critically analyse Ray's philosophy of film-making and his artistic techniques. The role of early 20th-century Bengali-Indian culture in the shaping of Ray's personality is informative.

759 Liberty and license in the Indian cinema.
Aruna Vasudev. New Delhi: Vikas, 1978. 221p. bibliog.

Developed out of a Sorbonne doctoral dissertation, this is a meticulously researched and cogently written book on Indian film censorship. The author provides a history of such censorship and a detailed account of individual fights for containing the powers of the censors. She argues that neither the constitution of the Censor Boards nor their manner of functioning has changed much over the years.

Publishing and journalism

760 Romance of Indian journalism.
Jitendra Nath Basu. Calcutta: Calcutta University, 1979. 617p. bibliog.

A detailed history of the growth of Indian journalism from the late 18th century to 1947. Basu divides the press in India into three broad categories: Anglo-Indian (controlled by Europeans resident in India), Indo-Anglian (English-language publications controlled by Indians), and vernacular. In addition to tracing the evolution of Indian journalism, the author provides sketches of leading journalists, Indian and foreign, who have made their mark on Indian journalism. The book has good sections on the efforts of the government to control the nationalist press.

761 The Indian press: profession to industry.
Arun Bhattacharjee. New Delhi: Vikas, 1972. 216p. bibliog.

A careful and balanced study of the Indian press. The first part discusses government pressure on the Indian mass media by curtailing freedom of the press and controlling the supply of newsprint. The second part examines the juridical, economic, and international aspects of the monopoly of wire services, both domestic and foreign. The third part analyses Indian dependence on foreign sources both in the distribution of news items and the purchase of printing equipment. Though published a decade ago, Bhattacharjee's analysis continues to be relevant.

762 **Book publishing in India.**
Kartar Singh Duggal. New Delhi: Marwah, 1980. 267p.
An insider's story of book publishing in India, by a leading Indian man of letters, publisher, and former director of the National Book Trust of India. The book has fifty short articles covering almost all aspects of publishing, from the author-publisher relationship to the import and export of all kinds of books. Included in the collection are profiles of sixteen publishers covering a wide range from speciality publishers to those for the mass market.

763 **Indian periodicals in print, 1973.**
H. N. D. Gandhi, Jagdish Lal, Suren Lal. Delhi: Vidya Mandal, 1973. 2 vols.
Alphabetical listing of 16,483 periodicals with language, date of first publication, frequency, and publisher's address. Volume 2 arranges these titles topically and by language. In addition there is a sponsoring institution index, a subject index, a list of cessations, and relevant statistical information. It is expected that supplements will be published to update the work.

764 **Mass communication and journalism in India.**
Dalpat Singh Mehta. Beverly Hills, California: Sage, 1980. 313p. bibliog.
A thoroughly documented book on the history of the press in India. There are chapters on press laws and the freedom of the press; newpaper, magazine, and periodical journalism; and a section on the latest controversies such as the UNESCO debate on the free flow of news between and among nations. The discussion of agencies which purvey official information is exceptionally good.

765 **A history of the press in India.**
Swaminath Natarajan. London: Asia, 1962. 425p. bibliog.
A well-written and analytical history of the press in India from its 18th-century beginnings to the report of the Press Commission of India in 1953. The author laments the departure of British journalists following Indian independence and readily admits that whatever their personal political persuasions, these journalists had very high professional standards which were lacking in the Indian-controlled press of the 1950's. Natarajan does an excellent job of analysing press-related legislation introduced by the Indian government through the 1950's.

766 **Indian Books in Print, 1979.**
Compiled by Sher Singh. Delhi: Indian Bibliographies, 1969- . irregular. 3rd ed., 1979, 3 vols.
Patterned on *Books in Print* and *British Books in Print*, this valuable publication has appeared in three editions. The first published in 1969 covered nearly 25,000 books in English published in India during 1955-67. The second edition included nearly 60,000 titles in English from Indian publishers that were in print in 1972. The latest edition, 1979, provides bibliographic information on about 75,000 books in English issued by Indian publishers remaining in print in 1977. The current edition is divided into three volumes - authors, titles, and subject guide. At the end of the third volume a list of publishers and their addresses is given. Despite the considerable time lag between editions, *Indian Books in Print* is an indispensable source of current Indian publications.

Mass Media. Newspapers and magazines

767 The emergency, censorship and the press in India, 1975-77.
Soli J. Sorabjee. London: Writers and Educational Trust, 1977. 61p.

A judicious account of how Mrs. Indira Gandhi harassed, subdued, and substantially tamed the Indian press in 1975. Until that time the Indian press were regarded as the freest in Asia. Sorabjee, a distinguised attorney, analyses Mrs. Gandhi's attempts under the Maintenance of Internal Security Act (MISA) to impose precensorship and other repressive measures on the Indian press.

768 Directory of Indian publishers.
Edited by Dinkar Trivedi. New Delhi: Federation of Publishers and Booksellers Associations in India, 1973. 591p. map.

This is the first comprehensive directory providing details of the book industry in India. It is divided into four sections: the first section, arranged by language, lists some 10,000 publishers; the second lists 1,000 public and corporate publishers; the third notes industry adjuncts - book designers, importers and exporters, printers, and foreign publishers' agents; and the last section is a geographical index to publishers.

Newspapers and magazines

769 Caravan.
Delhi: Delhi Press, 1940- . semimonthly.

A family-oriented literary and cultural review. Each issue contains short stories, articles of general interest, items on popular culture and other materials of interest to the entire family.

770 Economic Times.
Bombay: Bennett, Coleman, 1961- . daily.

Excellent coverage of the Indian economy. *Economic Times* is published simultaneously from Bombay, New Delhi, and Calcutta and has a combined circulation of over 60,000. Since 1972, *Economic Times* has issued the *Economic Times Annual*, a comprehensive survey of Indian finance, economy, and trade.

771 The Hindu.
Madras: National Press, 1889- . daily.

This highly respected daily has been known for its balanced editorial policy and extensive coverage of both national and international events. Its interpretive articles are widely quoted and its background surveys often kept for reference. As well as from Madras, it is published simultaneously from Coimbatore, Banglore, Hyderabad and Madurai. The only major newspaper with in-depth coverage of local south Indian events. An abbreviated overseas weekly edition is also published for foreign readers.

772 **Illustrated Weekly of India.**
Bombay: Bennett, Coleman, 1880- . weekly.
The most popular general interest weekly published in India, the *Illustrated Weekly* has the largest circulation it its class. Each issue contains one or more feature articles dealing with Indian life and culture, short stories, film and society news, one or more photo essays, and book reviews.

773 **India Today: the fortnightly newsmagazine.**
New Delhi: Thomson Living Media, 1975- . fortnightly.
Comparable in contents, style, and length to *Time* and *Newsweek*, this left-leaning newsmagazine has increased its circulation substantially in recent years. Investigative reporting is combined with a sensational style to enhance the magazine's popularity.

774 **Indian Express.**
Bombay: Indian Express Newspapers, 1953- . daily.
This daily, published simultaneously from ten major cities of India, has the largest combined circulation (over 500,000 copies) among Indian newspapers. Good coverage of political events in India, Pakistan, Nepal, and Sri Lanka.

775 **Indian Horizons.**
New Delhi: Indian Council for Cultural Relations, 1952- . quarterly.
The Indian Council for Cultural Relations, patterned after the British Council and the United States International Communications Agency, publishes this quarterly to promote understanding of Indian culture overseas. Each issue of *Indian Horizons* contains four or five articles generally written by Indian academics.

776 **Indian Review.**
Madras: Natesan, 1900- . monthly.
Indian Review was started in Madras as the south's answer to the *Modern Review*, which in the early 20th century reflected Bengali cultural renaissance. In recent decades *Indian Review* has shed its provincial image to become a highly respected general interest literary and cultural magazine.

777 **Link.**
New Delhi: United India Periodicals, 1958- . weekly.
Produced in the style of *Time* and *Newsweek*, this is a left-leaning, lively, informative, weekly news magazine. Though generally critical of western powers and capitalism, it provides useful, but opinionated, surveys of the economic and political situation in India and of events elsewhere which it considers relevant to India.

778 **Mainstream.**
New Delhi: Perspective Publications, 1963- . weekly.
Patterned after *Time* and *Newsweek*, this popular weekly strives to provide analysis of political and economic events, especially in India, from the liberal Indian perspective.

Mass Media. News digests

779 Modern Review.
Calcutta: Prabasi Press, 1907- . monthly.

One of the oldest general interest monthlies of India, in which articles by almost all the prominent public figures of 20th-century India have been published. It includes short essays on political, economic, literary, and cultural topics.

780 Onlooker.
Bombay: Onlooker Publications, 1939- . monthly.

This glossy coffee-table magazine was originally designed to reflect the 'westernized' bourgeois culture and values of India's metropolitan centres. Though the outlook of *Onlooker* has now become more Indian, its style still strongly reflects an upper-class affluent modern life-style.

781 Statesman.
Calcutta: Statesman's Press 1875- . daily.

The *Statesman* is published simultaneously from Calcutta and New Delhi and has a combined daily circulation of over 200,000. It has better coverage of local events of east India than any other major newspaper. For overseas clientele it publishes a weekly digest, the *Statesman Overseas Weekly*.

782 Times of India.
Bombay: Bennett, Coleman, 1961- . daily.

Times of India, the oldest major English-language newspaper, is published simultaneously from Bombay, New Delhi, and Ahmedabad. Typographically it is one of the best laid out and designed of Indian newspapers. Its Sunday edition, following the tradition of the London *Sunday Times*, carries a well-edited supplement and reviews of books and the arts.

News digests

783 Asian Recorder.
New Delhi: Recorder Press, 1955- . weekly.

A weekly news digest of Asian events modelled after *Keesing's Contemporary Archives*. The recorder is indexed quarterly and has annual and triennial cumulations. The arrangement is by country and, within country, alphabetically by subject. Entries are numbered serially with references given to previous entries on the topics. Very handy for current Indian events.

784 Data India.
New Delhi: Press Institute of India, 1974- . weekly.

Published by the Press Institute of India, this weekly covers important regional and national Indian events. Information is culled from newspapers, government reports, research papers, and trade and commerce bulletins. Sources of information are cited. Quarterly subject indexes with annual cumulations are issued. *Data India*'s coverage is broader than that provided by the *Indian Economic Diary* listed below.

785 **Indian Economic Diary: a weekly digest of Indian economic events with index.**
New Delhi: H. S. Chhabra, 1970- . weekly.
Provides a weekly digest of economic events in India. Information for the diary is obtained primarily from English-language Indian newspapers. Coverage usually includes national and local events, foreign trade, and Indian foreign economic affairs. Includes a quarterly subject index with annual cumulation.

Professional
Periodicals

786 Asian Affairs.
London: Royal Society for Asian Affairs, 1914- . thrice yearly.
The Royal Central Asian Society began publishing the *Royal Central Asian Journal* in 1914. In the 1970s both the name of the society and the title of the journal were changed to reflect more accurately the widening interests of the society. Interdisciplinary in nature, every issue of the journal carries one or two articles on India and a good book review section on South Asia.

787 Asian Survey.
Berkeley, California: University of California Press, 1961- . monthly.
This American monthly superseded the *Far Eastern Survey*. Most of its articles deal with contemporary developments and are based upon reports, interviews, and field research rather than standard documentary sources. Every year the first two issues survey major trends in Asian countries.

788 Bulletin of the School of Oriental and African Studies.
London: School of Oriental and African Studies, London University, 1917- . quarterly.
Though the coverage of the *Bulletin* is much wider than India, it is included here because of the recognized scholarly nature of its articles and its excellent book review section.

789 Gandhi Marg.
New Delhi: Gandhi Peace Foundation, 1957- . quarterly.
A journal devoted to the application of Gandhian philosophy and techniques to the social and economic problems of the world.

790 India Quarterly: a journal of international affairs.

New Delhi: Indian Council of World Affairs, 1945- .
quarterly.

India Quarterly offers both scholarly and general interest articles almost all
representing the point of view of the non-aligned nations in general, and of India
in particular. A substantial number of book reviews and occasionally a select
bibliography of Indian publications on political, economic, and social issues are
included.

791 Journal of Asian and African Studies.

Leiden, the Netherlands: Brill, 1966- . quarterly.

An interdisciplinary journal, published under the editorship of an international
board of Asian and western scholars. The emphasis is on social, political and
economic history. A good book review section.

792 Journal of Asian Studies.

Ann Arbor, Michigan: Association for Asian Studies, 1941- .
quarterly.

The major US scholarly journal on Asian studies. A good number of articles deal
with India. The emphasis is on the modern period: articles on Indology are not
included. It carries an extensive review of books, and a bibliographic supplement
is issued annually. Until 1956 it was known as the *Far Eastern Quarterly.*

793 Journal of Contemporary Asia.

Stockholm: Journal of Contemporary Asia, 1970- . quarterly.

A scholarly international quarterly devoted to Asian economic, political, and
social problems and conditions. The journal is left-leaning and has a sympathetic
attitude toward emerging Asian nations. Almost every issue carries an article on
South Asia. Some book reviews.

794 Modern Asian Studies.

London: Cambridge University Press, 1967- . quarterly.

British equivalent of the *Journal of Asian Studies* (q.v.). Contains fewer book
reviews than its American counterpart.

795 Monthly Public Opinion Surveys.

New Delhi: Indian Institute of Public Opinion, 1955- .
monthly.

The only Indian publication dealing exclusively with public opinion polls.
Publishes and analyses findings of research surveys conducted by the Institute on
political, social, and economic issues. Carries excellent election coverage.

796 New Quest.

Poona, India: Indian Association for Cultural Freedom,
1977- . bimonthly.

This bimonthly, published by the Indian Association for Cultural Freedom, carries
a wide range of scholarly articles on literary and political topics with India as its

Professional Periodicals

main emphasis. Original poems and short stories are included occasionally, and there is a book review section. Libertarian in outlook.

797 Pacific Affairs.
Vancouver, British Columbia: University of British Columbia Press, 1928- . quarterly.

The emphasis in this valuable quarterly is substantial treatment of contemporary topics relating to Asian and Pacific countries. Contributions are from the United States, Canada, and other Commonwealth countries. Excellent book review section.

798 Seminar: the monthly symposium.
New Delhi: Seminar Publications, 1959- . monthly.

Each issue is devoted entirely to a lively intellectual symposium on a single topic. Economic, political, and social issues are emphasized. At the end of the issue significant books on the topic under consideration are reviewed and a select bibliography is provided.

799 South Asia: journal of South Asian studies.
Nedlands, Australia: University of Western Australia, 1971- . biannual.

This interdisciplinary journal, which emphasizes modern history and social sciences, is the best scholarly serial publication from the South Pacific.

Libraries, Museums and Archives

800 **Brief directory of museums of India.**
Compiled by Usha Agrawal. New Delhi: Museum
Association of India, 1980. 3rd ed. 148p.
Entries are arranged alphabetically under state (or Union territory), and within
state by cities. Each entry provides name of the city; museum's name and
address; opening hours; types of collections; publications, if any; and availability
of guide services.

801 **Directory of research and special libraries in India and Sri
Lanka.**
Niharkanti Chatterjee. Calcutta: Information Research
Academy, 1979-80. 2 vols.
This two-volume directory provides information on 463 research and special
libraries in India and Sri Lanka. Each entry contains address, phone number,
year of establishment, subject of specialization, total number of volumes, annual
budget, name of head librarian, number of staff, branch libraries, and publications, if any.

802 **Directory of libraries and special collections on Asia and
North Africa.**
Robert Lewis Collison. London: Lockwood, 1970. 123p.
A list of 158 libraries in Britain and Northern Ireland describing their facilities,
Asian resources, and access rules. Libraries are listed geographically. There are
two useful indexes: one contains the names of special collections and all libraries
referred to in the text, the other is a subject index. The South Asia library group
is the dominant regional one in the collection.

Libraries, Museums and Archives

803 **Directory of special and research libraries in India.**
Calcutta: Indian Association of Special Libraries and
Information Centres, 1962. 282p.

Arranged alphabetically by name of library, this directory provides details on 173
special and research libraries in India. About 700 libraries for which full details
could not be obtained are also listed alphabetically by state. Separate indexes of
place and subject.

804 **Government archives in South Asia: a guide to national and**
state archives in Ceylon, India and Pakistan.
Edited by Donald Anthony Low, J. C. Iltis, Mary Doreen
Wainwright. London: Cambridge University Press, 1969.
355p. bibliog.

Over 300 pages are devoted to India in this comprehensive guide to South Asian
archives. The guide covers only the national and state or provincial archives.
District and subdistrict records, High Court records, private archival collections
and most of the holdings on microfilms are excluded. Each sketch provides a brief
history of the archive, access regulations, nature and extent of holdings, and
bibliographic references.

805 **Directory of cultural organisations in India.**
Compiled and edited by H. S. Patil. New Delhi: Indian
Council for Cultural Relations, 1975. 251p. bibliog.

Over 700 'cultural organisations' are listed according to the Dewey decimal classification system. Among the organizations included are museums, cultural societies, specialized schools, and research institutions. Each entry includes the address
of the organization, date of its establishment, its objectives and activities, and its
publications and library, if any. A separate institutional index, arranged alphabetically, and a place index are also provided.

806 **South Asian library resources in North America: a survey**
prepared for the Boston conference, 1974.
Edited by Maureen L. Patterson. Zug, Switzerland: Inter
Documentation Co., 1975. 223p. (Bibliotheca Asiatica, 12).

In-depth profiles of forty-three libraries, ranging from the Library of Congress to
several small colleges with special holdings on South Asia, based on responses
received to a questionnaire circulated by the Association for Asian Studies. Each
response includes a short history and current status report on the South Asian
programme; a summary of library holdings, special strengths, and languages
represented; and the library's use of the Library of Congress's acquisition programmes in South Asia.

807 **A guide to the India Office Library with a note on the India**
Office records.
Stanley C. Sutton. London: HMSO, 1971. 122p.

Manuscripts in the India Office Library, London, constitute the largest collection
of documents pertaining to South and Southeast Asia in the world outside South
Asia. This volume, written by a former India Office librarian, lists the major
collections and also includes a brief history of the library and information on its
book and pamphlet collection.

808 **A guide to western manuscripts and documents in the British Isles relating to South and South East Asia.**
Mary Doreen Wainwright, Noel Matthews. London: Oxford University Press, 1965. 532p.

This comprehensive guide covers both official archives and private papers in all the main British and Irish centres, including record offices, libraries, and learned institutions dealing with Afghanistan, Bangladesh, Bhutan, Burma, India, Nepal, Pakistan, Sikkim, Sri Lanka, and adjacent territories. India Office Library manuscripts are excluded on the assumption that any research student of modern South Asia would begin his studies in that library with its own extensive guides. Entries are arranged chronologically under individual depositories and are quite often remarkably full and detailed, extending to individual items. While holdings of the Public Records Office are covered in a general way, Cabinet Office records are not included.

Bibliographies, Abstracts and Indexes

Bibliographies

809 Accessions List, South Asia.
New Delhi: US Library of Congress, Delhi Office, 1981- .
monthly.

In 1981 the US Library of Congress accessions lists for South Asian countries were merged to form this monthly which records publications acquired from the area. Entries are arranged by country of publication. The monographic section under each country is divided by language of publication and under each language entries are listed alphabetically. Part 3 of each December issue contains cumulative author/title and subject indexes. This is an excellent source for current Indian scholarly publications.

810 BEPI: a bibliography of English publications in India.
Delhi: D. K. F. Trust, 1976- . annual.

This annual bibliography lists 'scholarly' and 'significant' English-language publications from India. Coverage has been substantially increased since 1976 and the latest year, 1979, contains 7,058 author, 5,103 title, and 10,907 subject entries. The author part constitutes the main section of the work and provides the fullest bibliographic information.

811 **South Asian history, 1750-1950: a guide to periodicals, dissertations, and newspapers.**
Margaret H. Case. Princeton, New Jersey: Princeton University Press, 1968. 561p.

The guide includes 5,431 items selected from 351 periodicals published between 1800 and 1965, and 26 composite works. Items are mostly in English and more than half of them are briefly annotated. Entries are divided into six sections - areas not primarily under British control, areas primarily under British control, nationalism and politics, economic history, social history, and cultural history. Also listed are 650 dissertations and a significant number of newspapers (341 English and bilingual and 251 Indian-language) published in South Asia and with the newspaper holdings and locations of various South Asian and western libraries.

812 **Catalogue of European printed books [of] the India Office Library.**
Boston, Massachusetts: G. K. Hall, 1964. 10 vols.

Volumes 1-6 contain entries for about 90,000 books in European languages held in the India Office Library in 1963. Volumes 7-9 are a subject index to volumes 3-6, and volume 10 notes the periodicals held by the library. Between 1867 and 1947 the India Office Library was a depository for all books and pamphlets published in India, thus this catalogue is an important reference tool for research in Indian studies.

813 **The social system and culture of modern India, a research bibliography.**
Edited by Danesh A. Chekki. New York: Garland, 1975. 843p.

5,475 books and articles, published between 1947 and 1974 and almost all in English, relating to sociology and social and cultural anthropology are included here and arranged in detailed classification.

814 **Cumulative bibliography of Asian studies.**
Boston, Massachusetts: G. K. Hall, 1969-73. 14 vols. (author bibliography, 1941-65, 4 vols., 1966-70, 3 vols.; subject bibliography, 1941-65, 4 vols., 1966-70, 3 vols.).

A cumulation of entries from the *Bibliography of Asian Studies* (and its predecessors), these volumes contain an extensive classified listing of books and periodical articles in western languages on all aspects of Asia. Over 600 periodicals devoted to Asian studies and a substantial number of non-area periodicals are indexed. Coverage from 1941-55 was limited to East Asia and, beginning with 1956, was extended to include South Asia. Some care must be used in consulting the subject bibliography because subject headings varied considerably over the years and were not reorganized or consolidated for the cumulation. The annual volume of the *Bibliography of Asian Studies*, published as a supplement to the *Journal of Asian Studies*, continues coverage after 1970.

815 **Annotated bibliography on the economic history of India, 1500 A.D. to 1947 A.D.**
V. D. Divekar (chief editor).   Poona, India: Gokhale Institute of Politics and Economics; New Delhi: Indian Council of Social Science Research, 1977-80. 4 vols. in 5. bibliog.

Prepared by the Gokhale Institute of Politics and Economics with financial assistance from the Indian Council of Social Science Research, this annotated bibliography, containing 31,484 items, is the most comprehensive source for the economic and social history of India, Pakistan, Bangladesh. Coverage includes selections from records, survey and settlement reports, gazetteers, acts and regulations, British parliamentary papers, reports of various committees and commissions, census reports, serials, books, periodical articles, and theses. Briefly annotated entries highlight the parameters of statistical information - its nature and the area and period covered. Coverage is limited to English-language printed material. A monumental work for the specialist.

816 **An anthropological bibliography of South Asia together with a directory of recent anthropological field work.**
Compiled by Elizabeth von Fürer-Haimendorf, Helen Kanitkar.   Paris: Mouton, 1958-70. 3 vols.

Almost 13,000 western-language items on South Asia are listed, though not annotated, in three volumes, the bulk of the items being on India. With the exception of census publications, government publications have largely been excluded. Items are divided into nineteen major regional sections and one general section, each section being further divided into six subsections: cultural and social anthropology, material culture and applied art, folklore and folk arts, prehistoric archaeology, physical anthropology, and miscellanea. An author index is given at the end of the each volume. The three volumes cover the period up to 1964. Helen Kanitkar has continued the work by publishing the first volume of the New Series covering the period 1965-69. The new series excludes physical anthropology and prehistoric archaeology and adds political sociology and socio-linguistics as subsections within the regional headings. Due to the regional arrangement and the much broader disciplinary coverage than the title indicates, the compilation has become perhaps the best bibliographical source for South Asian anthropological and sociological studies.

817 **Indian political movement, 1919-1971: a systematic bibliography.**
Compiled by Arun Ghosh, Ranjit Ghosh.   Calcutta: India Book Exchange, 1976. 499p.

As the title indicates, the bibliography covers the period from 1919 to 1971. This period is further divided into six subdivisions: 1919-33, 1934-39, 1940-47, 1948-55, 1956-64, 1965-71. Items are mostly in English. Author/subject indexes are given at the end. Excellent source for Indian political parties, especially 'parties less well covered in other bibliographies'.

818 **A guide to reference materials on India.**
Compiled and edited by N. N. Gidwani, K.
Navalani. Jaipur, India: Saraswati, 1974. 2 vols.

An ambitious, comprehensive, and exhaustive guide to reference materials on all aspects of Indian studies. Coverage includes materials in almost all languages of the world. There are about 20,000 items arranged in over 50,000 index entries. The arrangement in the main text is by subject matter, and most entries are fully annotated providing basic bibliographic detail, relevant information about previous editions, and published reviews. In spite of its enormous size, and the inclusion of some material which is out of date, this work is indispensable for the specialist as well as the librarian.

819 **India in English fiction, 1800-1970: an annotated bibliography.**
Brijen K. Gupta. Metuchen, New Jersey: Scarecrow, 1973. 296p.

This comprehensive annotated bibliography consists of 2,272 titles and covers English novels, tales, and short stories about India originally written in English or translated into English. For the convenience of the user, title and theme indexes are provided. Very useful for studying Indian fiction in English as well as the influence of Indian culture on western novels.

820 **Painting in South Asia: a bibliography.**
Ratan Pribhdas Hingorani. Delhi: Bharatiya Publishing House, 1976. 253p.

About 1,500 books and articles published up to 1972 dealing with South Asian paintings are indexed here. Titles are arranged under author index, anonymous works index, subject index, manuscript titles index, dated painting index, artists' index, index of patrons, sites index, and collections index.

821 **Indian National Bibliography.**
Calcutta: Central Reference Library, 1958- . annual.

This annual cumulative bibliography includes all books in English and other major languages published in India and required by law to be deposited in the National Library of India. Maps, music scores, periodicals, and newspapers (except for the first issue under a new title) are excluded. Author and subject indexes are provided.

822 **South Asia: a bibliography for undergraduate libraries.**
Edited by Louis A. Jacob (and others). Williamsport, Pennsylvania: Bro-Dart, 1970. 103p. (University of the State of New York, Foreign Area Materials Center. Occasional Publication no. 11).

Compiled under a US Office of Education contract, this bibliography is designed to assist librarians and scholars in developing undergraduate collections on South Asia. Each entry is graded according to its importance to undergraduate collections. The bibliography emphasizes titles in print and gives information about the reviews and annotations of these titles elsewhere.

823 **Bibliography of census publications in India.**
Compiled by C. G. Jadhav, edited by B. K. Roy
Burman. New Delhi: Office of the Registrar General,
Ministry of Home Affairs, 1972. 520p.

This bibliography provides the most comprehensive listing of all census publications through the 1961 census. Separate parts cover India, states and Union territories, and countries, like Pakistan and Burma, formerly covered by the Indian census. There are 2,820 entries and three appendixes, one of which provides useful information on pre-1850 population records.

824 **A bibliography of bibliographies on India.**
Compiled by D. R. Kalia, M. K. Jain. Delhi: Concept,
1975. 204p.

Compiled by two librarians in India, this bibliography has 1,243 entries, some of which are cited more than once. Most of the entries are for English-language publications. The main text is arranged by subject with a combined author-institution/subject-index following. Annotations are limited in number and are brief.

825 **National bibliography of Indian literature, 1901-1953.**
Edited by B. V. Kesavan, V. Y. Kulkarni. New Delhi:
Sahitya Akademi, 1962-74. 4 vols.

The bibliography lists over 60,000 items on social sciences and humanities in sixteen languages including English. Only those books having 'literary merit' or 'abiding value' are included. Arrangement is by language and within a language by author under broad subject headings - general works, philosophy and religion, social sciences, linguistics, arts, literature, history, biography and travel, and miscellaneous. All non-English entries have been romanized. At the end of each volume is a comprehensive title index.

826 **India: a critical bibliography.**
J. Michael Mahar. Tucson, Arizona: University of Arizona
Press, 1964. 119p.

The best annotated academic bibliography on India. It contains a carefully selected and descriptive list of 2,023 titles in English. Some of the titles are listed more than once to make various topical subsections complete units in themselves. A revised and updated edition is forthcoming.

827 **South Asian civilizations: a bibliographical synthesis.**
Maureen L. Patterson, in collaboration with William J.
Alspaugh. Chicago: University of Chicago Press, 1981.
853p. maps.

The focus of this bibliography is the Indian subcontinent plus the adjacent islands and Indian civilization including its extensions into Southeast Asia and beyond. The bibliography is limited to western-language works, principally English, but excluding Russian and other Slavic materials. This is a select bibliography of about 28,000 books and articles, arranged in a well-designed mix of chronology, topics, and regions. The outline of headings alone occupies 83 pages, indicating the comprehensiveness of the bibliography. The author index runs to over 100 pages, and the subject index, based on key words from headings, is 45 pages in length.

828 South Asian bibliography: a handbook and guide.
J. D. Pearson (general editor). Atlantic Highlands, New Jersey: Humanities, 1979. 381p.

A guide in two parts to works of reference providing information on Afghanistan, Bangladesh, Burma, the Himalayas, India, Maldives, Pakistan, and Sri Lanka. In the first part, eight bibliographical essays examine the importance of manuscripts and other unpublished materials in major libraries and archives of South Asia, Europe, and North America. In the second part, twenty-nine essays survey printed books, periodicals, newspapers, maps, and government publications by subject and by country. The guide lacks uniformity of style. Scholars have contributed bibliographical essays; librarians have generally provided lists of titles, annotated or not.

829 Women of South Asia: a guide to resources.
Carol Sakala. Millwood, New York: Kraus, 1980. 517p.

This book has nearly 5,000 entries on different facets of women's life in India, Bangladesh, Pakistan, Nepal and Sri Lanka. The first part indexes books, serials, published dissertations, articles, films, recordings, and individual contributions from important collected volumes of papers. Most of these entries are annotated. The second part consists of four reports describing library holdings, archival materials, and other research resources located in South Asia and abroad, principally in Great Britain. Full subject and author indexes are provided.

830 South Asia, a systematic geographic bibliography.
B. L. Sukhwal. Metuchen, New Jersey: Scarecrow, 1974. 824p.

10,346 books, articles and dissertations without annotations are arranged by country and subject matter. The emphasis is on geography. Tibet is included with India, Bangladesh, Pakistan, Sri Lanka, and Nepal. There is a separate author index.

Abstracts and indexes

831 Guide to Indian Periodical Literature: social sciences and humanities.
Gurgaon, India: Indian Documentation Centre, 1964- . quarterly.

This guide, modelled after the *Social Sciences and Humanities Index*, is published quarterly with an annual cumulation. It is a subject-author index to articles in the social sciences and humanities from selected English-language periodicals published in India. Since its inception the number of periodicals indexed has been substantially increased: volume 16 (1979) indexes over 400. A retrospective indexing plan is under way with the volume for 1963 appearing recently. A very useful source for current periodical literature.

832 **Index India: a quarterly documentation list on India of material in English, combining in one sequence, Indian newspaper index, index to Indian periodicals, index to composite publications, index to biographical profiles, index to book reviews, index to theses and dissertations, with separate author and subject indexes.**
Jaipur, India: Rajasthan University Library, 1967- .
quarterly.

The descriptive title indicates the broad scope of this comprehensive index. Over 1,000 periodicals and newspapers, as well as some composite works, are indexed. The book review index is quite substantial. Though listed as a quarterly, many issues appear on a half-yearly basis. The usefulness of *Index India* is reduced by the publication time lag which is about four years: last issue covers Jan.-Dec. 1979.

833 **Indian Book Review Index.**
Gurgaon, India: Indian Documentation Service, 1975/76- .

This index makes a substantial contribution toward establishing bibliographic control over book reviews, especially those published in Indian journals. The first volume (1975-76) incorporates about 3,000 review entries of nearly 1,200 books reviewed in 148 English-language journals (144 Indian, 4 non-Indian). Arrangement is by subject and within subject by author. Includes author and reviewer indexes. Nothing published after volume one.

834 **Indian Dissertation Abstracts.**
New Delhi: Indian Council of Social Science Research, 1973- . quarterly.

This quarterly journal is jointly sponsored by the Indian Council of Social Science Research and the Association of Indian Universities. The main emphasis of the coverage is social sciences: economics, education, management, political science, psychology, public administration, sociology, social anthropology, demography.

835 **Indian Press Index.**
Delhi: Delhi Library Association, 1968- . monthly.

A monthly index to about twenty-five English-language Indian newspapers including *The Hindu, Hindustan Times, Indian Express, Statesman,* and *Times of India.* All the signed and unsigned articles, special write-ups, editorials and important letters to the editor are indexed. Contains author and geographic entries. A quarterly supplement, *Book Review Supplement,* gives all the book reviews published in the indexed newspapers.

Index

The index is a single alphabetical sequence of authors (personal and corporate), titles of publications and subjects. Index entries refer both to the main items and to other works mentioned in the notes to each item. Title entries are in italics. Numeration refers to the items as numbered. As it is not always easy for the reader to determine under which element Indian names should be filed, all compound names have been indexed under the last element, e.g. Chopra, Prand Nath, with additional entries also given under the penultimate element for South Indian names such as Sivasankara Pillai, Thakazi.

Buddhism *contd.*
Chinese pilgrims, early period 83, 85
early period 83, 94, 96
European scholars 200
festivals 736−737
history 183, 187, 190−191, 196,
   199−200, 210
impact on culture 83
influence of Zoroastrianism 252
interaction with Hinduism, Gupta
   period 79
Madhyamika 193
Mahayana 191
monastic tradition 190, 192, 198
philosophy 272
psychological aspects 188
Tantric 187, 206
untouchables 182
women, early period 192
Buddhism in translations 184
Buddhism: its essence and
   development 187, 194, 196
Buddhist ethics: essence of
   Buddhism 198
Buddhist experience: sources and
   interpretations 184
Buddhist kingdoms 80, 183
5th-century accounts 72
Buddhist meditation 188
Buddhist monks and missionaries in
   India 190
Buddhist monuments 696
Buddhist nirvana and its western
   interpreters 200
Buddhist parables: translated from the
   original Pali 185
Buddhist religion: a historical
   introduction 184, 187, 196
Buddhist texts through the ages 184
Buddhist tradition in India, China and
   Japan 189
Budgets 495
Budhasvamin 616
Bueno de Mesquita, B. 369
Building materials 24
Bulletin of the School of Oriental and
   African Studies 788
Burger, Angela Sutherland 407
Burke, T. C. 244
Burlingame, Eugene Watson 185
Burman, B. K. R. 823
Burtt, E. A. 186, 194
Business
   autobiographical accounts 296−298
   Marwaris 308

periodicals 474, 476, 482, 533, 770,
   784−785
who's who 5
Business India 533
Businessmen
   local government 405
Bussagli, M. 671

C

Caitanya 227
Calcutta 58
Calcutta 23, 26, 58
   Black Hole incident 117
   management institute 599
   Marwaris 308
   politics 405
   women 355
Calendar
   Muslim 237
Calligraphy 684
Cambridge Economic History of
   India 486
Cambridge History of India 62
Cambridge Modern History 57, 62
Campbell, E. 201
Campbell, J. 681−682
Candrakanta abhidhana: a
   comprehensive dictionary of the
   Assamese language 168
Cape Comorin
   16th-17th century 73
Capitalism 489, 532, 540
   agriculture 553
Cappeller, C. 181
Car industry 524
Caraka 593
Caravan 769
Cardona, G. 156
Carpets 697, 701, 704
Carstairs, G. Morris 309
Carter, A. T. 330
Carvakas 269
Case, M. H. 811
Cashman, R. 750
Cassen, R. H. 144
Caste 8−9, 13, 148, 277, 280−281,
   283−285, 291, 295, 312, 327,
   329, 331−332, 334−337, 343,
   346, 547, 572
   Ambedkar, B. R. 378
   Brahmans 292, 299, 302
   economic role 504
   Hindu 275

210

214

216

East India Company 117
Eastern Europe
  aid to India 465
  technical aid 563
  trade with India 454
Eaton, Richard Maxwell 231
Ecology 22, 337, 342, 480
*Economic and commercial geography
    of India* 25
Economic and Political Weekly 475
Economic development 23, 379, 430,
    502, 505, 508, 511, 538
  impact on caste 328
  impact on employment 577
  impact on environment 22
  impact on family life 286
  impact on society 22, 307, 344, 504
  impact on tribes 324
  multinational companies 530, 540
  political factors 504
  regional industry 537
  role of agriculture 506, 546
  role of communications 559
  role of employment 506, 518
  role of energy 564
  role of foreign collaboration 539, 542
  role of import substitution 509, 519,
    521, 524
  role of industrial estates 541
  role of population control 142, 144,
    151
  role of savings schemes 513
  role of science 588
  role of science and
    technology 583−584
  role of steel industry 531
  role of water resources 566
  Telangana 422
Economic geography 14, 18, 20,
    22−26, 29, 33
  Mughal period 32
*Economic growth and technological
    change in India* 583
*Economic growth in China and India,
    1952-1970: a comparative
    appraisal* 492
*Economic Guide and Investor's
    Handbook of India* 536
Economic history 55, 59, 486−491,
    493−494
  bibliographies 811, 815
  colonialism 485
  famines 485
  maps 27
  periodicals 51, 791

*Economic history of India,
    1857-1956* 491
Economic planning 473, 477, 480, 484,
    488, 506, 508, 517−518, 536, 544
  Planning Commission 503, 510, 517
  political factors 503
  role of land reform 507
  social factors 503
Economic relations 451−452, 454,
    465−466, 469−470, 476, 481,
    497, 502, 508, 517, 523, 528, 534,
    536
  with Europe, 18th century 117
Economic Survey 495
Economic Times 770
Economic Times Annual 770
Economics of the black market 483
Economy 1−2, 4, 12, 21, 174, 276,
    280, 398, 453, 473, 477,
    479−481, 484, 495, 516, 536,
    795, 834
  14th century 74
  black market 483−484, 516
  British period 113, 117
  Buddhist views 195
  comparison with China's 492
  early period 82, 91, 97
  feudalism, early period 95
  Gandhism 257, 484, 789
  Gupta period 79, 89
  impact of bilateral trade 519
  impact of politics 518
  inflation 483
  Mughal period 108
  national income statistics 498
  periodicals 474−476, 478, 482, 515,
    533, 770, 777−779, 784−785,
    790, 793, 798
  role of FICCI 544
  role of Indian emigrants 525
  standards of living 496
  statistics 369, 474, 477, 482, 492,
    497, 499−501, 515
  tribal 323, 325−326
  urban 341
  villages 292, 334−336
*Economy and society: essays in Indian
    economic and social history* 487
Edgerton, E. 610
Edgerton, F. 610
Edicts, Asokan 96
Education 4, 148, 265, 280, 282, 288,
    334, 496, 600, 651, 805, 834
  (see also Universities)
  academic profession 597, 603

H

230

jewellery 699
land ownership 49, 115
maps 32, 103
politics 109
religion 109
society 109
Sufis 106
technology 107
Islamic separatism 114, 118, 125, 234, 238
Islamic world
relations with India 460, 462
Ismailiya Shia 232
Ismay, Hastings Lionel, Baron 120
Italian travellers' accounts
15th century 76
17th century 78
Ithna Ashariya Shia 232
Ivory 700
Iyengar, K. R. Srinivasa 384, 669
Iyengar, M. R. Rajagopala 618

J

J. P.: his biography 383
Jacob, L. A. 822
Jade 699
Jadhav, C. G. 823
Jaffrey, M. 746
Jain, D. 351—352
Jain, M. K. 824
Jain, M. P. 439
Jain, S. K. 256
Jaina path of purification 242
Jaina philosophy of non-absolutism: a critical study of Anekantavada 266
Jaina yoga: a survey of the mediaeval Sravakacaras 245
Jaini, J. L. 241
Jaini, P. S. 242
Jainism 9, 212, 241, 244—245, 269, 656, 670, 737
art 675, 679
Digambara and Svetambara sects 240, 242—243
history 240, 242
philosophy 266
Jajmani system 329, 335
Jammu and Kashmir
history 139
politics 419

Jammu and Kashmir: triumph and tragedy of Indian federalism 419
Jamshedpur
migration 324
Jan Sangh and Swatantra: a profile of the rightist parties in India 394
Jana Sangh 394, 407, 420
Jana Sangh: a biography of an Indian political party 394
Janata Party 361, 365, 383, 417—418, 420, 425, 462
Jannuzi, F. Tomasson 409
Japan
Buddhist texts 189
Japji 246
Jatra theatre 708
Jaunsar-Bawar region
polyandry 293
Java
Hindu expansion, early period 90
Jawaharlal Nehru: a biography. Volume 1: 1889-1947. Volume 2: 1947-1956 376
Jayadeva 609, 620
Jayakar, P. 704
Jayal, A. 731
Jayaram, K. C. 41
Jeffrey, R. 121
Jewellery 697, 699—700, 704
Muslim 237
Jha, P. S. 479
Jha, S. 164, 670
Jhabvala, R. P. 640
Jhangiani, M. A. 394
Jhaveri, M. M. 661
Der Jinismus 244
Jinnah, Muhammed Ali 111, 230
Jodhpur
railways 560
Johnson, B. L. Clyde 23
Johnson, W. L. 184, 187, 196
Jones, Betty True 711
Jones, C. R. 711
Jones, W. H. Morris 363
Jones, William 134
Jordens, S. T. F. 216
Joshi, B. R. 301
Joshi, H. 574
Joshi, N. C. 315
Joshi, P. C. 505, 549
Joshi, V. 574
Jotwani, M. W. 662
Journal of Asian and African Studies 791

234

235

N

244

251

254

259

Y

Map of India

Map of India

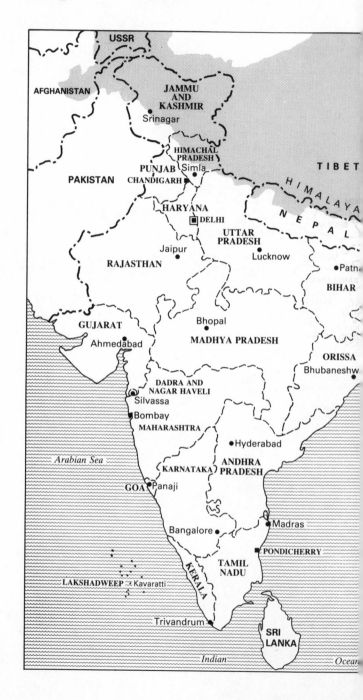

This map shows the
more important towns and other features.

CHINA

KIM

ARUNACHAL
PRADESH
Itanagar

BHUTAN

ASSAM NAGALAND
Gauhati
Kohima

Shillong
MEGHALAYA

Imphal
MANIPUR

BANGLADESH
Agartala
Aizawl
TRIPURA
MIZORAM

ST.
NGAL

cutta

BURMA

LAOS

Bay of
Bengal

THAILAND

CAMBODIA

ANDAMAN AND NICOBAR

Port Blair

DELHI	Capital
KERALA	States/Union territories
Trivandrum	Major towns
— — —	International boundaries
	Land over 3000 m

0   250   500 km